Ideas and Ideals of the Hassidim

Ideas and Ideals
of the
HASSIDIM

DR. MILTON ARON

The Citadel Press • *New York*

TO
Leona, Diane, Judith, and Heather

Contents

Contents

Acknowledgments

The author wishes to thank the following:

The Department for Education and Culture of the World Zionist Organization in Jerusalem for permission to quote from Eliezer Steinman's *The Garden of Hassidism*.

Schocken Books, New York, for permission to quote from Martin Buber's *Tales of the Hasidim*.

Louis I. Newman for permission to quote from his *Hasidic Anthology*.

The Jewish Publication Society of America, Philadelphia, for permission to quote from its edition of the Holy Scriptures.

The Viking Press, Inc., New York, and Irving Howe and Eliezer Greenberg for permission to reprint I. L. Peretz's "If Not Higher," in Marie Syrkin's translation, from *A Treasury of Yiddish Stories*.

Moshe Starkman for reading the manuscript in its first draft, for suggested additions, and for compiling the Bibliography.

M.A.

9

AND thou shalt love the Lord thy God with all thy heart, and with all thy soul, and with all thy might.

Deuteronomy 6:5

THOU shalt not take vengeance, nor bear any grudge against the children of thy people, but thou shalt love thy neighbor as thyself; I am the Lord.

Leviticus 19:18

LOVE thee Truth and Peace.

Zechariah 8:19

[1]
Jewish Universalism and the Teachings of Hassidism

THE PIETIST MOVEMENT known as *Hassidut* or Hassidism has
been the most influential Jewish religious movement from its
beginning in the second half of the eighteenth century, down to
our own times. It was started by Rabbi Israel Baal Shem Tov,*
whose name means "Possessor of the Good Name," in the
Podolyah Province of the Ukraine, and from there it spread out
to the whole of the Ukraine, parts of White Russia, and to
Poland, thanks to the efforts of the Baal Shem Tov's disciples,
among whom were many talented professional teachers.

The Jewish Pietists, known as Hassidim, had their origin
among scribes and teachers in the early days of the Second
Temple Era. Their devotional forms of prayer and ascetic, daily
living were emulated by groups and individuals in later eras and
in various countries. The *Hassidei Ashkenaz,* the Jewish Pietists
in Germany during the Middle Ages, added new forms and norms
of living, prayer, and study. The mystics of Safed, under the
leadership of their young teacher, Rabbi Isaac Ashkenazy, more
popularly known as Ari Hakadosh, prepared the spiritual way
for the later establishment of Hassidut which has been, for over
two centuries now, the most dynamic Jewish religious movement,
gaining new adherents wherever Jewish communities exist.

* Often called the Besht, an acronym of his name: *Baal SHem Tov.*

13

Hassidut owes its success to numerous factors, among them the emphasis on piety, not of the chosen, but of the broad masses of simple Jews; and the service of God through joy rather than sadness and self-mortification. Hassidut did not aspire to radical change in Jewish religious life, but emphasized practices, previously little known, to make the simple Jew feel beloved by God, and perhaps more so than the scholar, whose attitude towards the non-scholars was altogether negative.

The great sufferings of the Jews in various eras and lands, heightened the Messianic hopes of the Jews and they found solace in the prophecies of Isaiah and Micah. The Messianic hopes of the Jews were, on occasion, misused by ambitious individuals who posed as Messiahs. These false Messiahs caused many tragic events in Jewish history. When the Hassidut of Israel Baal Shem Tov began to gain followers, its opponents accused them of having established a new movement with a false Messiah. The accusation was groundless, because the Hassidim based their Messianic hopes on the compassionate Almighty's speedy fulfillment of the promises made through His servants, the Prophets.

According to one school of Jewish historians, the Modern Era in Jewish historic development began when the disciples of the Besht, and of the Gaon of Vilna, *went up* to the Holy Land; and not in the days when German Jews were granted civil rights.

The Hassidim explained, with supreme irony, the difference between themselves and their opponents, known as *Mitnagdim*, in the saying: "The pious Mitnagdim are afraid of transgressing against the Code of Laws, but the Hassidim are in fear of transgressing against God."

Hassidut created a literature of its own, mostly in the form of commentaries on the biblical portions read each Saturday and

on all of the Holidays. A number of Hassidic leaders also produced commentaries on parts of the Talmud and of the Code of
Laws. Hassidut has directly influenced the development of modern
Jewish literature in both Hebrew and Yiddish. Rabbi Nakhman
of Bratzlav was a master storyteller, and his tales, as recorded by
his disciple and scribe, Rabbi Nathan Shternhartz, are considered
as the dawn of a new era in the creation of Yiddish fiction. Rabbi
Levi Yitzkhak of Berdichev, the great defender of the Jews and
the accuser of the Almighty, was a poet in his own fashion.
Rabbi Meir of Premishlan and Rabbi Naphtali of Ropshitz were
humorists whose anecdotes and whimsical interpretations of
biblical passages are repeated to this very day.

Rabbi Levi Yitzkhak of Berdichev, who was a constant accuser of the Almighty and a defender of the Jewish people
against God's wrath, always stressed the principle that "whether
a man really loves God can be best determined by the love he bears
toward his fellow men." Rabbi Levi Yitzkhak usually stressed the
teaching of *Midrash Tankhuma:* "He who sustains God's creatures
is rewarded as though he had created them."

Rabbi Bunim of Pshyskha interpreted the biblical passage:
"Justice, Justice shalt thou pursue (Deut. 16:20)" as, we may
use only justifiable methods even in the pursuit of justice.

Among the great Hebrew and Yiddish writers who have
written stories of Hassidic content and in Hassidic form, are such
prose masters as I. L. Peretz, Yehudah Steinberg, Micah Yoseph
Berdychevski, Shmuel Yoseph Agnon, to mention only a few;
Hassidic leaders and their teachings have often been used by
modern Hebrew and Yiddish poets as subject matter for both
lyrical verse and narrative poems. The works of Martin Buber
have popularized Hassidut and its Masters among the readers in

Western countries, Jews and non-Jews alike. Eliezer Steinman, the great Hebrew-Yiddish novelist and essayist, has enriched Jewish literature with a whole series of books dealing with the masters of Hassidut and their teachings, from the Besht to recent times. The works of Hassidic masters are being re-published constantly in Israel and in the United States, and a number of distinguished historians and biographers have enriched Jewish research with excellent books on Hassidut and its creators. The interest in Hassidut is constantly growing among Jews in the English-speaking countries, and the intellectual Lubavitcher Hassidic school has been gaining followers among all classes of American Jewry.

Hassidism is in essence an ethical and esthetic interpretation of the divine ideals embodied in the 613 precepts of Judaism. It is the aim of the *Zaddik,* the true Hassidic Rabbi and teacher, to elevate the simple Jew to heights of piety, considering no one too low to ascend to the higher rungs of faith, piety, devotion and hope.

The Hassidic leaders made use of parables, and of song and dance to make their ideas better understood and to create fellowship among their followers. Their main aim was to elevate spiritually the simple masses and make them appreciate the lofty ideals inherent in Judaism.

In order to appreciate the teachings of Hassidut, it is important that we become familiar with some of the basic universal teachings of Judaism. Familiarity with Jewish concepts, in general, will make it easier for us to comprehend the life stories of various Hassidic leaders and their specific teachings.

All concepts of Universalism and Human Brotherhood are rooted in the Jewish concept of One God who is the Creator of the Universe and the Father of all mankind. No wonder that the Bible, the Book that is so deeply national Jewish in character, has become almost universally accepted as the main source of universal faiths, and the foundation of all that is encompassed by the terms "ethics" and "morality."

The German Jewish poet Heinrich Heine said wisely of the Bible that, "It is the great medicine chest of humanity."

The biblical Book of Psalms contains prayers for civilized people of all eras, ages and climates. Most poetry, lyrical poetry in particular, is an echo of what is found in the Psalms of King David, the "Sweet Singer of Israel."

The first words a Jewish child has to learn are contained in the SH'EMAH: "Hear, O Israel, the Lord is our God, the Lord is One" (Deut. 6:4). They are also the last words a Jew should say before he dies. The Oneness of God is the constant proclamation and the constant reminder to all mankind by Jews and Judaism, that it be recognized that the universal Creator is the Father all human beings have in common. All the blessings that Jews recite begin with the words "Blessed Art Thou, O Lord our God, King of the Universe."

Judaism emphasizes that the Almighty is the Lord of Peace, and He desires peace for all He created. In matters of feeding the hungry, clothing the naked, and healing the sick, Judaism stresses that one should imitate the Creator and bring help to those who are in need; making no exceptions and discriminating against no one.

The common descent of all human beings is emphasized by the great Sage Rabbi Meir in his statement that the earth from which Adam was created, had been collected from all parts of the entire world. In a much broader sense, this idea is developed in the *Mishnah:* "Therefore only a single man was created in the world, to teach us that if any man has caused a single soul to perish, Scripture considers it as if he had caused the whole world to perish; and if a man saves a single soul, Scripture imputes it to him as though he had saved alive the whole world. . . . For man stamps many coins with the one seal and they are all like one another; but the King of Kings, blessed is He, has stamped every man with the seal of the first man, yet not one of them is like his fellow. Therefore, everyone must say: 'For my sake the world was created' (Mishnah, Sanhedrin 4:5)."

Says Leviticus (19:18; 34): "Thou shalt love thy neighbor as thyself; and the stranger that sojourned with you shall be unto you as the homeborn among you, and thou shalt love him as thyself." The Sage Rabbi Akiba said: "This is a general principle in the Torah." Ben Azai said: "This is the book of the generations of Adam (Gen. 5:1) and is a greater general principle."

All members of the human race are judged on Rosh Hashanah, the birthday of Adam, which is the birthday of all humanity; and therefore the Universal New Year is the day of Judgment for all human beings.

Rabbi Khruspedai said in the name of Rabbi Yokhanan: "Three books are opened on New Year's Day; one for the perfectly righteous, one for the grossly wicked, and one for the intermediate class of people. The verdict of the perfectly righteous is promptly written and sealed for life; the verdict of the grossly wicked is promptly written and sealed for death; the verdict of the intermediate class is suspended from the New Year's Day till the Day of Atonement. If they prove themselves worthy, they are inscribed for life; if not, they are inscribed for death (Talmud Bavli, Rosh Hashanah, 16b)." On every Rosh Hashanah, the

Jews repeat the coronation of the Creator as King of the Universe, and they emphasize, in their prayers, that all which exists is dependent upon His grace and compassion.

At the Afternoon Service on the Day of Atonement, after the reading of the prescribed Torah portion (Lev. 18), the biblical book of Jonah is recited. The book tells how the prophet Jonah was punished because he fled from the responsibility to save the inhabitants of Nineveh. The Ninevehnites were not Jews, but the Jewish prophet also had obligations to non-Jews, since the Almighty is the Creator of all human beings.

Jewish traditional commentators on the Bible, basing their comments on Talmudic and Midrashic interpretations, took great care to emphasize that wherever Scripture uses the term "brother," in regard to everyone's obligation to moral and ethical behavior, the term includes also the believing non-Jew, for everyone who believes in God is thus a brother of the Jew. The non-Jew as well as the Jew is promised a reward in the World-to-Come, for enabling someone, by providing him with sustenance, to study the Torah and its laws, since if one enables somebody else to study, it is considered as if one studies the Torah himself.

Elijah said: "I bring Heaven and Earth as witnesses: Between Jew and Gentile, between male and female, between slave and servant, according to one's deeds the Holy Spirit rests upon him" (*Tannah D'bei Eliyahu Rabbah,* 10).

Emphasizing the Brotherhood of Mankind, the Midrash went so far as to state that only a calamity which befalls the Gentile peoples as well as the Jews is a real calamity; but trouble for Jews alone cannot be considered an affliction *(Devarim Rabbah 2)*.

According to Jewish tradition, the Patriarchs, Abraham, Isaac and Jacob, as well as Joseph and Moses, were sent by the Almighty

to wander in strange lands, so that they might have the opportunity to spread the knowledge of God among the nations of
the world and thus conduct a service for the welfare of all
humanity.

The Talmud, the Midrash, and the Zohar—the latter being
the central source of Jewish mysticism known as *Kabbalah*—
stress the point that Abraham taught the peoples of his time the
name of God, and they, in turn, taught the name of God to their
children. Thus, Abraham created a bond of unity among human
beings. Abraham's compassion included the inhabitants of the
sinful cities of Sodom and Gomorrah, for whom he pleaded with
God that He save them (Gen. 18:17–33). Abraham, considered
the greatest man of his time, proved his great humility by serving
three simple wayfarers, not knowing that they were Angels of
God in disguise (Ibid. 18:1–16). The Almighty promised that He
would remember the kindness, not of Abraham alone, but also
of his son Isaac and of his grandson Jacob, because they were
the first ones to proclaim Him before the entire world.

According to another Jewish tradition, all proselytes and all
God-fearing Gentiles are the descendants of the numerous children who were fed on the overflow of milk from Sarah's breasts,
after she had given birth to Isaac. In stressing this, Jewish tradition wishes to emphasize the symbolic kinship of all who trust
in the Almighty, whatever their racial origin or form of giving
testimony to their belief in the Creator of all.

Jewish election, the idea that the Jews are the Chosen People,
does not mean racial superiority, but a greater obligation because
of the divine merits of the ancestors of the Jewish people, the
Patriarchs. Pious non-Jews, according to Jewish teaching, will
share in the World-to-Come, and the righteous Gentiles are

placed in the category of the High Priests in the Holy Temple of God. The teachers of the Talmud and Midrash emphasized that "the Almighty rejects no human being. He accepts everyone; the gates of Heaven are constantly open and he who wishes to enter may do so." Rabbi Meir said: "How do we know that even a Gentile who is engaged in the study and practice of the Torah is like the High Priest? A passage teaches us: '. . . My statutes and mine ordinances which if a *man* do, he shall live by them' (Lev. 18:5). It is not written: Priests, Levites and Israelites, but '*a man.*' From this you infer that even a Gentile who is engaged in Torah, is like the High Priest (Talmud Bavli, Baba Kamma, 38a). 'Let thy priests be clothed with righteousness' (Ps. 132:9) means the righteous people among the nations of the world, for they are on this earth, priests of the Holy One, Praised be He." *(Tannah D'bei Eliyahu Zuttah, 20.)*

The tolerance of Judaism in regard to other monotheistic faiths, can best be explained by a Hassidic story concerning the young scholar who complained to his master that as soon as he ceased his daily study, inspiration left him. The Rabbi consoled him with the following explanation: "It is like a man who journeys through a forest on a dark night, and on part of the way is accompanied by a companion who carries a lantern. At length, they come to the point where their paths divide, and they must go on alone. If each carries his own lantern, he need fear no darkness."

So Judaism regards the other universal faiths. If they keep the light in their own lanterns, they will never be overtaken by the darkness of intolerance and idolatry.

Judaism teaches that since God made himself known to human beings by means of His compassion, all are obligated to walk in the ways of the Almighty and show kindness to all without distinction. According to Jewish ethics, emphasized often by the great teachers of Hassidut, we should dislike evil deeds, but not those who commit them, for even evil-doers are in the category of "Love thy neighbor." How much more is one obligated to show kindness and compassion for the weak and be on guard for their protection? Judaism stresses this in numerous ways and forms. Even in waging war, a Jew is prohibited from killing an enemy in an abominable manner; for the enemy is a human being, a child of the Almighty and created in His image.

According to Talmudic teaching, "the Holy One, Praised be He, does not rejoice over the downfall of the wicked." When the children of Israel walked on dry land and the pursuing Egyptians were drowning in the Red Sea, and Moses and the Israelites began to sing the song of thanks for the deliverance (Exod. chapters 14 and 15), the ministering angels wanted to sing their own song of praise to the Lord. He was angered and said to them: "My creatures, the Egyptians, are drowning in the sea, and you wish to sing?" (Talmud Bavli, Sanhedrin, 39b). And the Israelites were commanded: "Thou shalt not abhor an Egyptian, because thou wast a stranger in his land. The children of the third generation that are born unto them may enter the assembly of the Lord." (Deut. 23; 8–9).

The children of Israel were joined by other peoples in singing the song of deliverance when they heard of the Egyptian defeat and of the destruction of the Egyptian idols. The non-Jews joined the Israelites in singing harmoniously: "Who is like unto Thee, O Lord, among the mighty?" (Exod. 15:11).

According to traditional interpretations, the Ten Commandments were handed down in the desert, in a place that belonged to no particular nation, so that all peoples might be given the opportunity to adopt the Ten Commandments as their very own.

Rabbi Yokhanan said: "What is meant by the passage 'The Lord gave (happy) tidings; they were published by the messengers, a numerous host' (Ps. 68:12), is that every single utterance which went forth from the mouth of the Almighty, was heralded into seventy languages."

It was taught in the academy of Rabbi Ishmael: "Like the hammer that breaketh the rock in pieces" (Jer. 23:29); meaning "that just as the hammer strikes the stone into a multitude of pieces, so every utterance which proceeded from the mouth of the Holy One, Praised be He, was heralded into seventy languages." *(Talmud Bavli, Sabbath, 88b.)*

At the dedication of the Holy Temple in Jerusalem, King Solomon implored the Creator that in the house which was to become His abode on earth, the prayers of all the world's inhabitants should be answered: "Moreover, concerning the stranger that is not of Thy people Israel, when he shall come out of a far country for Thy name's sake—for they shall hear of Thy great name, and of Thy mighty hand, and of Thine outstretched arm—when he shall come and pray toward this house; hear Thou in Heaven, Thy dwelling place, and do according to all that the stranger calleth to Thee for; that all the peoples of the earth may know Thy name, to fear Thee, as doth Thy people Israel, and that they may know that Thy name is called upon this house which I have built." (I Kings, 8:41–43).

In the special "Hallel" psalms, recited at the beginning of the new month and during the major Jewish festivals, the smallest of all psalms is a call to all humanity to join in the worship of the Lord (Psalm 117), and the beginning of the psalm next to it

(Psalm 118) includes in the responsives the statement of the God-fearing Gentiles present at the Temple Service:

> O praise the Lord, *all ye nations*
> Laud Him, *all ye peoples*
> For His mercy is great toward us
> And the truth of the Lord endureth forever, Hallelujah.

> O give thanks unto the Lord, for he is good,
> For His mercy endureth for ever.

> So let Israel now say:
> For His mercy endureth for ever.

> So let the House of Aaron now say,
> For His mercy endureth for ever.

> *So let them now that fear the Lord say:*
> For His mercy endureth for ever.

The seventy bullocks that were sacrificed during Succoth (Tabernacles), as commanded in the Book of Numbers (chap. 29), were offered "for the sake of the seventy nations" (*Talmud Bavli,* Succoth, 55b) that were in existence during Temple times. The Sage Rabbi Joshua Ben Levi said; "Had the peoples of the world known what the Holy Temple meant for their existence, they would have surrounded it to watch that it never be destroyed by an enemy."

Job, the tragic hero of the biblical book bearing his name, is not considered by the Sages to have been a Jew. On the contrary, Job is considered the greatest pietist among the righteous Gentiles of the world.

In ancient times, the Jews did not place any obstacles in the way of those who wanted to become proselytes to Judaism. Historic developments, after the rise of Christianity and later of

Mohammedanism, made Jewish missionary activity both hazardous for the Jews and unnecessary from the standpoint of belief in the Universality of God.

All Jewish festivals are "in remembrance of the exodus from Egypt," which was joined by a "mixed multitude" of non-Israelite slaves. A number of great Jewish leaders in the era of the post-biblical Tanaitie teachers during the era of the Second Temple and after its destruction, were of non-Jewish descent, such as Shemaia and Abtalion, Rabbi Akiba and Rabbi Meir. The great Sage Hillel, known as Hillel the Elder, formerly a pupil of Shemaia and Abtalion, was known for his great humility, while Shammai, Hiller's partner in the last of the five *"Zugot"* (Pairs) who were the original transmitters of the Oral Law, was known for his strictness. The rigorous attitude of Shammai and the humility of Hillel are usually illustrated by a Talmudic description of the different attitude of each to Gentiles who had decided to enter the Jewish fold:

"Our Rabbis taught: A heathen once came before Shammai and said: 'How many Torahs have you?' Shammai replied: 'We have two: The Written Torah and the Oral Torah.' The heathen then said to him: 'In the Written Torah I believe Thee, but in the Oral Torah, I do not believe thee. Make me, therefore, a proselyte on condition that you teach me the Written Torah only.' Shammai rebuked him sharply and sent him away angry. The heathen then appeared before Hillel, and the latter made him a proselyte. On the first day, Hillel taught the Hebrew letters Aleph, Beth, Ghimmel, Daleth. On the morrow, Hillel reversed the order of these letters. 'Thou did not teach me so yesterday,' said the proselyte to him. 'True,' said Hillel, 'but dost thou not rely upon me with the Oral Torah?'

"On another occasion, it happened that a heathen appeared before Shammai and said: 'Convert me to Judaism but on condition that thou teachest me the whole Torah while I am standing upon one leg.' Shammai drove him off with the builder's measure he held in his hand. Then the heathen appeared before Hillel, and he made him a proselyte, and said unto him: *'That which is hateful to thee, do not do unto thy neighbor.* This is the whole Torah, and the rest is merely its commentary.'

"Again it happened that while a heathen passed by the rear of a synagogue, he heard the voice of a scribe who was saying: 'And these are the garments which they shall make: a breastplate, and an Ephod and a robe' (Exod. 28:4). 'For whom are these?' asked the heathen. 'For the High Priest,' replied the scribe. So the heathen said to himself: 'I shall go and become a proselyte on condition that I be made a High Priest.' He came before Shammai and said to him: 'Make me a proselyte upon condition that you make me a High Priest.' Shammai drove him away with the builder's cubit which he held in his hand. The heathen then came before Hillel. The latter made him a proselyte, and said to him: 'Is it possible for one to be made a king unless he knows the court ceremonials? Go, study first the court ceremonials.' The proselyte thereupon went and learned the Torah. When he came to the passage, 'And the stranger that cometh nigh shall be put to death' (Num. 3:10), he asked: 'For whom is that passage meant?' Hillel replied: 'Even for David, King of Israel.' Then the proselyte came to the following conclusion: 'If for the Israelites, who are called the Sons of God, and, on account of God's love shown to them, were called *My Son, my firstborn, Israel* (Exod. 4:22), a warning is written, *'And the stranger that cometh nigh shall be put to death,'* how much more does this apply to the

mere proselyte who came but with his staff and traveling bag?'
He went to Shammai and said to him: 'Am I then elegible to
be a High Priest? Behold, it is written in the Torah: *'And the
stranger that cometh nigh shall be put to death.'* He then went
to Hillel and said to him: 'O, thou forbearing Hillel, many blessings rest upon thy head, because thou has brought me under the
wings of the Divine Presence.'

"Later, all of the three proselytes happened to meet in one
place and they said: 'O, the impatience of Shammai could drive
us out of this world, but the patience of Hillel brought us under
the wings of the Divine Presence' *(Talmud Bavli, Shabbath,
31–a)."*

The patience and humility of Hillel were practiced by the
Hassidic teachers in order to elevate the simple masses to the
heights of devotion, faith and brotherhood.

It is related that the Besht consoled a bereaved mother with a
story about a princely proselyte: "A woman who had long
yearned in vain for motherhood, at last gave birth to a son. But
after two years of happiness, she lost her child. Thereupon the
Baal Shem Tov told the weeping mother the story of a childless
king in a distant land who had vainly consulted all his magicians
on how he might secure an heir for his throne. Finally one of them
advised him to forbid the Jews of his realm to exercise their
faith; for only the prayers born of their despair would be able to
move God to give him a son. The king issued the prohibition.
The pious community was shaken with grief and terror. The
dreadful cries of the Jews rose to heaven. Then one of the
transfigured souls in Paradise was seized with compassion and
came before God, offering to return from the nether spheres as
the son of the king.

"The prince was born; but because his soul was supernal, he stood so high above all men that his father could find no teachers who would be able to do him justice; until a stranger instructed him in the Jewish faith and he, burning with Holy fervor, abandoned the palace and became a Jew.

"When, after the Prince's death, the soul whose compassion had moved it to sacrifice itself for Israel, stood before the Divine Tribunal, only a trifling charge was brought against it: that it had spent the first years of his life amid the pomp and worldly vanity of a royal court. In order to atone, it would have to descend to earth once more, to be nursed by a pious Jewess. The Besht asked the sorrowing mother: 'Dost thou, pious woman, regret having nourished a sainted soul for two years?' "

The concluding adoration of each of the three daily Jewish prayers emphasizes the hope in the Messianic spiritual redemption of humanity.

"We therefore hope in Thee, O Lord our God, that we may speedily behold the glory of Thy might, when Thou wilt remove the abominations from the earth, and heathendom will be utterly destroyed; when the world will be perfected under the kingdom of the Almighty, and all the children of flesh will call upon Thy name, when Thou wilt turn unto Thyself all evil-doers upon earth.

"Let all the inhabitants of the world perceive and know that unto Thee every knee must bow, every tongue must swear allegiance. Before Thee, O Lord our God, let them bow and worship; and unto Thy glorious Name let them give honor; let them all accept the yoke of Thy kingdom, and do Thou reign over them speedily, and for ever and ever. For the kingdom is Thine, and to all eternity Thou wilt reign in glory; as it is written in Thy Torah: 'The Lord shall reign for ever and ever' (Ex. 15:18). And it is said: 'And the Lord shall be King over all the earth; in that day shall the Lord be One and His name One.' " (Zech. 14:9).

II

R. Israel Baal Shem Tov:
In the Shade of the Lord

"The Lord is thy shade" (Ps. 121:5). Just as the shadow does what the human being does, so the Almighty conducts himself according to the deeds of every human being.

(Sefer Mevasser Tsedek.)

R. ISRAEL, the son of Eliezer, the Baal Shem Tov, the Possessor of the Good Name, appeared in Jewish life—"became revealed" according to Hassidic terminology—during a critical period in the life of Eastern European Jewry. The pseudo-messiah Sabbatai Zvi (1626–1676) had ended his adventurous career by adopting the Mohammedan faith, thus causing great disappointment among the naive masses who had believed that the Messianic redemption was at hand because of the great sufferings experienced during the massacres of the 300,000 Jews by the Cossacks (1648–1649), under the leadership of the Ukrainian "Hetman" Bogdan Chmielnitzky. The adventurous activities of another pseudo-messiah, Jacob Frank (1726–1791), also brought additional havoc in Jewish Life. Frank and his closest followers adopted Catholicism, and, in their vengeful activities against their opponents within Jewry, heaped various false accusations against the Jews and their teachings, leading to the burning of the Talmud. According to tradition, R. Israel Baal Shem Tov participated in the disputations of the Jews with the Frankists. Nevertheless, the deterioration of

Jewish life in Poland, in the Ukraine, and in the provinces of Podolyah and Vohlynia, took on catastrophic proportions. It was in these days that the Besht, as the Baal Shem Tov is called in the Hebrew abbreviation of the name, established his Hassidic movement. In the beginning, many believed Hassidut to be just another pseudo-messianic sect, and this is the reason why even at the outset Hassidism had to face the counter-actions of opponents, known under the Hebrew name, *Mitnagdim*. Strong as the opposition was, however, even greater was the determination of the early Hassidim to spread the teachings of their beloved master to console and elevate the masses who had been neglected by the scholars. The latter were too absorbed in their studies to interpret Jewish religious law to pay attention to the needs of those who had to observe the clarified precepts.

Israel ben Eliezer, the "Possessor of the Good Name" (1700–1760), was born in the Podolyan-Ukranian town of Okup where he acquired his first knowledge of basic Jewish studies, including the teachings of Jewish mysticism, known as Kabbalah.

Tradition relates that when Israel was very young, there lived in the vicinity of Vienna, the Austrian capital, a mystic named Adam Baal Shem. He possessed a book of mystic teachings, and one day when he realized that he would soon die, he commanded his son to journey to Okup and present the book to young Israel. Soon after, in order to prepare himself for the great task before him, Israel left for Brody, a city of great scholars where he had a better chance to continue his preparations for the future. Acting as mediator in disputes, his abilities to bring peace among men gained him the position of a teacher's helper in a local "kheder," as the one-room Jewish schools were called. R. Ber of Mezritch, upon whose shoulders fell the yoke of leadership after the passing of the Besht, later told his disciples: "I wish people would kiss the Holy Torah in the same manner the Besht used to kiss the children when he gathered them to bring them to their studies." After Israel married the sister of aristocratic, scholarly R. Gershon of Kutov, who had opposed the match, the couple settled in a village between Kosov and Kutov, and there they derived their livelihood from the sale of clay and bitumen. Israel secretly continued his studies, and when by coincidence the Rabbi of Kolomiya visited Israel's home, he was greatly impressed by his manner of prayer and his general way of life. Israel spent many solitary hours in the surroundings forests, and when necessary brought healing to the sick and succor to the distressed. Among his important activities in those days was the collecting of large sums of money "for the ransoming of captives", to bail out needy Jewish innkeepers who had been arrested by the lordly village owners for failure to pay the annual rental.

At the age of thirty-six, R. Israel settled in Tlust where he became popular as a healer and helper. From Tlust, he moved to Medzibozh, and among the followers and disciples that gathered around him there, were some pietists older than himself. But they became his Hassidim after he expounded the new ways of serving God with joy rather than by means of fasting, asceticism and other forms of self-mortification. Some of those who became his followers had previously been among his bitterest opponents. Among those who joined the Besht, were R. Ber, the Maggid (Preacher) of Mezritch; R. Yaakov Yosef of Polonoah, later the author of Hassidic works and the first biographer of the Baal Shem Tov; R. Pinkhas of Koretz; and R. Nakhum of Chernoble—all of whom in later years gained popularity as Hassidic leaders in their own right.

The Besht had one daughter, Odell, and an only son, Zvi, who had been asked by his father not to engage in rabbinic activity. Odell married R. Yekhiel Ashkenazi, and she was the mother of three children, two of whom became Hassidic leaders: R. Barukh of Medzibozh and R. Moshe Khayim Ephrayim of Sadilkov. Odell's daughter, Feigeh, married R. Simkha, son of the pietist R. Nakhman of Horodenka, one of the Besht's earliest disciples. To R. Simkha and Feigeh was born a son whom they named Nakhman, in later years known as R. Nakhman of Bratzlav, the great master of story-telling and ethical teachings.

When the Besht became ill and realized that his end was approaching, he consoled the disciples who had gathered around his bed: "I am not worried at all, for I know that I am leaving through one door and entering through another door."

The Besht himself left no books, but his teachings were written down by his disciples, chiefly by R. Yaakov Yosef of Polonoah, and gathered also by his grandson Moshe Khayim Ephrayim. Many had assumed that the prolific writer, R. Yaakov Yosef, would become the heir of the Besht, but the Baal Shem Tov himself named R. Ber of Mezritch to take over the leadership after his demise.

TEACHINGS OF THE BESHT

From what he advised others to do, we know of the Besht's schedule:

"Be very punctual always to arise at midnight, and turn your nights into days. A person should sleep several hours during the day so that he need only little sleep during the night."

He disapproved strongly of self-importance and haughty behavior on the part of the scholars. Criticizing the conceit of the learned, he insisted that certain scholars were so engrossed in their studies that they often forgot that there is a Creator and that human beings are his children.

Knowing that he was being scoffed at, and that the same fate was in store for his spiritual heirs and disciples, he warned them against fear of others and simultaneously cautioned them against seeking undue honor and popularity:

> Be absolutely indifferent to popular approval or disapproval. . . To achieve this indifference, practice constant devotion to the Creator, which leaves little opportunity for petty thoughts. . . If you wish to live long, don't become famous.
> *(S. Setzer: R. Yisroel Baal Shem Tov, New York; A Treasury of Jewish Quotations, New York, 1956.)*

The Besht was not considered a great scholar, and there is some doubt whether his learning was above mediocrity, but he had great understanding of both the spirit of Judaism and the spiritual needs of the simple Jewish masses. He taught them faith and hope by means of joyously lifting oneself and one's fellows from daily reality to the pietistic reality of Love of God and happy brotherhood. While accepted rabbinical teaching was the teaching of religious law, the Besht's Hassidism added emotion to the practice of Jewish law. R. Mendel of Kotzk, himself one of the great Hassidic teachers of his time, epigrammatically characterized the difference between the Hassidim and their opponents, the Mitnagdim: "The Hassid is in fear of Heaven; the Mitnaged is in fear of the *Code*" (Jewish religious laws).

The Besht said of himself and of the *Tsadikim,* his pious followers and heirs to leadership:

> I came into the world to show another way, to cultivate love of

God, of Israel, and of the Torah, and there is no need for fasting
and mortification.

The *Tzadik* must descend to the level of the people, to make
them understand the word of God.
*(Kether Shem Tob; Baruch of Mezbizh, Butzina de Nehora, 1880;
A Treasury of Jewish Quotations, New York, 1956.)*

R. Nakhman of Bratzlav, one of the greatest figures Hassidut
has produced, said of his great-grandfather, the Besht, that he
knew the language of the violin. R. Nakhman echoed this in a
story that had been told by the Besht's grandson, R. Moshe-
Khayim Ephrayim of Sadilkov:

"I heard this from my grandfather: Once a fiddler played so
sweetly that all who heard him began to dance, and whoever came
near enough to hear, joined in the dance. Then a deaf man who
knew nothing of music, happened along, and to him all he saw
seemed the action of madmen—senseless and in bad taste."
(Buber: Tales of the Hasidim, Early Masters, p. 53.)

The Besht often told folk-stories to his disciples. Once, noting
their surprise, he told them the following parable:

"A king sent his son to take charge of a fortress situated near
the frontier. He informed him that the enemy was planning an
attack in the near future, and instructed him to store within the
fortress all food procurable. If he could not secure food of superior
quality, he was to fill every storehouse with food of poor grade.
Though the king's counsel did not seem necessary to him, the prince
obeyed. The siege of the fort continued a long time, and the coarse
food in the end proved the safeguard against surrender.

"Likewise, my friends, store in your memory those common tales
I narrate to you, as well as the teachings which seem to you pro-
found. In your work among the people, everything will prove
useful."

(Meoroth Ha Gedolim, p. 11; Newman: Hassidic Anthology, p. 345.)

Great religious thoughts of a universal character are imbedded in the teachings of the Besht about knowledge of God and about the values of prayer and faith. In his teachings, he stressed that in His manifestations, the Creator is often concealed and He reveals Himself in acts that to humans seem concealed; and so when someone comprehends even a small part of the unity of the Almighty, he comprehends His entire unity.

> People should get to know what the unity of God really means. To attain a part of this indivisible unity is to attain the whole. The Torah and all its ordinances are from God. If I, therefore, fulfill but one commandment in and through the love of God, it is as though I have fulfilled them all.
> *(Solomon Schechter: Studies in Judaism, Vol. I, p. 29.)*

An echo of the Besht's reaction to the forces in Jewish life which opposed his teachings, is found in the following statement:

> "I have made all things equal in my eyes, because 'I have set the Lord always before me' (Ps. 16:8). It is immaterial to me whether I'm praised or abused. I've reached a state of absolute equanimity, because of my all-absorbing consciousness of God, which leaves no room for concern with anything else."
> *(Tzavatt Ribash, 1797.)*

Talking to himself, he asked: "I wonder, O body of mine, that up to now you have not yet crumbled because of fear of the Almighty?"

The Besht conceived of prayers as windows to Heaven and the entire world as a prayer-house. Therefore, "A man needs no fixed place to say his prayers, no synagogues; among the trees of the forest, everywhere one can pray." (S. A. Horodetzky: Leaders of Hassidism, London, 1928, p. 10). Prayer, if offered from the heart and for the sake of Heaven, even though the worshipper does not know its meaning, ascends on high and pierces the firmament." (Or Yesharim).

According to the Besht, a joyful prayer is certainly more acceptable to the Almighty than a prayer in sadness and weeping, but whatever the character of the prayer, one should remember to pray for the redemption of the soul that is in captivity to the evil inclination. He explained:

> Pray not for material prosperity: a partition rises when the material is introduced into the spiritual.
> *(S. A. Horodetzky: Leaders of Hassidism, London, 1928, p. 10.)*

> The main thing in worship is the feeling of oneness with God, the ecstasy with which one serves Him and studies Torah, the attitude which is free of selfish motivation.
> *(Keter Shem Tov.)*

> Before you can find God, you must lose yourself. If a man after prayer be conscious of the least pride or self-satisfaction . . . then let him know that he has prayed not to God but to himself. And what is this but disguised idolatry?
> *(Solomon Schechter: Studies in Judaism, Vol. I, p. 30.)*

Warning his disciples against prayers without sincerity, the Besht stressed that spiritual bastards are born when the beautiful and holy words of prayer become mixed with one's unbecoming thoughts. "One moment of worship, motivated by joy and love, is better than a hundred fasts . . . And when God wants to punish man, He deprives him of faith." *(Derekh Ha Emunah U Masseh Rav; Keter Shem Tov.)*

The Besht interpreted a biblical passage:

"But from thence you will seek the Lord thy God; and thou
shalt find Him if thou search after Him with all thy heart and
with all thy Soul" (Deut. 4:29), means that only from "thence,"
from the place where one finds himself at the particular time, even
if it is not a high place, even from "thence" one can find God and
attach himself to the Blessed Name.
(Tzeror HaHayim.)

The Besht also warned his followers against relying too much
even on their own leaders, no matter how great their piety. He
quoted from the Holy Scriptures to substantiate his statement,
"Happy is the people that know the joyful shout, they walk,
O Lord, in the light of Thy countenance." (Ps. 89:16). The
Besht explained the passage with a parable: "Once upon a
time there was a country that had a single mighty warrior. All
inhabitants relied on that valiant man and none engaged in
military training. Suddenly a war broke out, and the clever
enemy stole, one by one, each of the weapons that had been
prepared for him. So the entire population came under the
enemy's domination." And this is what the Psalmist meant:
When the people do not rely upon an individual hero, but "they
know the joyful shout" of battle, then "they walk in the light"
towards their Sovereign, and they do not rely upon individual
heroes."

While the Besht emphasized the importance of the individual,
he also reminded his disciples of the specific limitations of man,
which would place him on the level of animals if he were not
to exercise self-control. Just as the human being is limited to
a specific size, he said, so is everything in his mind also limited
to specific measure; but all human tasks have an inner purpose.
One should learn pride, but not become proud; one should learn

anger, but never become angry; likewise one should learn all other forms of human behavior. Everyone has to emulate the Almighty Who combines the strictness of law with the utmost compassion. True, human thought is tied to the human body. It is nevertheless open to impressions from the heavenly world.

"There are two kinds of vision: physical and spiritual. He who sanctifies his eyes and does not look where he is not supposed to, he is blessed in time with spiritual vision. But he who contaminates his eyes loses the ability to see things in a spiritual manner."

The Besht stressed that all human desires and pleasures can be sublimated into positive deeds, just as the love of parents for their children gives them courage to face the difficulties of family life, and thus such love enhances the existence of the world. This is why the Almighty has given us the spark that is transformed into the flame of love. The same is true of other human feelings and desires, since all are a result of the sparks of holiness. Opposing the excessive fasting and self-denial practised by many pietists of his time, the Besht taught his followers to enjoy both the wonders and mysteries of the world, since "everything above and below is one unity." Explaining the character of miracles, he said: "Anything that happens for the first time in nature, is a miracle, but after that it becomes a part of nature." *(Keter Shem Tov.)*

It is related:

A naturalist came from a great distance to see the Baal Shem and said: "My investigations show that in the course of nature the Red Sea had to divide at the very hour the children of Israel passed through it. Now what about that famous miracle?" The Baal Shem answered: "Don't you know that God created nature?

And he created it so that at the hour the children of Israel passed through the Red Sea, it had to divide. That is the great and famous miracle!"
(Buber: Tales of the Hasidim, Early Masters, p. 71.)

Emphasizing that life in this world is not only a means to gain a place in the World-to-Come, in after-life, but also an end in itself, the Besht dwelt often on the necessity of joy so that the stresses of life be lightened and sweetened. He illustrated it with a biblical passage: "And when they (the Israelites) came to Marah, they could not drink of the waters of Marah, for they were bitter" (Exod. 15:23). Yet not the waters were bitter, but there was bitterness within them, so the waters tasted bitter."

Since sadness interferes with faith and prayer, said the Besht, one may cry only through happiness. One should always be joyful and believe wholeheartedly that the Divine Radiance watches over him (Tzavaat Ribash); thus those who live joyfully, live according to the desire of the Almighty.

If the vision of a beautiful woman, or of any lovely thing, comes suddenly to a man's eyes, let him ask himself: whence this beauty if not from the divine force which permeates the world? and why be attracted by the part? better be drawn after the All! . . . Such perception of beauty is an experience of the Eternal.
(Tzavaat Ribash, A Treasury of Jewish Quotations.)

Who speaks of worldly matters and religious matters as though they were distinct, is a heretic . . . Pleasures are manifestations of God's love. . . . The important thing is not how many separate injunctions are obeyed, but how and in what spirit we obey them.
(Solomon Schechter: Studies in Judaism, I, pp. 28–29.)

"Consider and see that the Lord is good" (Ps. 34:9) is a passage often quoted by the Besht.

In his opposition to extensive fasting, practiced by many pietists of his time, the Besht emphasized that one can worship God even by means of eating in such a manner that the food becomes a form of thanksgiving, and the table is transformed into an altar. He also explained that:"People should take special care to be healthy. When someone is ill, no matter how meritorious are his deeds, he is not in a position to serve God properly." *(Keter Shem Tov).*

> Said the Besht: "When you eat and take pleasure in the taste and sweetness of the food, bear in mind that it is the Lord who has placed into the food its taste and sweetness. You will, then, truly serve Him by your eating."
> *(Midrash Ribash Tov, Hassidic Anthology, p. 86.)*

According to the Besht, in every garment a person puts on, every kind of food he eats, every vessel he uses, he enjoys the life-factor, the vitality that is contained in all things. In truth, everything possesses attributes of all that is present in the world; but the human being has the free will, the power of choice to incline towards the elements he desires.

The precept "Love thy neighbor as thyself" (Lev. 19:18) is a fundamental teaching in Hassidut, and the Besht conveyed it in different forms. He voiced the thought that the human being was created with two eyes, so that with one eye he could see his own faults and shortcomings, and with the other eye, he could see virtues of his fellows.

> It is not good for a man to be alone, for he cannot know his own defects. By observing the acts which he dislikes in a fellowman, he can see his own defects as in a mirror. He would not have been given the opportunity to note his comrade's offense if he had not been unconsciously guilty in some degree of the same offense.

Likewise, if a man is disturbed in his study or worship by his neighbor's revelries, it is a sign from Heaven that his interest has been turning in the wrong direction, and he should commence afresh with the proper intention.

(Keter Shem Tov, p. 21–B; Newman: Hassidic Anthology, p. 430.)

Once the Besht said to a man of great piety: "How can you reprove others for their wrong-doings if all your life you live separated from human beings and you do not even know what their sins consist of? *(Amtakhat Binyomin)*. The wise man learns from the deeds of others. Just as when a man who looks into the mirror, notices his own blemishes, so when one sees a deficiency in someone else, he realizes that he also possesses something of the same" *(Toledoth Yaakov Yoseph)*.

The Besht expounded the idea that if one judges his fellow favorably, he will find a way to influence him favorably. In addition, every human being is judged in heaven according to the verdicts he pronounced against others when he noticed them committing transgressions. Why so? Because such people forget that they have committed the very same sins for which they demand punishment for others. Those who preach to others about exemplary behavior, while they themselves behave quite differently from what they preach, are like brooms: they clean floors and pavements, but they themselves remain dirty.

Preaching ethical behavior, the Besht expounded ideas on the various aspects of human characteristics and deeds.

There is no sphere in heaven where the soul remains a shorter time than in the sphere of merit; there is none where it abides longer than in the sphere of grace (love).

One should not consider himself more important than the next man as regards piety and the service of the Almighty. The worm

serves God with all its strength. Let everyone remember that he is
not better than the worm and that all are dependent on the Creator
who gave them all power that they possess.

If you have a strong desire to abuse someone, abuse yourself;
and if you wish to praise someone, praise God. There is no room
for God in him who is full of himself.

Silence is better than talk because in silence one can think of
God's greatness, but when one talks, no matter how important
the subject, there usually creeps in a desire to show one's own
importance.

*(Tzavd'ath HaRivash: Solomon Schechter: Studies in Judaism,
Vol. I, p. 31; J. S. Minkin: Romance of Hassidism, p. 371.)*

The Besht's disciple and heir to the leadership of Hassidism,
R. Ber, the Maggid (Preacher) of Mezritch related a biblical
interpretation by his master:

"Truth springeth out of the earth" (Ps. 85:12). If truth grows so
easily, then why is truth so rare? Because no one wishes to bend
down to pick up the truth. To find truth, one must bend down
humbly. . . . What does it mean when people say that truth goes
all over the world? It means that truth is driven out of one place
after another, and must wander on and on.

(Darash Tov, p. 10; Tales of the Hassidim, Early Masters, p. 71.)

Realizing the frailties of the human body against the powerful
forces of desire and passion, the Besht crystalized the idea of
repentance without self-punishment. He proclaimed that everything draws sustenance from God's Divine Presence; that is why
evil can be a rung in the ladder to good if the possessor of evil
inclinations will choose to use it properly. The miser can devote
his time to study since he needs not much to sustain him materially; a bit of pride is not unbecoming to a scholar, and firmness
is necessary in battle against blasphemers.

The bad is often a chair for the good. In each movement of man there is the Creator . . . even in evil. Sinners are mirrors. When we see in them faults, we must realize that they but reflect the evil in us. Each penitent thought is a voice of God. Sometimes the evil inclination leads one astray by giving him the feeling of guilt for a serious transgression and this causes the person great sadness which interferes with his service to the Almighty. One should understand this trick of the evil inclination, and, instead of being saddened, serve God with greater joy and he will be forgiven the transgression which was probably minor but the evil inclination made it seem to have been of great importance.

(Tzavaath HaRivash; S. Schechter, Studies in Judaism, I, p. 31.)

The Besht used a parable to illustrate how negative physical passion can be turned into a positive quest for knowledge:

Once upon a time there was a king who wanted his son to learn various sciences. So he hired a number of scholars to be his tutors. When the prince had made no progress, all the tutors were disappointed and left the palace, except for one tutor who refused to give up. Once the prince saw a beautiful maiden and he desired to possess her. So the scholar complained about it to the king. The king replied: "Since my son has a desire for the physical, the very same desire can lead him to knowledge and wisdom." Later, the king ordered that the beautiful girl be brought to the palace, and he commanded her that if the prince asked her to give in to his passion for her, she should refuse unless he would first acquire the knowledge of one science, and every time she should repeat the same condition. The maiden did so, and because of the prince's physical desire, he became a learned man.

(Keter Shem Tov.)

The Besht interpreted a biblical passage in a symbolic manner: "When thou goest forth to battle against thine enemies, and the Lord thy God delivereth them unto you, and thou carriest them away captive" (Deut. 21:10), what is meant is that when you are in continuous battle with your enemy, which is the evil inclinations, you can 'carry them away captive' and learn from them how to conduct battles; and the perseverance that they use to capture you, you can likewise use to capture them.

When everyone will redeem his soul from captivity to the evil inclinations, the general redemption will take place, assured the Besht. The very same assurance is given by Hassidut to its followers in our own generation.

III

R. Dov Ber, Heir to the Besht
And First of a Dynasty

AFTER THE PASSING of the Besht, his spiritual heir, R. Dov Ber the Maggid (Preacher), moved the center of Hassidism from Medzibozh to Mezritch, but not without some opposition. In the beginning, a group of the Besht's disciples forced his son R. Zvi to be his father's heir, but within the year he notified the Hassidim that he had seen his father in a dream and was told by him that R. Ber should take his place. R. Ber's legs were crippled and he had to use crutches. Commenting on this defect, the Besht said of his disciple: "I know that this bear has sick legs, but he has strong hands to take human hearts and bring them under the wings of God's Divine Presence."

R. Ber (1704–1772) was born in Lukatch, where his father was a teacher of small material means. At an early age, Ber was sent to Lvov (Lemberg) where he studied in the Yeshiva (Academy) of R. Yaakov Yehoshuah, a Talmudic giant whose work *Pnay Yehoshuah (The Face of Joshua)* is still studied and relied upon by scholars of traditional Judaism. After his marriage, R. Ber moved to Torchin and later became a teacher in a nearby village. In his spare time, R. Ber broadened his knowledge and devoted many hours to the study of Jewish mysticism. Being a gifted speaker and interpreter of Jewish laws, morals and ethics, he was given the position of Maggid at Torchin. Later he occupied the same position, first in Koretz and then in Dubno. He was among the early disciples of R. Israel Baal Shem Tov, and his gifts as a preacher helped him spread the teachings of Hassidut from the Ukraine to other Jewish population centers in Eastern Europe. His own great scholarly attainments influenced other scholars to join the new movement. Among R. Ber's disciples were a number of young men who became, in time, Hassidic leaders in their own right, such as R. Nakhum of Chernoble, R. Levi Yitzkhak of Berdichev, R. Shneur Zalman of Ladi, later founder of the Khabad-Lubavitcher intellectual trend in Hassidism; also the brothers R. Zusheh of Annipol and R. Elimelekh of Lizhensk, and the brothers R. Shmuel Shmelkeh and R. Pinkhas Hurwitz. R. Ber's disciples wrote down his teachings which later were published in the volumes *Maggid Devorov L' Yaakov* (*He Declareth His Word Unto Jacob*, Ps. 147:19), *"Or Torah"* (*Light of the Torah*) and *Or HaEemet* (*Light of the Truth*). R. Ber was the first of a Hassidic dynasty that has been continuous to our own day. He had an only son, Avrohom, who because of his great piety and asceticism, was known as "Avrohom Malakh" (Abraham the Angel). R. Avrohom's partner in his studies was young Shneur Zalman of Ladi; but generally the son of the Maggid lived in seclusion and self-mortification, contrary to his father's Hassidic opposition to such forms of service to God.

R. Ber prayed with great fervor. He was once asked about the source of his fervor in prayer and service. R. Ber replied: "He who needs fire looks for it in the ashes."

About R. Ber's ways of leading the simple people among his Hassidim, the following story is related:

During his stay in Mezritch, the Rabbi of Kolbashow saw an old man come to the Great Maggid and ask him to impose penance on him for his sins. "Go home," said the Maggid. "Write all your sins down on a slip of paper and bring it to me." When the man brought him the list, he merely glanced at it. Then he said, "Go home. All is well." But later the rav observed that Rabbi Ber read the list and laughed at every line. This annoyed him. How could anyone laugh at sins!

For years he could not forget the incident, until once he heard someone quote a saying of the Baal Shem: "It is well-known that no one commits a sin unless the spirit of folly possesses him. But what does the sage do if a fool comes to him? He laughs at all this folly, and while he laughs, a breath of gentleness is wafted through the world. What was rigid, thaws, and what was a burden becomes light." The rav reflected. In his soul he said: "Now I understand the laughter of the Holy Maggid."

(Buber: Tales of the Hasidim, Early Masters, p. 109.)

According to R. Ber's teachings, the will of God and the will of the true Tzadik complement each other because the will of the true Hassidic leader agrees with the will of the Almighty.

As the number of Hassidim grew, R. Ber felt that the burden of leadership was too heavy upon him: Once he cried out the question: "Have I really sinned so much as to be punished with great popularity?"

Preaching the necessity of appreciating what the Creator has prepared for human beings, the Maggid told his followers that by making use of God's bounties and by changing them into forms fit to be used by humans, everyone thus becomes an associate of the Almighty in continuing the creative process (*Or HAEmet*). And while it is true that there are many idol-worshippers in the world, there are, nevertheless, sparks of holiness even in idolatry, because the whole world is full of God's glory. In this sense, he conveyed the following thoughts:

The whole world is divinity. The world rests on divinity and we walk in divinity. There is divinity in everything; divinity sustains everything. The Holy One, blessed be He, has vested himself in this low world. Yet, there are people who believe that the Holy One, blessed be He, does not permeate this earth. But this is because of the great light that He brings into the world. It is comparable to a great light that blinds a person so that he is unable to see.

Everything in the world is full of divinity. The Holy One, blessed be He, is called "Ein Sof" (Without End): He is not called "Ein Reshit" (Without Beginning). If He were without beginning, we should not be able to speak about Him at all. After all, our conception of Him is by virtue of His creations which is but a beginning and not an end.

The Holy One, blessed be He, is called "Rest" for the term "movement" does not apply to Him at all. For movement applies only to a thing which is bounded by time and place. But the Holy One, blessed be He, is called "Rest" for concerning Him there is no conception of movement or of time.

Were it not for the active force of Creation, the whole world would be nothingness. For that reason, therefore, the Universe and everything therein is but an active force of God.

Every Heavenly Gate requires the proper key to open it, namely the proper prayer with sincere intention. This, however, is a slow process. Let us act like the thief who breaks through every door without keys. Let us open all Gates of Heaven by breaking through our hearts of flint.

Evil, too, is good in that it is the lowest degree of perfect goodness, but when man sins thereby it becomes truly evil. The broom, for example, has some goodness in it. Although it is of a low degree, it is nonetheless good.

(Keter Shem Tov, p. 18–A; Newman: Hassidic Anthology, p. 474; Steinman: The Garden of Hassidism, pp. 165–169; Buber: Tales of the Hasidim, Early Masters, p. 103.)

While the Besht generally used parables about a king and his children, in order to illustrate the attitude of God to humanity and the relation of human beings to God, R. Ber used parables about a father (God) and his actions as regards the children (Humanity) that he had brought into the world.

"But from thence ye will seek the Lord thy God, and thou shalt find Him. You must cry to God and call him 'father' until he becomes your father."

A child riding a hobby-horse, derives great pleasure from it, although unlike the horse that carries man, it is the child here that carries the horse. The child's father who rejoices in his child's pleasures, helps him and is always ready to give him a stick in order to provide joy to his son. Similarly, with the *Tzaddikim* who desire to lead the world, and the Holy One, blessed be He, derives great satisfaction from the joy that His followers derive from their leadership.

When a father sees his child from a distance, playing with children of his own age, he approaches him. And when the child espies his father it at once leaves off the games and childish occupations and runs after his father calling him: "Father, father." But when the father sees his son running after him, he pretends not to notice him and continues on his way in order to increase the child's yearnings for him so that he may continue to call: "Father, father." This gives the father great pleasure in that he perceives the wisdom of the child who is prepared to leave off his games, and it shows that nothing is so important to him as his love for his father. The father, however, tries to hide himself from him, in order to induce the child to spurn his childish occupations and to follow him. But this sense of pleasure is followed by a sense of pity in the father's heart in that he has disturbed his child's enjoyments and games. But the father's joy at beholding his son's love for him passes over also to the son. It follows, therefore, that the great joy of the father which passes over also to the son, was brought about by means of diminution and contraction: in that the father, to begin with, diminished and hemmed in his love for his child and the child reduced his childish ways. The Holy One, blessed be He, also created the world by means of diminution, because of his great love of us. And when we reduce our mundane pleasures for the sake of our love for the Lord, we cause Him satisfaction, and from Him pleasure in great profusion passes over to us.

There is the parable of the boy who joined a group of unruly children with whom he ran about in wild chase, so that a thorn entered his foot. This caused him a little pain. Came his father and wanted to remove the thorn from the leg, but the child did not allow him to touch it for fear that the extraction might be very painful. But the father took him in his hands and removed the thorn from his leg against his will. In the child's opinion the father acted cruelly toward him, because the pain of extraction is greater than the pain of the thorn entering the flesh. In truth, however, this was a healing and not a torture, because if the thorn had not been removed a festering wound would have ensued in the leg. One can see, therefore, that the father's fear cannot be compared to the child's fear. The father feared lest the wound suppurate and fester, the child feared the remedy. If, however, the child had understanding, his fear would have been on a par with his father's concern.

This we gather from the verse: "What doth the Lord thy God require of thee, but to fear the Lord thy God," namely, that thou shalt have the same fear as thy Father in Heaven. And just as He is concerned about thy future, be thou also concerned. This is the true meaning of "Fear of Heaven."
(Steinman: The Garden of Hassidism, p. 169–171.)

R. Ber knew human psychology, and used the first chapters of the biblical Book of Genesis to illustrate and explain negative traits. He maintained that in every human being are to be found the characteristics of Cain and Abel, of the Generation of the Flood and of the Generation of the Tower of Babel. Cain and Abel are the essence of jealousy; the Generation of the Flood means human lust; the Generation of the Tower of Babel symbolizes the passion to be honored. But every human being is also part of God Above. Man was created last so that he is rooted in all the worlds created before him, and a human being's thoughts are called "The World of Freedom."

Therefore, one should separate himself from physical desires and strive for spiritual heights, reaching unity with the Almighty; thus he will really become a human being. Why so? Because the human being is a part of God above, and when he attaches his thoughts to the higher spheres, it enables him to know what transpires there. Every human being is a small world in himself and, being a microcosm, he should consider himself as one of the Upper World. Compared to the world above, this world is but a mustard grain, and when one acts properly, he should not mind whether others like it or not, because their love or hate is of no value at all. Whatever a person sees, he should endeavor to draw from it the proper conclusion.

Fear of God, stressed R. Ber, is awe of majesty and not fear of punishment. A person should always have the realization that the good he does here, in this world, causes great joy in the Upper World. Every human being is himself a small world. He possesses spiritual attributes, one different from the others, but all are rooted in the Upper Worlds of spirituality (*Or HaEmeth*).

A man's kind deeds are utilized by the Lord as seed for the planting of trees in the Garden of Eden; thus, each man created his own Paradise. The reverse is true when he commits transgressions.

Vitality is but a spark of the Holy One, blessed be He. It is an offspring of God the King. It is the desire of the spark to cleave to its Father and Maker.

Whatever man sees or hears is not just casual. Everywhere there are holy sparks that are constantly yearning to be united with their source. Each spark desires to be united with and cleave to its like, such as love to love, and splendour to splendour.

Man must study pride but not be proud; he must study anger but not give way to anger himself, and similarly with all human traits. For he must be perfect in all the attributes of the Holy One, blessed be He, and God Almighty has the trait of justice tempered with mercy.

(Eser Arot, p. 32; Newman: Hassidic Anthology, p. 1 Steinman: The Garden of Hassidism, p. 167–169.)

In the volumes of *Maggid Devorov L' Yaakov, Or Torah* and *OR HaEmet,* the following ideas of R. Ber are included in different formulations:

I. As regards the ways and actions of the Almighty, many people are to be compared to the backwoodsman who comes to town and notices the tailor at work. He notices the tailor is shearing into pieces a roll of silk, and he begins to shout hysterically that the tailor is destroying the material. The backwoodsman does not realize that to cut the silk is an act of improvement.

II. Everything that God created for the world we live in, is a vessel of great wisdom. When one is merited to comprehend intellectually the Infinite, it means that the Divine Presence has been revealed to him.

III. Through faith, the truth within himself makes a person become properly clothed and he is able to motivate his deeds. This means that faith is transformed into a vessel for truth.

IV. When you look at a vessel, you should realize that the material it is made of has very little value, but its beauty is a result of the inspiration of the person who formed the vessel.

v. When one sees a beautiful woman, let him think that if she were dead, she would not be beautiful. So he must realize that beauty is a result of Divine power. Why should one attach himself to a part of beauty when he can attach himself to the source of and root of all the worlds that all beauty comes from?

vi. Every letter in the alphabet is a world by itself, and God's spirit dwells separately in each letter. The words one utters are the garments of his thoughts, and when a person is speaking he reveals the thoughts in his mind. Words and intentions are a unity of mind and soul. Thought always strives to become voice in order to be expressed by means of words.

vii. Joy without thought is folly and mockery.

viii. Satisfaction from eating comes to the human being from the spiritual strength within the food and not from its bodily form. Thus the pleasure from eating a meal is not physical but spiritual. This means that also in this world we can attain the joys of Paradise.

ix. Where there is division, there must be quarrel and war.

x. The end of a thing is its purpose. When one sees something happen, he does not understand immediately the reason for it, but in the end, the purpose becomes clear.

R. Avrohom HaMalakh, (1741–1776) the ascetic-angelic, only son of R. Ber, wished to live the life of the pietists in the form of pre-Besht Hassidic hermits. His behavior rather than his teachings gained him the great esteem which he did not seek.

R. Avrohom said:

"I have learned a new form of service from the wars of Frederick, king of Prussia. It is not necessary to approach the enemy in order to attack him. In fleeing from him, it is possible to circumvent him as he advances, and fall on him from the rear until he is forced to surrender. What is needed is not to strike straight at Evil but to withdraw to the sources of Divine power, and from there to circle around Evil, bend it, and transform it into its opposite."

Once he visited his father-in-law in Kremnitz. The most distinguished members of the congregation assembled to welcome the holy man. But he turned his back on them and looked out of the window at the mountain at whose foot the city lay. Among those waiting for him, was a man very much aware of his own learning and intent on his own importance. He said impatiently: "Why do you keep staring at the mountain? Have you never seen anything like it before?" The rabbi answered: "I look and am amazed to see how such a lump of earth made much of itself until it grew into a tall mountain."
(Buber: Tales of the Hasidim, Early Masters, pp. 115–116.)

While the angelic R. Avrohom preferred a way of life that only the chosen among the pietists could follow, his son E. Sholem Shakhneh, whose residence was in Prohibisch, blazed the trail to create for Hassidic leadership a form of modesty that would be concealed in outer forms of living befitting the scions of royal families. As a result of Sholem Shakhneh's belief, his son, R. Israel of Ruzhin and his descendants, gave their form of Hassidic leadership the aura of Princes and Dukes. In time, this sparkling form of a Tzadik's life caused a great schism within Hassidut. The wounds have long since healed, and the descendants of R. Ber, spiritual heir of the Besht, occupy a foremost place among the Hassidic Masters of our time. The same dynasty begun by R. Ber of Mezritch, has given modern Hebrew and Yiddish literature several of its most creative spirits in poetry and prose.

IV

R. Yaakov Yoseph:
In the Shadow of the Besht

R. Yaakov Yoseph HaKohen Katz (? –1794) was already
a prominent Rabbi and an eminent scholar when he joined the
group of disciples that surrounded the Besht. The year and place
of his birth are unknown. He had occupied rabbinic positions in
the towns of Shargorod, Rashkov and Polonoah, and is usually
mentioned as the Polonoah Rabbi. He joined the Besht after
having been, for a long time, among his strongest opponents, and
his own piety included fasting and self-mortification in general.
The Besht influenced the much older R. Yaakov Yoseph to join
him in the new way of serving the Almighty with joy and by
making use of all that the world possesses to thank God for His
gifts to humanity. Even after R. Yaakov Yoseph joined the
Besht, it was difficult for him to give up his previous forms of
ascetic behavior. The founder of Hassidut was so happy that R.
Yaakov Yoseph became one of his disciples, that he called him
"Yosseleh," the diminutive of his second name. Once the Besht
cried out in elation: "Master of the Universe! I do not ask to
be rewarded in the World-to-Come for my deeds, but for my
having given you such a Yosseleh."

Because of his having joined the Hassidim, R. Yaakov Yoseph
was driven out of his Rabbinic position in Shargorod. He was a
man of the pen and of the book rather than a leader. Therefore,

it is understandable why the Besht picked R. Dov Ber, the Preacher of Mezritch, to be his heir, instead of R. Yaakov Yoseph.

As is still the custom among writers of traditional scholarly works, the author's name is often included in the title of his work. It took R. Yaakov Yoseph some thirty years to write the source book of Hassidism entitled *Toledot Yaakov Yoseph* (*The Generations of Yaakov Yoseph*). The title is based upon the fusion of two different parts in a biblical sentence: "These are the generations of *Jacob, Joseph* being seventeen years old . . ." (Gen. 37:2). In this work, are embedded the teachings of the Besht. After its publication, the book was ordered burned by the leaders of the Mitnagdim, the opponents of the Hassidim. He wrote three other works in whose titles his name is included: *Ben Porat Yoseph* (*Joseph Is a Fruitful Vine,* based on Gen. 49:22); *Tsofenat Panneah* (*And Pharaoh called Joseph's name Tsofenat Paaneah,* ibid. 41:45) and *Ketonet Passim,* meaning "*Coat of Many Colors*" ("Israel loved Joseph . . . and made him a coat of many colors" Ibid. 37:3). Most teachings of the Besht are known thanks to R. Yaakov Yoseph's talent as a writer. He understood well that the Maggid of Mezritch was better suited than himself for the position of Hassidic leadership, and, announcing his loyalty to R. Ber, he stated: "The Divine Presence took its pouch and left Medzibozh for Mezritch." R. Yaakov Yoseph died in 1782. To this very day, he is popular in Hassidic lore as the "Toledot," which is the first word in the title of his chief work.

R. Yaakov Yoseph was the first Hassidic writer to formulate the role of the Tzadik, the spiritual leader, vis-a-vis his followers. He explained that just as the heart is inward and is the vitality of the body, so are the Tzadikkim the vitality of the world.

The other inhabitants of the world are the bodies that cover the soul like a garment. "The Tzadikkim are the soul and life of the world, and the other people are the body that clothes the soul." (Toledoth Yaakov Yoseph).

The great Hassidic author embodied in his teachings the idea that simple faith and humility make a person satisfied with bare necessities; and because he needs so little in this world, his share in the World-to-Come is very great.

The pleasure of communion with God is beyond the natural pleasure of human beings, and this can be attained only through suffering and by overpowering the evil inclinations.

Punishment from Heaven, underlined R. Yaakov Yoseph, often comes in the form of taking away from a person his confidence and his faith. His bitterness and his doubts are the visible signs of the punishment meted out to him.

> The aim of man is to be the Temple of God.

> Fasting and penance sadden, while devotion is only through joy.

> All our exercises in piety are only introductory to our union with God.

> Since God knows the thoughts of every individual, why are prayers necessary? Because words are needed to create vessels to draw abundance from above.
> (Toledoth Jacob Joseph; S. A. Horodetzky: Leaders of Hassidim, London 1928, p. 31. A Treasury of Jewish Quotations, New York, 1956.)

But what is this world of ours and what is the place of the human beings in it? R. Yaakov Yoseph dwelt on this problem and in various parts of his works he tried to answer the question. He asserted that this world is but a stamp-impression of the World Above. Everything that exists in the Upper World is

to be found in the human soul. The soul descends to this world
that it may attain perfection with the help of the limbs of the
human body. This world is a ladder which is set up on the earth
to prepare for the World-to-Come, so that it's top reaches the
Heights of Heaven. The body of a man is not the man himself;
it is only his garment. Body and soul need each other, as do
husband and wife, because each is only a half-part of a human
being. It is often the case that pleasure of the body causes displeasure for the soul; and pleasure of the soul causes pain to
the body. R. Yaakov Yoseph formulated the same idea twice in
his *Toledot* and in the work *Ben Porat Yoseph:*

> This world is like Jacob's ladder. It is set up on earth and its
> top reaches Heaven (Gen. 28:12). The human beings are the
> Angels of God ascending and descending on the ladder to fulfill
> errands of the Almighty. No one stands constantly on the same
> rung. Often a human being descends in order later to ascend. There
> is no pleasure in living without evil desires and without good
> desires. R' Jacob Joseph made use of a parable about the man who
> learned the trade of a silversmith. He wrote down all details but
> forgot to include in the list that one has to kindle a fire to do
> work. The spark of inspiration is always a necessity.

> This world is a stamped replica of the world above—a ladder
> standing upon the earth, to prepare for the World-to-Come. The
> top of the world-ladder should be made to reach Heaven. Every
> human being is an ascender or a descender. Either he goes up or he
> steps down. All letters that make up words are spiritual vessels. He
> who seeks pleasures, realizes soon that constant pleasure is no
> pleasure at all.
> (*Toledot Yaakov Yoseph; Ben Porat Yoseph.*)

Commenting on the biblical precept, "Thou shalt love thy
neighbor as thyself" (Lev. 19:18), R. Yaakov Yoseph asked:
"How is it possible to love one's neighbor if he is evil and

love the wicked person?" And he gave the answer: "See to it
that he is like yourself, and then he will become like yourself."
(Toledot Yaakov Yoseph.)

"No leaven be seen in thee, neither . . . in all thy borders"
(Exod. 13:7). Let nothing stale or sour be seen in you, and you
will not see it in others.

One must not pass all the time in study; one must also seek inter-
course with people.
*(Toledot Jacob Joseph; Tzofnat Paaneah; S. A. Horodetzky: Leaders
of Hassidism, London, 1928, p. 33; A Treasury of Jewish Quotations, New York 1956.)*

Ethical living, by means of subduing lust and overpowering
one's own evil inclinations, are often accentuated in R. Yaakov
Yoseph's teachings. Interpreting biblical passages, he embodied
in his comments his thoughts on the subject of original sin. He
asserted that before Adam sinned, he wore garments of light,
but later he had to wear garments of skin. The evil inclination
is very, very old, he wrote, and it came long before the good
inclination which is to man like a young child born to him in
his old age. The evil inclination now changes into garments, but
in the Messianic era, it will be transformed into a holy angel.
In his youth, a man is in the category of power. Later, when old,
he enters into the category of kindness and compassion.

"Lusted lust" (Num. 11.4). When dulled by surfeit, people
crave desire for pleasure even more than pleasure itself. The body
likes physical pleasures, and when the pleasures are repeated, they
become ordinary, but to spiritual pleasures there is no end.
*(Toledot Yaakov Yoseph; A Treasury of Jewish Quotations, New
York 1956.)*

R. Yaakov Yoseph paid much attention to social behavior.

"When three people are having a conversation, and one leaves them, the two remaining should avoid speaking evil of him. In such cases it is better that all three go simultaneously in different directions." He also stressed the negative character of pride, arrogance, and jealousy, as well as the necessity for peace among men. His maxims and general rules of conduct included the following:

I.   An arrogant person hates everyone. The same is the case with someone who is envious.

II.   No human being is worthy enough to hate someone else. He is permitted to hate only his own baseness and his own evil desires.

III.   The haughty person negates every one and interferes with the coming of the Messiah.

IV.   The Messianic Era will be ushered in only with the disappearance of the haughty and the vulgar.

V.   He who is not jealous enjoys physical peace as well as emotional well-being.

VI.   Peace is more important than truth.

"Who shall ascend into the mountain of the Lord? He that has clean hands and a pure heart." (Ps. 23:3,4). And just as a man who climbs a high mountain divests himself of his heavy clothing and all superfluous burdens, so he who ascends the path of the Lord must shed all sins and cares and be clean of hands and pure of heart. "We are taught: It is a great 'Mitzwah' (precept) to achieve peace between two men who quarrel (1. Peah, 1; Mishnah, 1.) I will tell of an even greater 'Mitzwah'; namely to make peace between your body and your spirit, so that materialism does not conquer the spirit."
(Steinman: The Garden of Hassidism, p. 159; Newman: Hassidic Anthology, p. 311.)

[V]

Teachers, Disciples, and Descendants

SOME SIXTY men of various age groups were among the original disciples of R. Israel Baal Shem Tov, founder of Hassidut. A biblical verse has been applied by Hassidic lore to depict their roles in establishing the Hassidic movement: "Behold, it is the litter of Solomon; Three score mighty men are about it, of the mighty men of Israel" (Song of Songs, 3:7). Among the sixty were also several who had formulated their own ways of pietist devotion before they heard of the Besht, joining his ranks after they met him later and "smelled his flask." They are considered to have been among the original teachers and founders of Hassidism. Some had previously been among the opponents of the Besht, but they later became the most diligent defenders and steadfast propagandists of his teachings. Among the Besht's original disciples were also founders of Hassidic dynasties whose members added to the Besht's teachings or paved new ways of Hassidic devotion and practice. They, in turn, had their own followers from whose ranks came successors in Hassidic leadership.

Foremost among the Besht's contemporaries and originators of Hassidic forms, was R. Pinkhas Shapiro of Koretz (1726–1791), descendant of a noble family of Talmudic giants and of martyrs for the Jewish faith. He was born in Shklov, White Russia, and in his early youth gained fame as a great scholar whose attainments included expert knowledge of the Jewish philosophy which had been created in the Middle Ages. As the result of a false accusation against his father, R. Abraham Abba Shapiro, the family escaped from Shklov and settled in Miropol, Vohlynia.

R. Pinkhas began to formulate strict rules of ethics and piety, and he influenced those close to him to adopt his ways of behavior. R. Abraham Abba, who had come from a Lithuanian Mitnagdim environment, full of opponents of Hassidism, once visited the Besht, and he became so impressed with what he had seen and heard that he prevailed upon his son, Pinkhas, to join the leader of the new movement. In the beginning, the disciples of the Besht regarded with suspicion the scholarly "Lithuanian" who insisted on his own rigid forms of piety, but the Besht himself considered it a great accomplishment that R. Pinkhas had joined his circle. Because he lived in Koretz for a number of years, he became known as R. Pinkhas Koretzer, but later he moved to Ostrah, a city known for its great rabbis and scholars. Late in life, he decided to settle in the Holy Land, but on the way to realize this wish, he stopped at the city of Shepetovka. There he become ill and died at the age of sixty-five. His main teachings are included in his works, *Midrash Pinkhas* and *Nofeth Tzufim (Honey from the Honeycomb)*.

In his teachings, R. Pinkhas preached universal love, even love of the most sinful people in humanity, because only such love can hasten the coming of the Redeemer. He was very fond of song, believing that if the pious sang beautifully, it would be possible to influence God to leave Heaven and make His abode among human beings on earth. The spiritual kinship among men he likened to choral singing, one helping the others to raise their voices.

R. Pinkhas used to say and pray: "Protect me, O Lord, that I should not be wiser than pious . . . I would prefer that the soul leave my body rather than utter a lie with my mouth . . . When people realize that to utter a lie is just as sinful as committing adultery, the Messianic days will begin." He emphasized in his teachings that one can really be considered a Tzadik, a saintly person, if he does not possess even a speck of evil within himself and does not see any evil in others. The less one talks, the nearer one comes to sanctity and joy. "Sadness is rooted in haughtiness, because one thinks that he deserves what he desires. All desires of a human being must have a cause, but pride is without cause or reason."

The biblical passage dealing with Creation—"And God said; 'Let there be light' (Gen. 1:3)—R. Pinkhas interpreted as, "Since Creation, the world is full of light, but as a result of idle talk, a screen is formed. It is similar to the sun's rays through the clouds. During prayer, the clouds disperse and after prayer they gather again."

In regard to pride, R. Pinkhas insisted that to commit a transgression one has to do something so that the transgression becomes a fact. But there is one transgression that needs no physical effort. This is the transgression of pride. One simply lies stretched out on his couch or in his bed, yawns with self-importance and says to himself: "I am great!" Nevertheless, it is possible to learn humility from pride, for pride is so humble, that it enters into the hearts and minds of even the lowliest.

Speaking of human pride, R. Pinkhas illustrated it by telling of the behavior of royalty: "When a king takes off his crown, he hangs it upon a hook. Why not place it on another person's head? Because the other person would pretend that he also is a king, but a hook remains a hook without pretense."

R. Pinkhas also taught proper behavior as a means of influencing people to change their ways for the better: "When I wish to reprove someone, I mention to him words of wisdom that give him spiritual inspiration, as Scripture teaches us: 'Wisdom preserveth the life of him that hath it' (Eccles. 7:12). And wisdom is an aspect of the soul. Even by telling anecdotes, we can influence a person to change his ways for the better. But in our times, some people just reprove someone so that he repent, but the person is unable to do so by himself without the help of others."

On various occasions, R. Pinkhas underlined the necessity of brotherly love:

"There is something precious in every human being. Thus, when one prays without having in mind his fellowmen, his prayer is not acceptable. Therefore, everyone should try to express love in over-abundance. The world has too little of this attribute, so let's each fulfill the need by supplying individually what is lacking in the world.

Commenting on how to acquire the knowledge of God and serve Him truly, and on the problems of sin and sorrow, humility and daily tasks in general, R. Pinkhas stressed the following teachings:

It is possible for everyone to know who serves the Lord truly and who is thoroughly evil. This knowledge is attained through God, Who includes everyone in Himself. The world is identical with God.

In our code, we read that we should not avoid the proper religious rites because we are ashamed of those who ridicule us. This means that we should not be ashamed to perform any religious rite. How do we know this? We learn it by observing those who scoff at us. If they are bold in their ridicule of those who serve the Lord, how much bolder should we be in serving Him!

If man did not sin, the Lord would have no occasion to employ His attributes of mercy, compassion, and the like, but only his attributes of justice. Therefore, it follows that even sinners please the Lord: they bring into play His worthiest attributes.

Sadness and bitterness are the result of pride. The proud man who suffers tribulations cannot understand how a person of his quality merits tribulations. But the humble man accepts whatever betides with calmness and philosophic resignation.

If a man honors you, he considers himself less important than you at the moment, and he thereby becomes a better man than you. The more he honors you, the more he actually grows at your expense. How then can you feel pride at being showered with honors?

A man may often live out the entire span of his life for the purpose of performing a single Mitzwah or gaining a single chosen end.

In all things there is a direct light and a reflected light. What a father gives his son is in the category of a direct light, which is compassion; and what the sons give their father is in the category of reflected light, which is justice. And people say: One father can maintain ten sons but ten sons often fail to maintain one father. (*Middash Pinkhas; Nofet Tzufim; Mifaloth HaTsadikkim; Newman: Hassidic Anthology; Steinman: The Garden of Hassidism.*)

R. Pinkhas of Koretz is considered to have been an associate rather than a disciple of the Besht. He was physically of miniature

size and was called admiringly in the diminutive, R. Pinkhasl.
But to his followers he was a spiritual giant, "R. Pinkhas the
Great!"

The Canadian Yiddish poet, Yaakov Yitzhak Segal (1896–
1954), whose ancestor R. Yaakov of Annipol was a teacher of the
Besht before the latter "became revealed," and who himself spent a
part of his early youth in Koretz, dedicated to R. Pinkhas several
of his masterpieces in verse. Following are two of Segal's Koretzer
Poems based on lore about R. Pinkhas, in translations that do not
measure up to the greatness and beauty of the original. The two
poems are from the book, *Seffer Yiddish* (*The Book of Yiddish*)
published in Montreal in 1950.

I. *Little R' Pinkhas*

R' Pinkhas never travels anywheres,
He became an ordinary Jew like all other Jews.
He goes daily to pray in the shoemakers' Synagogue,
And he refuses to be called "Rabbi,"
But plain and simple: R' Pinkhas.
Jews are embarrassed and saddened,
And have yet a stronger urge to call him "Rabbi,"
Because his radiant and holy countenance
Has become more radiant and holy.
His eyes are full of heavenly secrets.
His tranquility—compassion and fear.
He argues with the Jews of Koretz:
"All of you know me, brother—Jews,
"Moshe-Mordecai, and David, and Yaakov-Elyeh,
"So why should you call me 'Rabbi'?
"And how long is the limit to be a Rabbi?
"I have taught all of you
"The alphabet, the vowel-points and the Pentateuch,
"And now I wish to sit in comradeship with you

"Under the pointer of the World Creator.
"We are all His pupils,
"All of us are His adherents.
"Aren't we all His Hassidim?"
Jews are standing with lowered eyes.
Jews are standing in fearful silence.
And more radiant becomes R' Pinkhasl,
The simplest of all Hassidic Rabbis,
The most Jewish of all Jews.
Perhaps it is impermissible to say so?

II. *The Koretzer*

The Baal Shem Tov had his own Synagogue,
The Berdichever, the Bratzlaver—each his Synagogue,
The Anipoler, the Maggid of Mezritch,
Everyone—a Synagogue for his family of Hassidim.
But the Koretzer, R' Pinkhasl,
The most quiet Rabbi, and the most quiet Jew,
He had a little Synagogue, low and downhill,
Neither for an entire community, nor for a Hassidic congregation,
But a little Synagogue—for all manner of Jews,
The smallest Synagogue—for all manner of Jews.
This meant: For every Jew who came as a stranger,
And as if by miracle—so did Jews relate—
His legs themselves led him thereto,
To the little Synagogue of the saintly Koretzer.
And Jews whispered quietly, secretly, with their eyes,
So that a strange ear should not, God forbid, overhear,
That when Messiah, King David, God willing,
Ascends from his wanderings to our place,
He will also come on the old road,
And the first doorpost kiss,
Recite the first Afternoon-Evening prayers,
At R' Pinkhas Koretzer in the low Synagogue.

When R. Yaakov Yoseph of Polonoah, later the author of the first Hassidic work, *Toledot Yaakov Yoseph,* had long been a disciple of R. Israel Baal Shem Tov, the latter once exclaimed that the Almighty should reward him for having given Him such a "Yosseleh." R. Pinkhas of Koretz expressed himself similarly about the greatest among his own disciples, "Raphaelkeh," the unique Hassidic leader, R. Raphael of Bershad (? –1827). R. Raphael was not simply very pious and very humble, but piety and humility personified. Many adherents followed in his footsteps in various parts of Podolyah. To utter even a white lie, or to do anything that is a fraction of deviation from humility, was considered, among Bershder Hassidim, the most unpardonable transgression, as was the slightest show of pride. The souls of haughty people enter into bees, R. Raphael reminded his Hassidim, that's why the buzzing of bees sounds like a drawn out "I, I, I."

It is related that R. Raphael of Bershad never accepted any gifts from his followers. He refused to sit in the pew nearest to the Torah Ark, a seat usually reserved for the Rabbi in every Synagogue. On the contrary, he prayed near the exit where were standing the water-carriers, the wood-choppers and the others who could not afford to buy seats for themselves. This was not done by Raphael as a lesson in behavior, because any form of show was considered by the Bershader a cardinal sin, but as a result of R. Raphael's conviction that his own prayers might have a slight chance to reach the Gates of Heaven if taken aloft by the prayers of those with broken hearts, caused by various day-to-day hardships. When eating, R. Raphael never bent down to the plate, but brought the spoon to his mouth; and he never sat at the oven to warm himself, believing that warmth causes sluggishness. He was against talking when there was no reason for it and explained that, "Those who talk a lot eventually tell lies. Avoid unnecessary talk, so you will avoid the untruth. In his prayers, every one should insert a special plea that the Almighty lead him in the Path of Truth."

In regard to pride, R. Raphael expounded a biblical passage: " 'The Lord reigneth; he is clothed in majesty' (Ps. 93:1): When one is motivated by pride, he takes, so to speak, part of God's clothes and acts against the infinite, because human pride also has no limits."

Symbolic of R. Raphael's teachings dealing with love of fellow-humans and of one's being hopeful of his own good capabilities, are the following expressions:

> Love the man of wickedness. Why? Because he will then love you, and love will unite his soul and yours. As a consequence, inasmuch as you hate wickedness, you will transfer your hate to him, thereby causing him to repent and turn from evil to good. A man should not think contemptuously of his ability to do good. Let him but choose and God does the rest. Is there any limit to God's ability?
>
> (Midrash Pinkhas, p. 44, 51; Newman: Hassidic Anthology, p. 97; 220.)

R. Raphael's dovotion to the truth cost him his life. It once happened that a man who had been accused of a crime was sentenced to death. When the family of the man appealed to save his life, Russian judicial authorities replied that if the Hassidic leaders, R. Moshe of Savran and R. Raphael of Bershad would swear to it that the man was innocent, he would be freed. R. Moshe, believing that the saving of a human life is of greater importance than the fear of perjury, was ready to swear although he was not sure whether the man was innocent or not; but R. Raphael refused to do so, not being moved even by the pleas and tears of the sentenced man's wife and children. The night before the morning when the testimony under oath was to be given, R. Raphael locked himself in a room, and he wailed in prayers to God that He take his soul rather than force him to testify in favor of someone without knowing the exact truth. The Hassidim who were keeping watch all night outside R. Raphael's home and those who stayed at their own homes, prayed and cried, each man separately. After daybreak a messenger brought the news that the sentenced man had confessed to his crime and no oath of the two Rabbis was necessary. When joyful Hassidim broke into R. Raphael's room to tell him that it was no longer necessary for him to swear in court, they found him dead. And the Bershader Hassidim became more devoted to the truth than ever before.

When R. Menakhem Nakhum of Chernoble (1730–1798) visited Medzibozh for the first time to talk with the founder of Hassidut in order to find out whether he should join him and the circle of his disciples, the Besht said to his wife after the first chat with the guest: "Keep an eye on that man . . . he is a thief . . . he wants to steal all the heavenly rewards which are the shares of others."

R. Nakhum was both a great Talmudic scholar and a man of great deeds. He is recorded in the history of Hassidut as R. Nakhum "The Great," and as "The Little Baal Shem Tov." He was the founder of a Hassidic dynasty that is in existence in our own days, mostly in the United States.

R. Nakhum was born in the Vohlynian town of Narinsk. When he was still a child, his father, R. Tzvi, died and his paternal uncle, also named Nakhum, became the nephew's guardian. Recognizing young Nakhum's intellectual abilities, the uncle sent him to study in a Lithuanian Yeshiva where he soon gained fame as a scholar. Being of a poetic nature, young Nakhum also studied Kabbalah, the sources of Jewish mysticism. After his return home, he married and became a teacher, practicing ascetism not only because of material want but also as an outcome of his great piety. After visiting the Besht, he became one of his adherents. Being a gifted speaker, R. Nakhum became a Maggid (Preacher). This enabled him to visit many places to spread the teachings of Hassidut, and also to collect funds for various purposes, chiefly as dowry for the daughters of the poor, and for the ransoming of Jewish innkeepers who had been unable to pay, in time, the rentals to the owners and had been kept in prison. Later he was given the position of Rabbi in the city of Chernoble.

Even at the time when R. Nakhum was already the leader of many Hassidim, he refused their gifts and was satisfied with the bare necessities of life. His only son, R. Mordecai, who became a Hassidic leader during R. Nakhum's lifetime, had a taste for the better things in life. When the father once visited R. Mordecai's home and noticed all the trappings of material wealth, it caused him great pain and he reproved him gently for having forsaken the way of modest living.

In his preachings and teachings, which are included in his books, *Yismakh Leyv* and *Meor Aynayim* (meaning *"Rejoiceth the Heart* and *Light of the Eyes,* based on Prov. 15:30: 'The light of the eyes rejoiceth the heart"*), R. Nakhum dealt with the problems of wealth and poverty, goodness and sin, and various aspects of behavior in general:

Between poverty and wealth I always choose poverty. It is the best shield against egotism and against every evil of the spirit. It is the least costly, the most easily attainable; it need not struggle against jealousy and competition; it need answer no questions or suspicions; it is understood without comments and without explanations. I beg of you, my good friends, not to deprive me of this great treasure.

I have greater fear of good deeds which bring me pleasure than of transgressions from which I derive no benefit whatever.

When a man stands on the roof of a house and espies a precious gem on the ground, he cannot come by it except by going down to where it lies, picking it up and bringing it up with him. Similarly, with the Zaddik; he sometimes falls down in order that he may be able to uplift the fallen souls.

The seriousness and depths of man's queries are to be measured according to the infractions of his soul. When a man is guilty of a transgression by cunning and conceit his query will be great. Thus it is a failing for a person to ask serious questions. Yet there are fools who pride themselves on posing difficult questions.

There is goodness in everything.

Darkness, too, was created, and when light came, darkness was swallowed up by the light and disappeared. For it is the desire of darkness to be included in and consumed by the light.
(Steinman: The Garden of Hassidism, pp. 156–158; Newman: Hassidic Anthology, p. 324; S. A. Horodetzky: Leaders of Hassidism, London, 1928, p. 40.)

R. Mordecai (? –1837), also known as R. Motteleh, the diminutive of his name, became a mass leader of Hassidim, but unlike his father, R. Nakhum, believed that beautiful living surroundings enhance the prestige of the teacher in the eyes of his followers. Not only the simple people, but even great scholars were among his followers. His teachings were published post-humously in the book *Liqqutei Torah, (Torah Selections)*.

Although R. Mordecai's Hassidic Court was far different from the modest looking centers established by his predecessors, his teachings were in the tradition of the Besht and his disciples. His poetic nature was given expression in relating his experiences and in his attitude towards the closest among his followers. During one of his chats with his Hassidim, R. Mordecai told them that when he once visited the graves of R. Dov Ber, the Maggid of Mezritch, R. Zusheh of Annipol and R. Leib, the Reproving Preacher of Polonoah—their places of burial being in the same row—he felt in his nostrils the aroma of Paradise. On another occasion, he turned to one of his disciples, a great scholar with a sharp mind, and he said to him: "Put your head upon my heart and it will be good for both of us." Complimenting the scholars among his followers, he stated: "It occasionally happens that one who is a disciple in this world, becomes a teacher in the Heavenly World."

R. Mordecai cautioned his Hassidim against pessimism if reality was not in harmony with their wishes, and emphasized: "One should never be overpowered by sadness about anything but believe that whatever happens is for his own good, as it is written, 'Out of the mouth of the Most High proceeded not evil' (Lam. 3:38). One should avoid anger, flattery and lies. When one utters a lie, being accustomed to do so, he should not hesitate because of shame to confess: 'I have just told a lie'; and say so on every occasion until he is weaned from lying."

Preaching brotherhood and understanding, he said: "People wash their hands before they sit down to eat. But how could people sit down casually and eat the food supplied by the Creator before having cleansed their mouths of the malice and vulgarity they used against their fellow-men?"

Speaking of divinity, he formulated the following thoughts:

"1. Divinity within a man is limited because a man is limited in his ability to receive it.

"2. Divinity has no limit, but finite man cannot comprehend this.

"3. Divinity created matter so that man, composed of matter and soul, may have a conception of it. It follows, therefore, that all matter may be likened to a parable by means of which Divinity can be understood."

(Isaac Even: Fun Rebes Hoif I, p. 33; Newman: Hassidic Anthology, p. 83.)

According to the R. Mordecai's wish, he was buried in the town of Anatevka, near Kiev. He was the father of eight sons, and all of them became Hassidic leaders: R. Aaron in Chernoble; R. Moshe in Karistichov; R. Yaakov Israel in Hornosteipol, later moving to Cherkass; R. Nakhum in Makariv; R. Abraham in Trisk; R. David in Vasilkov, later transferring his Hassidic Court to Talnah; R. Yitzkhak in Skvira and R. Yokhanan in Rakhmistrivka. The dynasty of R. Nakhum of Chernoble adopted the family name of Twersky. This dynasty of Hassidic teachers also produced a number of literary men, among them the Yiddish poet Avrohom Twersky and the Hebrew-Yiddish novelist and essayist Yokhanan Twersky. Shmuel Abba Horodetzky, the historian of Hassidut, was, through both his parents, a descendant of R. Israel Baal Shem Tov, R. Pinkhas of Koretz, R. Nakhum of Chernoble and R. Nakhman of Bratzlav.

The success of the Besht's Hassidut in its early days was in the largest measure due to the fact that Maggidim were among the early disciples of the Baal Shem Tov. One of them was R. Yehudah Leib, the "Reprover" of Polonoah (? –1811) where he occupied the positions of cantor and preacher. He may have been the first to influence the local rabbi, R. Yaakov Yoseph Katz, to join the Besht's circle. The Reprover visited many communities, and he won the hearts of the simple masses by his criticisms of the haughty behavior of the scholars and by his emphasis on the beauties of simple living under the guidance of precepts about brotherly love, and the principles of ethics and morality. The contents of his teachings are depicted in the collection, KOL ARYEH (meaning *Voice of the Lion;* because his Hebrew-Yiddish name Yehudah-Leib alludes to the king of the animal world.)

R. Yehudah-Leib interpreted the biblical passage: "Thou shalt surely rebuke thy neighbor, and not bear sin because of him" (Lev. 19:17), as meaning that a rebuke has to be through love and not through hatred; that is why the first part of the same passage warns that, "thou shalt not hate thy brother in thy heart"; and when someone reproves others, he should include himself among those being rebuked.

R. Yehudah-Leib certainly did practice what he preached. Speaking of earthly desires and evil inclinations, the Reprover declared: "One should not blame other things for the passions and desires that motivate human beings. It is not wealth that is at fault, but love of money; not honor, but love of honor. The Messiah will love everyone and point out virtues even in the most evil people. He who finds virtues in everyone, possesses a Messianic attribute."

A preacher and the son of a preacher, was R. Yekhiel Mikhel of Zlochov (? –1787). His father, R. Isaac of Drohobitch, became one of the followers of the Besht after many years of opposition to him, and he influenced his son to join the Besht's circle of disciples.

R. Yekhiel Mikhel was born in Brody, and he held the position of Maggid in his home town and later in other communities, including Zlochov, dying at the time he was preacher in Yampol.

The Maggid of Zlochov lived in great want, and he believed that since he wished to be poor, the Almighty provided him with the portion he desired. He said: "I have never wanted something that I did not possess, because as long as I did not have it, I was certain that I did not need it."

Upon another occasion, he said: "When one joins his own prayers to the prayers of others who are poor or afflicted, he may be certainly considered among those who are attached to the Creator."

Speaking of conceit, he stated: "All manner of conceit, every form of pride, creates a barrier between a person and the Almighty, since those who are full of pride are always thinking of their personal 'I' while forgetting that 'I' is permissible only to God alone."

Symbolic of R. Yekhiel Mikhel's own manner as a preacher, and of his chats with the circle of his closest disciples, is the following pronouncement: "One should never put the shame on even a man who is notorious for his wickedness. Pray for your enemies that they be granted a good life. This is a service which is greater than prayer."

The Maggid of Zlochov had five sons—they were called "The

Five Cedars"—and each of them became a Hassidic leader in his own right. One of the sons, R. Yitzkhak-Itzikle of Radzivil, often repeated his father's teachings and he maintained that, "those who are attached to the Almighty, have no earthly personal desires."

One of the disciples of the R. Yekhiel Mikhel, the Maggid of Zlochov, was R. Mordecai of Neskhiz (? –1800), a descendant of Don Yitzkhak Abarbanel (1437–1508), Portuguese and later Spanish diplomat before the expulsion of the Jews in 1492, and one of the greatest Jewish scholars of the Middle Ages. In his early youth, R. Mordecai escorted his teacher on a journey to visit R. Dov Ber, the Maggid of Mezritch, successor of the Besht. He became a businessman, but because of his great Talmudic knowledge, was influenced to embrace a rabbinic career. Before settling in Neskhiz, he occupied rabbinic positions in Leshnov, Kovel and Ludmir. One of his three sons, R. Yaakov Aryeh, later became Rabbi of Kovel. Of his other sons, R. Yoseph was Rabbi of Hrubyeshov and later of Ustillah, and R. Yitzkhak inherited his father's chair in Neskhiz.

R. Mordecai coupled his rabbinic activities as spiritual leader and magistrate of the local community with the activities of a Hassidic teacher, and he became widely known as a "Tzadik" who could even perform miracles. Speaking to one of his sons, R. Mordecai explained that a real "Tzadik" is one who knows when a woman in his vicinity is in pains of childbirth, takes part in her sufferings, and, with his prayers, hastens the birth of her infant.

In his teachings, some of which were published in the collection *Rishpei Eysh* (meaning *Flames of Fire*), R. Mordecai emphasized the greatness of unswerving faith in God, the importance of subduing evil instincts by constant battling against them, and the benefits that all humanity derive from each person's individual repentance. He asserted: "With the power of faith, it is possible to resurrect the dead, to transform silver into gold and to change all ways of nature. He who has faith, does not fear anything and nothing will harm him."

"The human being sleeps regularly, but the evil instinct is always awake."

"Everyone should believe that for his benefit alone the entire world was created, and repent for his wrong-doings until he will force all humanity to repent."

His son and heir, R. Yitzkhak, interpreted the passage "Love thy neighbor as thyself" (Lev. 19:18), in the following manner: "When one sees a fault in someone else, he should not hate him for it but consider it as a reminder that he should examine his own shortcomings, and consequently he will not hate his neighbor. By correcting his own deeds, one observes the commandment to love his neighbor."

The book *Toledot Yitzkhak* (meaning *The Generations of Isaac*) is a resume of his teachings.

Among the very last disciples of the Maggid of Mezritch, was Rabbi Tzvi Hirsh of Nadvurnah (? –1801). He had been a preacher in Dolinah before settling in Nadvurnah to occupy the same position there. His extraordinary ethical standards and humility, and his great scholarship drew to him many followers, and R. Yitzhak of Radzivil, son of R. Yekhiel Mikhel of Zlochov, was one of his closest disciples. He wrote three books, namely: *Tzemakh Adoshem LeTzvi*, meaning *The Growth of the Lord be Beautiful, Siftay Kedoshim*, meaning *The Lips of the Holy*, a commentary on Psalms; and *Millay DeAvot,* an Aramaic title meaning *The words of the Fathers,* a commentary on the Mishnah-tractate, *Peerkay Avot,* popularly known as *Ethics of the Fathers,* which is traditionally studied on Sabbath afternoons, between Passover and Rosh HaShanah, the Jewish New Year.

It is understandable why R. Tzvi Hirsh wrote commentaries on "Psalms" and *Ethics of the Fathers.* The first enabled him to emphasize important matters of prayer and piety; the second gave him full opportunity to stress principles of morality and behavior in general.

"It is written: 'O ye that love the Lord, hate evil' (Ps. 97:10). This means that those who really love the Lord, hate all that is evil, the earthly matters of this world and the desires to attain them, since such matters are outright evil."

Commenting on the passage, "Man doth not live by bread only, but by everything that proceedeth out of the mouth of God" (Deut. 8:3), R. Tzvi Hirsh clarified his belief that vitality is not in the bread itself, but "proceedeth out of the mouth of God"; the Almighty said that there should be bread, so it came into being.

God's punishments, he insisted, are not punishments at all, but purifications and healings of the soul. Only fools are more afraid of the medicine than the illness. And that is why it is written: "May the fear of Heaven be upon you" (Talmud Berakhot, 28–B), and not the fear of punishments.

"Just as the shoe protects the foot, so the body protects the soul from being soiled by worldly realities; and just as before one goes to sleep, he takes off his shoes, so the soul takes off the body-protection as it departs for its resting place."

R. Tzvi Hirsh warned against permitting stark reality to influence one to sadness. He said of himself: "It is a sin to be pessimistic and to be overpowered by worry. My only worry is that I am often terribly worried."

It is true that R. Israel Baal Shem Tov, his successor R. Dov Ber of Mezritch, and R. Yaakov Yoseph of Polonoah, laid the foundations of Hassidism, but due credit and honor must also be accorded to other Tzadikkim and teachers who were their contemporaries; likewise, recognition must be given to their own disciples as well as the disciples of their disciples and to their descendants, who broadened and illuminated the teachings of their Masters, winning for Hassidut the hearts and minds of larger masses. Such were the men whose thoughts and words were summarized in the review just concluded.

VI

Three Sets of Brothers
And Three Different Disciples

DURING THE Persian rule of Cyrus the Great, five sets of leading teachers, called "Zugot" (Pairs), laid the foundations of Jewish spiritual life and daily behavior in the crucial times of the Second Commonwealth, which had been established in Judea in the year 586 before the Common Era, after the return from Babylonian exile. The Second Commonwealth lasted until the year 70 of the Common Era, when the Second Temple in Jerusalem was destroyed by the Romans. In the early days of the Second Commonwealth, Jewish spiritual life was formulated by the members of a legislative body known as the *Anshay Knesset HaGedolah,* the Men of the Great Assembly. From their ranks, came the Scribes, the spiritual leaders who taught and interpreted the Mosaic Torah-laws to the inhabitants of the then existing several towns and numerous villages. Those teachers established the group of pietists known historically as The First Hassidim, and it was as a result of their teaching endeavors that the Jews had the courage to go into battle against the pagan Syrian Greeks in the first known war for religious freedom. Under the leadership of the Maccabeans who were of the priestly Hasmonean family, the Jews were victorious, the Holy Temple was cleansed of pagan symbols which had been placed there by the idol-worshipers, and the Feast of Lights, called *Hanukah,* was instituted to commemorate the triumph over the enemies from without and the pro-Greek assimilationists from within.

During the national spiritual development of the Second Commonwealth, the Great Assembly of 120 members was replaced by the Sanhedrin,—a name rooted in Greek—or Supreme Council, consisting of seventy-one members. The Sanhedrin was a synthesis of a religious parliament, a Supreme Court and an Academy of learning. The early heads of the Sanhedrin were the "Five Pairs" or Zugot, one of each pair serving as *Nassee,* the equivalent of President, and the other as *Av Bet-Din,* or "Father of the Court," the equivalent of Chief Justice. The seat of the Sanhedrin was in the "Hall of Hewed Rocks" on the Temple Mount. Some members were appointees of the ruling head in Judea at the specific time, others were disciples ordained by Sanhedrin Sages to take the places of those who had died. The last one of the five sets of "Pairs" which headed the Sanhedrin were the friendly and kind Hillel and the strict-rigorous Shammai. Those who followed in the separate footsteps of the last two teachers, formed the House of Hillel and the House of Shammai. It is related in the pages of the Talmud:

> Since the disciples of Shammai and Hillel, who did not serve their masters sufficiently, grew in numbers, differences increased in Israel, and it seemed as if the one Torah had become like two Torahs.
>
> The Houses of Shammai and Hillel fought over their differences for three years. One claimed that "The Halakha (Traditional Law) is according to our interpretation," while the other claimed "The Halakha is according to our interpretation." Then was heard a Heavenly Voice which announced: "Both interpretations are the words of the Living God, but the Halakha is according to the House of Hillel." If either of the interpretations are the words of

the Living God, why were those of the House of Hillel merited that the Halakha should be established according to their interpretations? Because they acted gently and submissively, and they always studied their own opinions together with the opinions of the House of Shammai, and mentioned the interpretations of the House of Shammai before their own.

Although the House of Shammai and the House of Hillel were opposing each other, what one declared to be prohibited, the other proclaimed as permissible, this did not restrain those of the House of Shammai from marrying women from the House of Hillel, as it did not restrain the House of Hillel from marrying women from the House of Shammai, to teach that they practiced love and friendship one to the other in order to fulfill what is said, (in Zechariah 8:19): "Love ye truth and peace."
(Sanhedrin 88-B; Eyruvin 13-B; Yevamot 14-A.)

Some of the events related above, found their repetition in the development of Hassidut. Just as in the Sanhedrin of old, so later did Hassidut have its own "Pairs," sets of brothers, as will be related in this chaper. In a later chapter, will be told the story of the battle of one Hassidic "House" against another—the battle of Tzanz against Sadigorah—where long after the fire and smoke of battle had disappeared, descendants of the participants in the struggle arranged marriages between sons and daughters of both dynasties, in the pursuit of love and peace.

Among those who stood around the Besht in the last hours of his early life, were his two grandsons, Moshe Khayim Ephrayim, for brevity called only by the last of his three names, and Barukh, the younger of the two. Both were the children of Odell, the Besht's only daughter. Ephrayim was about twelve at the time, and had been the Besht's joy by demonstrating his scholarship at an early age. The proud grandfather boasted of young Ephrayim's knowledge in letters to his brother-in-law, the great Talmudist R. Gershon of Kutov, and to others. When little Barukh was seven, he realized that his grandfather was no more, and he began to weep bitterly. R. Pinkhas of Koretz was perhaps touched more by the crying of the little boy than by the Besht's demise. Little Barukh was taken, for a short time, to Mezritch where his traditional education was begun under the guidance of his grandfather's successor. But the small-sized R. Pinkhas, who was residing at Ostrah in those days, could not forget little Barukh's crying, and he had him brought to his house, showering him with love and affection while leading him into the realms of Jewish spirituality. In time, the two brothers themselves became Hassidic teachers and the uncles of a genius among the masters of *Hassidism:* R. Nakhman of Bratzlav, son of their sister Feigeh. R. Ephrayim (1737–1800) was later a resident of Sudilkov, being the Rabbi of the local Jewish community. R. Barukh (1750–1810) settled in the Podolyan town of Tulchin, known in Jewish history as the place in which occurred one of the most ferocious massacres perpetrated by the Ukrainian Cossacks under the leadership of Bogdan Chmielnitzky in 1648–1649. Years later, R. Barukh moved his Hassidic court to his home town, Medzibozh, where his grandfather had established the first center of the Hassidic movement.

R. Ephrayim refused to accept any gifts from followers who had to come to Sudilkov to see the Besht's grandson and to be blessed by him. He preferred to sustain his family on the meager salary he received from the community as its spiritual guide and magistrate. He wished to be left alone so that in his spare time he could record the teachings of his saintly grandfather and the dreams he had dreamt on various occasions of meetings with the

Besht and of chats with him. He recorded all this in a book titled *Deggel Makhne Ephrayim (The Standard of the Camp of Ephrayim)*, based on Numbers 2:18, which was published posthumously. As is the custom in Jewish tradition, authors of generally accepted or exceedingly popular works are not known by their personal names, but by the full or abbreviated titles of their books. Just as R. Yaakov Yoseph Katz, author of the first Hassidic work, *Toledot Yaakov Yoseph,* has been known in the Hassidic world as "The Toledot," so has R. Ephrayim of Sudilkov, author of *Deggel Makhne Ephrayim,* the second of the early Hassidic works, become historically known as *The Deggel,* or *The Standard.*

In contrast to R. Ephrayim, his younger brother, R. Barukh, did not believe that he had to practice upon himself the statement of the Sages that "poverty is as becoming to Jews as a red ribbon or a red rose on the nape of a white horse." But he did believe that God had created poverty so that the wealthy could be able to give charity, and in particular not neglect the children of the poor; since from the ranks of the poor, new Torah teachers arise. It was true that R. Barukh had material riches, and he often made trips to the various cities and towns where his Hassidim gave him money as "redemption" payments. But in R. Barukh's Hassidic Court there was always "open house" for those in need, and he secretly assisted poor young scholars. R. Barukh once visited Sudilkov and while spending the Sabbath in his brother's home, he noticed that R. Ephrayim was so poor that his wife used candlesticks of clay for the kindling of the Sabbath candles. He argued against such surroundings for a grandson of the Besht. Answering his brother's suggestion that he too make trips for the purpose of collecting "Ransom"—contributions from the

Hassidim,—R. Ephrayim replied: "It is better that I stay home and my candlesticks be far away than that I wander to far places and my candlesticks stay at home." R. Ephrayim's wife, believing that there was some substance to her brother-in-law's criticism, once did accept, secretly, a money gift which she made use of to buy silver candlesticks. When R. Ephrayim noticed her put out the new candlesticks, he exclaimed: "Before this I also had light on the Sabbath, now the light is all yours!"

R. Ephrayim's aim in life was to record for posterity all his grandfather's teachings, and to live by them. R. Barukh's descent from the founder of *Hassidut* gave him a feeling of self-importance, so that he considered those of his contemporaries who were leaders of Hassidim as unworthy of the task.

R. Barukh was, like his brother, a man of love and humility, but he often had fits of uncontrollable anger which frightened his followers; or he sank into great sadnesses which were equally frightening. Did he, too, long for a life of seclusion and reflection, like his brother Ephrayim's? Was he tired of touring the cities of the Hassidim and of the commotion that his visits caused in various places? Had Hassidic reality become repelling? A scholarly jester and prankster, Hersheleh of Ostropol, was brought to R. Barukh's court, and whenever the master fell into deep sadness, Hersheleh did his best to pull him out of it, and he often succeeded.

There are some similarities between the teachings of R. Ephrayim and R. Barukh. The latter wrote no books, but his words and comments are recorded in the collection *Bootzina Dinhorah,* a title in Aramaic meaning *The Bright Light,* symbolic name for a wise person. The collection appeared years after R.

Barukh's demise. The specific spiritual similarities between the two brothers, also underscore the differences between them. R. Ephrayim wrote:

> The deeds of a human being are like a stream. When its bed is clean, the waters flow swiftly. If one's deeds are in the spirit of sanctity, they are acts of purity, like a clean, flowing stream.

> Truth is constantly humiliated by being thrown on the ground, as it is written: "It cast down truth to the ground" (Dan. 8:12). Therefore, he who strives to be near the truth, has to lower himself to the dust to pick it up, and from the ground, he can ascend to the loftiest heights.

> Every human being can be divine because his soul is part of God above and he possesses not only a part of Divinity but its entirety. He who wishes to cleave to truth, has to become as low as dust in order to pick up the truth. This is the meaning of the Scriptural teaching that "Truth springeth out of the earth" (Psalms 85:12).

> Everyone can examine the blemishes of others but not his own. And this is like the parable about a certain man who had an ugly looking wife. Because of the quantity of jewelry and clothes she always wore, the wife considered herself very beautiful, therefore she was very haughty. A clever friend gave the man a mirror as a gift and told him to place it in front of his wife's bed. When she awoke in the morning and saw her face reflected, she was seized by great fear and cried out: "Woe to me, I am seeing a devil!" Said the husband: "You are the devil, when you are not wrapped in fancy clothes and you don't wear your jewelry." From that day on, the wife was no longer prideful. The moral of the story: Whenever one sees an unbecoming thing, he should understand that from Heaven it was shown to him that he possesses within himself a speck of the unbecoming. He should then examine his own behavior, and with a broken heart correct his actions.
> *(Deggel Makhneh Ephrayim.)*

And now some of the recorded thoughts and words of R. Barukh:

Two are alike: God and love of God, because both have no limitations.

All things in the world wish to become uplifted by human beings. So when a person is ill and he needs medicines made of herbs and other things, he should believe that by his taking the medicine he elevates their ingredients. Truthfully, God could heal every sick person without the necessity of medicines, and He renews Creation of the world every day, and in His hands are the souls of all the living. What He created was done for His own glory, but all medicines, and the various forms of knowledge and science, have to become uplifted by man when he is in need of something, and he does uplift them by faith in God's unity.

People are very careful not to swallow a live ant, but they are not careful at all about swallowing a human being.

The world looks brightly illuminated for those who are not deep in it, but very dark and gloomy for those who are sunk into it.

Every person should consider himself a vessel that takes into itself whatever its owner pours into it, whether wine or vinegar.

It is related that once, when an admiring guest complimented R. Barukh on being a "beautiful preacher," he commented: "It is better to speak less than to speak beautifully."

Because of his strong attachment to his grandfather's lore, R. Barukh was opposed to the new roads in Hassidic teachings, and he expressed himself particularly against R. Shneur Zalman of Ladi, founder of the *Khabad* school, which stressed Wisdom, Understanding and Knowledge.

Not long before his death, R. Ephrayim left Sudilkov for

Medzibozh. When he passed away, he was buried near the sepulchre of his grandfather, the Besht. His brother, R. Barukh, died eleven years later. Although there were vast differences between the two in character and behavior, the teachings of both are imbedded in living Hassidut.

The wealthy villager Eliezer Leepeh was known in the entire region of Lvov (Lemberg) both for his great piety and for his great deeds, which included the providing of free lodging and food for transient strangers, and the "ransoming of captives," the bailing out of innkeepers who had been imprisoned for being in arrears in their payments of rent to the owners, members of the Polish gentry. Although his was the only Jewish family in a village populated by illiterate and exploited Galician-Ruthenian peasants, Eliezer Leepeh and his likewise pious and compassionate wife saw to it that their seven sons "learned to swim in the sea of the Talmud," as did the bright boys who lived in the towns and larger cities. Two of the sons, Elimelekh and the younger Zusheh, were attached to each other far more than to the other brothers. Their spiritual affinity and poetic longings led them to study in unison the intricacies of Kabbalah and walk the labyrinths of Jewish mysticism. During one of the Kabbalah sessions, the younger, Zusheh, turned to his older brother and posed a problem:

"According to what we have now studied, the souls of all generations of human beings, including our own, were present in Adam. How come that we permitted him to eat the fruit from the Tree of Knowledge?"

"We acted wisely," replied Elimelekh, "for had we stopped Adam, he would have imagined that he was himself the Creator."

The minute observances of the traditional laws and the fulfilling of the precepts of the Torah, were not enough for the longing hearts of the two brothers. Later, when they had become familiar with the teachings of Hassidut, its aims and its forms, Elimelekh and Zusheh decided to visit Mezritch, seat of the Maggid R. Ber, successor of R. Israel Baal Shem Tov, and join the circle of his disciples, which they did.

The Maggid R. Ber once was asked to mediate a dispute between the brothers Elimelekh and Zusheh. One said that a person must first of all be very humble, so that in his own humility, he will realize the greatness of the God. The other said that first one must observe the greatness of the God and thus he would recognize his own insignificance as a mere mortal of flesh and blood. The Maggid replied: "Both opinions are the words of the Living God, but the first form of humility is greater than the second."

Elimelekh and Zusheh learned much during their stay in Mezritch and shared all the joys of being Hassidim. But both had still to fulfill all their needs of soul-purification and to tread the roads of the humble. What did they, the sons of a wealthy family, know of hunger and want and what it meant to have no bed to sleep in? In the meantime, the Maggid died, so Elimelekh and Zusheh decided to "practice exile." For some six years, they wandered from town to town, from village to village, sustaining themselves with what people offered them. They were often thought of as ordinary lazy tramps and they suffered in silence many indignities visited upon them by fun-loving Jews and non-Jews alike. But they also learned much about human sufferings and human needs, as well as about human behavior in general. When the days of their "practicing exile" came to an end, the two brothers separated, each going in a different direction to spread the teachings of Hassidut and to establish families of their own.

R. Elimelekh (1717–1787) settled in Lizhensk, which in time became the fountainhead of Hassidut for all Galicia. Of his three sons, one later was his father's successor and the other two became spiritual leaders in other cities. Some of his very close disciples later established Hassidic Courts of their own in various places. R. Elimelekh was author of the book *Noam Elimelekh,* meaning *Elimelekh's Delight;* an allusion to what is related in the biblical Book of Ruth about Elimelekh and his wife Naomi, her name meaning "Delight." In Hassidic writing, the book *Noam Elimelekh* ranks in importance together with such works as *Toledot Yaakov Yoseph,* by the Besht's biographer, *Maggid D' vorov l' Yaakov,* containing the teachings of the Besht's successor, and *Deggel Makhne Ephrayim,* by the Besht's grandson.

It is related that when R. Shneur Zalman, founder of the HABAD school in Hassidism, once visited a scholar who was a Mitnaged, an opponent of the Hassidic ways, the scholar boasted that he had received a book titled *Noam Elimelekh,* and as soon as he recognized that its author was of the Hassidim, he threw the book under the table. R. Shneur Zalman retorted: "I can tell you about the author. If you threw him under the table, he would also take the indignity in silence."

R. Elimelekh often visited various places to preach on Hassidut and its teachings, and he used human psychology to influence those who came to hear him. It was his custom to enumerate publicly, various sins he supposedly had committed, acting so in order to influence others to repentance. When R. Elimelekh enumerated his transgressions, many in his presence began to tell of their own sins and vowed to repent in the manner that R. Elimelekh asked them to.

R. Elimelekh once visited Apta, and there he was the guest of the local Rabbi. The host entered unnoticed into the room where R. Elimelekh was staying, and he overheard a dialogue the guest was having with his own self:

"You're a sinner and therefore not worthy of a share in the World-to-Come. Nevertheless, you will be given a share. The Almighty is very charitable. In the World-to-Come, there is no eating and no drinking. So what acts of charity can the Almighty practice in Heaven besides forgiving the sinners their transgressions?"

Before his daily morning devotions, R. Elimelekh recited a private prayer of his own: "Lord of the Universe. Grant our hearts the ability to see in our fellow humans only their virtues and not their shortcomings." Later this prayer was inserted into numerous Hassidic editions of the Jewish prayerbook.

Noam Elimelekh consists of commentaries on the weekly Torah portions which are read publicly in the Synagogues during the Sabbath Service. Interpreting biblical passages, he expressed many thoughts and ideas concerning faith, piety and good deeds in general:

A person should constantly be under his own observation, so he will be able to judge himself whether he is really pious. Negative thoughts may often pass his mind, but he drives them away because he does not need them.

Those who witness the performance of a trick, know that it is only a trick, but those who witness a miracle are awed to such an extent, that even believers in miracles are surprised at what they have seen!

God said to Abraham: "Get thee out" (Genesis 12:1). Everyone has to get out to search and seek in order to recognize in everything the greatness of the Almighty. Thus he will be merited to possess wisdom and understanding to comprehend things on high. One has first to purify his acts to reach such a level of knowledge and understanding.

"And he (Jacob) rose up that night and took his two wives" (Gen. 32:23). It seems to me that all humans have two wives each. One is the wife that the Creator has given him to be fruitful and multiply, and the other wife is his holy soul that is constantly reaching out to her former heavenly place. The physical wife often helps to fulfill the cravings of the spiritual wife, his soul. Every man also has two concubines, the animal spirit and the evil inclination, and they interfere. But when a man cleanses himself and breaks the material and evil desires, even the evil inclination is transferred into goodness, and thus he can serve God with both his good inclination and his evil inclination.

"Take thou also unto thee the chief spices" (Exod. 30:23), and offer a sweet savour unto the Lord by everyday deeds.

When someone is overpowered by a desire to enforce discipline, let him begin to think of his own acts in the days when he was young, and he will eventually say to himself: "My own sins have brought me to this irritability." And so in other matters, let him remind himself of his own evil acts, and thus he will conquer and break the power of evil inclination.

R. Elimelekh had an only daughter, named Miriam. They were attached to each other, and he often related to her his experiences when he had been a village boy, and various incidents during his wanderings together with her uncle R. Zusheh. After R. Elimelekh was "called to the Academy on High," his disciples consoled themselves by listening to her repeat what her father had told her, mixed with various teachings that were not included in the work *Noam Elimelekh*.

After R. Elimelekh and R. Zusheh finished the years of "performing exile," and after various new experiences for R. Zusheh, the latter settled in Annipol.

Born and educated in the home of a wealthy villager, R. Zusheh (? –1800) had been marked to live in want for some additional years. He was convinced that want was the most precious gift that God had given him for an inheritance on earth. It is related that R. Zusheh was once in the Synagogue, full of joy, when a relative came in and interrupted him with the news that his wife and children at home were crying of hunger because he had failed to provide food for them. He replied: "They have good reason to cry, for they are relying on me, a mere human being, instead of relying on Almighty God."

When already a famous Hassidic leader, R. Zusheh was often plagued by illness, but he outlived, by fifteen years, his older brother, R. Elimelekh. The humility R. Zusheh learned during his wanderings never left him. For himself, he preferred fear of God in place of love of God. Once he prayed fervently: "Lord of the Universe, I love You very much, but I feel no fear of Thee. Grant me that I should fear you very much, in the manner that a pure angel fears Thee." Immediately a great fear filled his heart. Terrified, he hid underneath the bed, and began to cry: "I beg of You, Master of the Universe, let me love You in the manner I am accustomed to," and his fright evaporated immediately.

Although himself extremely pious, he emphasized on numerous occasions: "I love an evil person who knows that he is evil, much more than I love a pious person who knows that he is pious." His religious fervor often reached such outpouring of the emotions, that it was difficult to revive him. So he performed special charitable deeds in the hope that it would protect him from an untimely death. Thoughts of death constantly engaged his mind because of his physical condition. He explained his fears: "I am not worried that I might be asked in the World-to-Come why I was not as great as Moses; my answer is prepared: There could be only one Moses, not two. But I am worried lest they may ask why I was not Zusheh, the Zusheh I could have been had I really tried. To this question I will have no answer."

On a specific occasion, he bent down to the ground and said with a sigh: "Earth, earth, you are better than I, but I have the audacity to step upon you. But there comes a time when I will lie underneath you."

R. Zusheh was not a man of the pen, but his disciples recorded his teachings in their own books. The teachings were later gathered into a single volume titled *Menorat Zahav,* meaning *The Golden Candlestick,* the name being based on a biblical passage: "And thou shalt make a candlestick of pure gold" (Exodus 25:31). R. Zusheh had two sons. One, R. Tzvi Menakhem, succeeded his father in Annipol; the other, R. Israel Abraham, became Rabbi at Charno-Ostrah.

The recurring subjects in the teachings of R. Zusheh, are love of fellow-men, love of truth and humility without bounds.

Falsehood is the only transgression that Scripture warns to keep away from: "Keep thee far from a false matter" (Exodus 23:7), which means that not only should one avoid falsehood, but actually take steps not to be near it altogether. The moment one utters even a single word of untruth, he becomes far from the Creator. One should talk to everybody with friendship and respect. When one hears words of praise, he should retire into a hiding place and worry why people praise him for qualities he does not possess. When one is humble, he is guarded against being misled.

It had been the contention of the Mitnagdim, the opponents of the Hassidim, that the new movement had no great scholars in its ranks. The truth was that few distinguished Talmudists were among the early teachers and their disciples. As time went on, however, and the movement gained in prestige and influence, the number of Talmudic giants in its ranks became greater. Among the disciples of the Maggid of Mezritch, were two such giants of the younger generation; Shmuel-Shmelkeh, for brevity called only by his second name, a diminutive of the first name, and his brother the younger Pinkhas, both sons of R. Tzvi-Hirsh Halevy Hurwitz, Rabbi of Chortkov, and a Talmudist of renown in those days. The father had, years before, befriended a young man who had come to Galicia from Frankfurt-on-the-Main in search of a livelihood among his Eastern European brethren. This young man later returned home. After the passage of a long time, his son, according to Hassidic lore, established the financial dynasty known as the Rothschild family.

When the brothers, Shmelkeh and Pinkhas had reached maturity, they decided that the time had come for them to go of their own free will, and be "exiled to a place of Torah-learning" and "become covered with dust sitting at the feet of scholars." In their search of learning, they got as far as Vilna, the "Jerusalem of Lithuania," where resided the great giant of Talmudic knowledge, the *Gaon* R. Eliyahu, who was the spiritual leader of the Mitnagdim, the stiff-necked opponents of the Hassidim, and of their "frivolous ways." The Hassidic movement had by then already begun to penetrate the citadel of its opponents. After their scholarly discussion with the Gaon, Shmelkeh and Pinkhas managed to find the gathering place of the Hassidim, and from them they heard details about the Maggid R. Dov Ber, spiritual heir of the Besht, and of the ever-growing number of his disciples and followers. Shmelkeh and Pinkhas, eager to see everything and eager to learn, set out on their pilgrimage to Mezritch. They were favorably impressed.

It is customary among the Talmudists, when a young scholar meets an older one, that the younger starts the conversation by posing a question or expounding a point of law. So at their first meeting with R. Dov Ber, Shmelkeh and Pinkhas started the discussion on the opinion of the Talmudic Sages that "just as a man should bless God for the good, he should also bless Him for the bad," and accept the bad with joy. "But how is this possible?" asked the two brothers of R. Ber. He told them to go to the House of Study and ask Zusheh for the answer. They went to look for him, and when they found Zusheh seated in a corner behind the furnace, they repeated the Maggid's advice. Zusheh, who had experienced many trials and tribulations, was surprised: "I cannot understand why our Honorable Teacher picked on me to answer your question. Only a person who has suffered much in his lifetime, can tell you how someone could accept joyfully even the bad. As for me, I have never had a bad day in my life, thank God." And then Zusheh went on to answer the question of the young scholars. He pointed out that although the Matriarch Sara had many difficulties in her life, as the great bible-commentator Rashi explained, all of Sara's years had been equal because she accepted without complaint, joyfully and with love, all that God had willed for her.

It is believed that Zusheh's answer, as well as his exceptional humility, influenced the two brothers to become Hassidim and disciples of the Maggid.

As time passed on, R. Shmelkeh (1726–1778) and R. Pinkhas (1730–1805), were each given a rabbinic position. The older one was Rabbi Ritchevol and of Shinyave, and the younger became Rabbi of Vitkov and Lekhovitch. R. Shmelkeh and R. Pinkhas were known for their great wisdom and learning. To R. Shmelkeh, flocked many young men who had become attached to Hassidut, and in time some of his disciples became great Hassidic leaders themselves, among them R. Moshe Leib of Sassov and R. Yitzhak Isaac of Kaaliv.

It came to pass that at the same time two Jewish communities were each in search of a Rabbi, the community of Nicholsburg in Moravia (now part of Czechoslovakia), and the community of Frankfurt-am-Main, then a free city in Germany. According to Hassidic lore, Meir Anshel Rothschild, founder of the financial dynasty, knowing that the Rabbi of Chortkov, who had been his father's benefactor, had two learned sons, recommended that one of them be invited to become the spiritual leader of the Frankfurt Jews. A double problem of etiquette had to be solved. Neither of the two communities wished to outbid the other, and each waited until the other should first take one of the two brothers, so that it would be able to take the other. In addition, R. Pinkhas waited for his older brother to decide first which of the two offered rabbinic positions he would take; and R. Shmelkeh, considering his younger brother a greater scholar than himself,

wanted R. Pinkhas to choose first. So they betook themselves to
Mezritch to ask their teacher, the Maggid, to mediate the case.
While they were standing at the Maggid's door, he overhead
them argue as to who should enter first, one offering the honor
to the other. R. Dov Ber called out in a loud voice: "Let the
Rabbi of Nicholsburg enter first, for he is the older." So. R.
Pinkhas understood immediately that he, the younger, was to
accept the Rabbinic position in Frankfurt.

When R. Shmelkeh left Ritchevol for Nicholsburg, he took
with him the most beloved among his disciples, Moshe Leib, a
student young in years, but in piety and good deeds a spiritual
contemporary of the pietists of all the generations before him.
The great hopes that R. Shmelkeh placed on Moshe Leib were
later realized in the fullest measure.

R. Shmelkeh and R. Pinkhas were destined to be the first to
transplant Hassidut into Central and Western Europe.

When R. Pinkhas arrived in Frankfurt, young and old of the
Jewish community went to the outskirts to meet him. He was
surrounded by a multitude and actually carried into the city. Later,
when asked to comment on the extraordinary welcome he had
been given, R. Pinkhas replied: "I imagined that it was my
funeral, and was being carried in a casket, with the entire community escorting me to the cemetery."

R. Shmelkeh established a great Talmudic Academy in Nicholsburg and his Yeshivah produced a line of rabbis and scholars,
although he had to overcome great opposition to his Hassidic
teachings. The residents of Frankfurt, however, including non-
Jews with strong feelings of local patriotism, were proud that
their Rabbi was of the calibre of the great scholars who had
preceded him in the position. Many needy Gentiles turned to

R. Pinkhas for assistance since he devoted so large a part of his time and energies to charitable endeavors. In his teaching he also stressed the importance of charitable acts, maintaining that "the rich should be grateful to the poor, because if there were no needy people, those who are wealthy would have no occasion to be rewarded for their charitable deeds."

In his work *Paanim Yaffot*, meaning *Pleasant Countenance*, which is a commentary on the Five Books of Moses, written in the manner of Hassidic teachings, R. Pinkhas stressed the following: "When one does a deed of kindness, mercy or charity, he should realize that the other person reciprocates. But if one refuses to help his fellow, someone else may help him, and he who refuses, has lost a divine mission. Whatever one possesses was given to him from Heaven, only to help others."

In addition to brotherly love, R. Pinkhas stressed human equality: "The Holy One, blessed be He, does not differentiate between the great and the small, as He is Himself Incomparable. Therefore, even the most humble person should not consider himself so insignificant as to believe that he is not worthy to ask of the Creator what he needs."

Numerous rabbis and scholars in general turned to R. Pinkhas with problems on points of Jewish law. His contributions to Jewish jurisprudence are contained in the volumes *Hafla'ah*, meaning *Distinction*, and *HaMikneh*, dealing with forms of *Possession*.

R. Shmelkeh outdistanced his younger brother in mass popularity, since in addition to leading a Yeshiva, he also was engaged in Hassidic teaching and activity, becoming himself a symbol of ethics, love and humility.

R. Shmelkeh taught that it is not permissible to make distinctions in regard to love of human beings. Once, when asked how he found it possible to love someone who is wicked, he replied: "Every human being possesses a spark of the Almighty. I have compassion for the Creator that a spark of His is captive in evil."

R. Shmelkeh often stressed that one should never utter unkind words about other people:

"One should not engage in spreading rumors and lies; never make use of flattery and hypocrisy, never put anyone to shame, and never be ashamed of those who mock him. One should always have a special fund for charitable purposes."

It is related that a poor man, the descendant of a noble family, came to him for assistance. Since R. Shmelkeh had no money, he gave the poor man a ring, advising him to sell it. When the wife came home and found out what he had done, she began to cry: "You have given away so priceless a ring!" R. Shmelkeh left the house to look for the poor man to whom he had given the ring. When he found him, he told him with joy: "I have been told that it is a ring of great value. You can get for it a very large sum of money."

The question was asked: How is it possible to fulfil the precept: "And thou shalt love thy neighbour as thyself" in a case of the neighbour who does you harm? But this can be explained by logical inference. All the souls are included in the soul of the first Adam, thus all human beings derive from one soul and all souls are infused in bodies derived from one body. Sometimes a man may inadvertently strike himself. But will that man take a stick in order to punish the hand with which he struck himself? Surely, that is inconceivable. Similarly, in the case of a man who repays evil for evil, thus causing double injury to himself. On the contrary, man must always think that everything comes through Divine Ordinance and that the Holy One, blessed be He, has many

agents and agencies. One must not vent one's anger on a messenger; one must not hate him.
(Steinmann: The Garden of Hassidism, p. 182.)

Among the numerous tales about R. Shmelkeh, there is one about his command appearance before the Austrian Empress, Maria Theresa. During the audience, he kept his head lowered and did not look at her. When she reproached him for his manners, he replied: "I am looking at the ground from which I was created and to which I will return."

Like his younger brother, R. Shmelkeh wrote commentaries on Jewish Law. His Hassidic teachings are included in the volumes, *Divray Shmuel,* meaning *The Words of Samuel,* and *Shemen HaTov,* meaning *The Precious Oil;* the Hebrew word *"Shemen"* being an abbreviation of *Shmelkeh Nicholsburger.*

Father of Widows, Orphans, the Sick and the Needy, is the long title that Hassidic lore and the historians of Hassidism have applied to the life and activities of the extraordinary R. Moshe Leib of Sassov (1744–1807). He is usually mentioned simply as "The Sassover," as if no other Hassidic leader living later in the same city could claim so close an attachment to its name.

Before R. Moshe Leib became a master of Hassidic followers, he was himself attached, for almost a decade and a half, to R. Shmelkeh, being the latter's closest disciple.

R. Moshe Leib was born in Brody, a city connected with the first activities of the Besht. In his early youth, he became a disciple of R. Shmelkeh. Thanks to his master's encouragement, he developed into a great Talmudic scholar, and his inborn humility was increased by the great deeds of his beloved teacher.

After living for a number of years in Apta, R. Moshe Leib moved to Sassov, and followers by the hundreds came regularly to see him, to listen to his discourses and receive his blessings.

R. Moshe Leib used to say that the very first words in the Holy Scriptures—"In the beginning God created" (Gen. 1:1)—teach that the beginning of all knowledge is to know that God created everything, and from this knowledge one can proceed to learn more and more about the greatness of the Almighty. Particularly is the knowledge of the Creator important for the poor people, because the rich depend upon their wealth, but the poor have no one to depend on but God alone. On the other hand, wishing to emphasize the importance of charity, R. Moshe Leib went so far as to say that, "There are times that for the love of God one should not display faith in the Almighty. When a poor man comes to you in time of need, don't tell him piously that God who sustains all Creation, will also help him in need. You should rather think, that if you don't help him, no one else will. And when one helps a wicked person, he should not regret it. If God helps us, although we are not worthy, so we should likewise not judge the worthiness of a person who needs our help."

R. Moshe Leib himself practiced much more than he preached. By sundown, he distributed for charity all the money he had accumulated on that particular day, explaining that if money remained in his home, he would have a sleepless night.

Once he gave away to an evil man all the money in his possession. When the Hassidim asked him why he had done so, he replied: "He is not a good man, nor am I. If I give charity to an evil man, the Almighty will repay me measure for measure and He will also be charitable to me although I am not a good man."

The Sassover had to be notified about every case of illness among the children of the city, so that he would be able to visit everyone of them separately. He was particularly busy on the day of a *Yaarid,* the country fair, to which the peasants brought their produce and where horses and cattle were bought and sold. R. Moshe Leib, realizing that the peasants who came to the fair would also make use of the visit in town to see the tricks of circus men, and in the meantime would forget that their animals had to be given food and water, personally saw to it that the animals did not suffer from hunger or thirst, and that the hard-working peasants enjoyed themselves without being punished by the Compassionate Father in Heaven for causing suffering to His dumb creatures.

Basing his actions on the Jewish traditional teaching that everyone should imitate God in regard to other human beings, R. Moshe Leib taught that acts of charity must be coupled with acts of understanding. It is related that once, after midnight, when he was engrossed in the study of the Talmud, a drunkard knocked at the window and asked to be admitted. R. Moshe Leib felt annoyed by the interference, and decided not to open the door. But suddenly he began to argue against his own decision: "If you, Almighty God, tolerate drunkards in this world, then it is necessary that he should be here, and I will also tolerate him." Then Rabbi Moshe Leib admitted the man.

Teaching his followers to avoid every form of quarrel, R. Moshe Leib asserted that a person gains greater merit by remaining silent in the face of insults rather than by torturing his body with fasting and self-affliction in general, with the aim of obtaining rewards in the World-to-Come.

Having had contacts with human beings of different character, beginning with little children and ending with those of bad reputations, R. Moshe Leib said that he had, "learned three things from the behavior of a child and seven things from the behavior of a thief. A child, when awake, never rests; when it wants something, it cries; and as soon as its wish is fulfilled, it becomes happy without a trace of any sadness left. A thief does his main work at night; he works every night in order not to waste time; whatever is in his power to do, he does; he gives away no secrets; he never gives in, even when beaten; he is loyal to his fellow thieves; and what he accumulates during a lifetime, he loses within an hour."

The teachings and deeds of R. Moshe Leib were recorded in tiny "paperbacks," small printed brochures, and in the books of his important disciples. His own writings and what had been written about him, were later gathered in the three-part collection *Khidushey RaMaL*, meaning *The Novel Interpretations of RaMaL;* the last word in the title being an abbreviation of the name *R'Moshe Leib*.

The tales about the humility of R. Moshe Leib Sasover and about his charitable deeds in secrecy, inspired the great Yiddish-Hebrew writer, Isaac Leib Peretz, to create one of the gems of Yiddish fiction. It is the story *If Not Higher,* in which "The Sassover" is called "The Nemirover," and an anti-Hassidic Lithuanian Jew is the additional hero. Peretz's story is as follows:

> Early every Friday morning, at the time of the Penitential Prayers, the Rabbi of Nemirov would vanish.
>
> He was nowhere to be seen—neither in the synagogue nor in

the two Houses of Study, nor at a "minyan." And he was certainly not at home. His door stood open; whoever wished could go in and out; no one would steal from the rabbi. But not a living creature was within.

Where could the rabbi be? Where should he be? in heaven, no doubt. A rabbi has plenty of business to take care of just before the Days of Awe. Jews, God bless them, need livelihood, peace, health, and good matches. They want to be pious and good, but our sins are so great, and Satan of the thousand eyes watches the whole earth from one end to the other. What he sees he reports; he denounces, informs. Who can help us if not the rabbi!

That's what the people thought.

But once a Litvak came, and he laughed. You know the Litvaks. They think little of the Holy Books but stuff themselves with Talmud and law. So this Litvak points to a passage in the "Gemarah"—it sticks in your eyes—where it is written that even Moses, our Teacher, did not ascend to heaven during his lifetime but remained suspended two and a half feet below. Go argue with a Litvak!

So where can the rabbi be?

"That's not my business," said the Litvak, shrugging. Yet all the while—what a Litvak can do!—he is scheming to find out.

That same night, right after the evening prayers, the Litvak steals into the rabbi's room, slides under the rabbi's bed, and waits. He'll watch all night and discover where the rabbi vanishes and what he does during the Penitential Prayers.

Someone else might have got drowsy and fallen asleep, but a Litvak is never at a loss; he recites a whole tractate of the Talmud by heart.

At dawn he hears the call to prayers.

The rabbi has already been awake for a long time. The Litvak has heard him groaning for a whole hour.

Whoever has heard the Rabbi of Nemirov groan knows how much sorrow for all Israel, how much suffering, lies in each groan. A man's heart might break, hearing it. But a Litvak is made of iron; he listens and remains where he is. The rabbi, long life to him, lies on the bed, and the Litvak under the bed.

Then the Litvak hears the beds in the house begin to creak; he hears people jumping out of their beds, mumbling a few Jewish words, pouring water on their fingernails, banging doors. Everyone has left. It is again quiet and dark; a bit of light from the moon shines through the shutters.

(Afterward the Litvak admitted that when he found himself alone with the rabbi a great fear took hold of him. Goose pimples spread across his skin, and the roots of his earlocks pricked him like needles. A trifle: to be alone with the rabbi at the time of the Penitential Prayers! But a Litvak is stubborn. So he quivered like a fish in water and remained where he was.)

Finally the rabbi, long life to him, arises. First he does what befits a Jew. Then he goes to the clothes closet and takes out a bundle of peasant clothes: linen trousers, high boots, a coat, a big felt hat, and a long wide leather belt studded with brass nails. The rabbi gets dressed. From his coat pocket dangles the end of a heavy peasant rope.

The rabbi goes out, and the Litvak follows him.

On the way the rabbi stops in the kitchen, bends down, takes an ax from under the bed, puts it in his belt, and leaves the house. The Litvak trembles but continues to follow.

The hushed dread of the Days of Awe hangs over the dark streets. Every once in a while a cry rises from some "minyan" reciting the Penitential Prayers, or from a sickbed. The rabbi hugs the sides of the streets, keeping to the shade of the houses. He glides from house to house, and the Litvak after him. The Litvak hears the sound of his heartbeats mingling with the sound of the rabbi's heavy steps. But he keeps on going and follows the rabbi to the outskirts of the town.

A small wood stands behind the town.

The rabbi, long life to him, enters the wood. He takes thirty or forty steps and stops by a small tree. The Litvak, overcome with amazement, watches the rabbi take the ax out of his belt and strike the tree. He hears the tree creak and fall. The rabbi chops the tree into logs and the logs into sticks. Then he makes a bundle of the wood and ties it with the rope in his pocket. He puts the bundle of wood on his back, shoves the ax back into his belt, and returns to the town.

He stops at a back street beside a small broken-down shack and knocks at the window.

"Who is there?" asks a frightened voice. The Litvak recognizes it as the voice of a sick Jewish woman.

"I," answers the rabbi in the accent of a peasant.

"Who is I?"

Again the rabbi answers in Russian. "Vassil."

"Who is Vassil, and what do you want?"

"I have wood to sell, very cheap." And, not waiting for the woman's reply, he goes into the house.

The Litvak steals in after him. In the gray light of early morning he sees a poor room with broken, miserable furnishings. A sick woman, wrapped in rags, lies on the bed. She complains bitterly, "Buy? How can I buy? Where will a poor widow get money?"

"I'll lend it to you," answers the supposed Vassil. "It's only six cents."

"And how will I ever pay you back?" said the poor woman, groaning.

"Foolish one," says the rabbi reproachfully. "See, you are a poor sick Jew, and I am ready to trust you with a little wood. I am sure you'll pay. While you, you have such a great and mighty God and you don't trust him for six cents."

"And who will kindle the fire?" said the widow. "Have I the strength to get up? My son is at work."

"I'll kindle the fire," answers the rabbi.

As the rabbi put the wood into the oven he recited, in a groan, the first portion of the Penitential Prayers.

As he kindled the fire and the wood burned brightly, he recited, a bit more joyously, the second portion of the Penitential Prayers. When the fire was set he recited the third portion, and then he shut the stove.

The Litvak who saw all this became a disciple of the Rabbi.

And ever after, when another disciple tells how the Rabbi of Nemirov ascends to heaven at the time of the Penitential Prayers, the Litvak does not laugh. He only adds quietly, "If not higher."
(Translated by Marie Syrkin)

In the early period of Hassidism, the movement had a mystery man in its service. His name was Leib Soreh's, meaning Leib the Son of Sara (1730–1791). Why was he called by his mother's name? It is related that when Sara was young, she lived with her parents in a village somewhere in Germany. Sara was considered the most beautiful girl in the entire region. But she paid no attention to the compliments about her looks, and after finishing the daily household chores under the direction of her mother, and in her spare time, in general, she listened to how the elderly teacher R. Yoseph instructed the boys and to the stories he told them after teaching hours. Admiring the old teacher, Sara observed carefully all his doings, and came to the realization that R. Yoseph practiced, in secret, the very same forms of piety which he told when relating the great *Tzadikim* of the past. The German nobleman who owned the village where Sara lived, had a young, debauched son, and the fellow, becoming aware of Sara and her extraordinary beauty, decided that she must become his wife. When Sara rejected his proposals, he threatened her with kidnapping. On one occasion Sara told her parents and the elderly teacher of the young nobleman's desire, and right then and there she pleaded with R. Yoseph to marry her. She confessed that she had noticed the secret ways and deeds of the teacher, and would consider it a great honor to become his spouse. In the beginning, R. Yoseph was astonished at the suggestion of the young and beautiful Sara, but after she had emphasized several times that the actions of the young nobleman were a threat not only to herself, but to all Jews in the region, the old man agreed to her proposal, and after a hastily arranged, secret wedding ceremony, R. Yoseph and his young wife escaped from Germany, settling in the Vohlynian city of Rovno. There Sara gave birth to a boy. Since R. Yoseph was a descendant of R. Yehudah Leib Ben Betzalell, known in history as the miracle-performing Talmudic giant, *MaHaRal* (1515–1609) who created a human figure made of clay and gave him a living soul to act on behalf of the Jews in time of persecution, R. Yoseph named his son after his famous ancestor. The boy was called Leib for short. Old R. Yoseph died not long after the son came into the world, and young Sara took it upon herself to lead the boy in the path his father would have wished. Everybody knew him as Leib, the son of Sara.

When Leib Soreh's was in his late teens, he joined the Hassidic circle of R. Israel Baal Shem Tov. The Besht entrusted young Leib with the secret missions he himself used to perform when he was younger: providing bail for Jewish innkeepers who had been arrested for inability to pay their landlords in time. After the Besht passed away, his successor the Maggid of Mezritch, R. Dov Ber, entrusted R. Leib with the same missions. It was R. Leib Soreh's custom to visit all the country fairs to which came Jewish merchants and villagers. He usually rented an empty store, but he put no wares on its shelves. When people came in and asked what he sold, he replied: "Mine is the best merchandise! I am selling trust in the Almighty!" On such occasions, R. Leib gathered information about suffering innkeepers and he made contact with people of means to supply him with the necessary funds for the "Ransoming of Captives." The credentials of the Maggid R. Dov Ber were of great help, but soon R. Leib Soreh's own personality was considered the best recommendation and guarantee.

R. Leib Soreh's once approached the wealthiest man in a certain town asking him to contribute to the fund for the "Ransoming of Captives." The rich man was a miser, and when he refused to contribute, R. Leib Soreh's gave him a brief lecture:

"Look here, my dear fellow, the earth we step on is dust: the table that we sit around is also rooted in dust; the mansion of the wealthy man is built by dust; his money and gold were mined from the dust; the wealthy man himself was created from dust; his money is certainly the dust of dust. Are you, my dear friend, really so fearful of dust?"

On another occasion, R. Leib Soreh's explained briefly his philosophy on the life of humans and faith in God:

"People are constantly complaining that life is short. Are seventy years of life as easy as a straw to pick up? Does the cow live longer? And how about the life of the creeping things? The lifetime of a fly is but a single day in human life. Nevertheless, the human being is full of complaints. Do many days, months and years of life mean a long life? No, longevity means many accomplishments; and every one who directs his own heart towards it, becomes attached to the Eternal and he will no longer taste the taste of death."

In connection with his activities, R. Leib traveled a great deal, and one of his trips took him as far as Hungary. Once, while on the road, he noticed a little boy tending a flock of geese and overheard him murmuring, in prayer, and singing to himself. R. Leib stopped and listened to the boy's Yiddish prayer-song:

/

> God in Heaven!
> If You had
> A flock of geese,
> I would very gladly
> Take care of them,
> Free of charge.

R. Leib, strongly impressed, struck up a conversation with the boy. Answering the stranger's questions, the boy replied that his name was Yitzkhak Isaac, but people usually called him Isaacle; he was eight years old, and since his father was dead, he tended geese to help his widowed mother. R. Leib decided then and there to "ransom" Isaacle from the geese, and asked the boy to take him to his mother. Being a man of the world and a gifted talker, R. Leib Soreh's persuaded the widow Reizelle to be separated for a time from her only son. Mentioning his own childhood as an orphan, R. Leib promised the mother that he would take Isaacle to Nicholsburg, to live there in the home of R. Shmelkeh and study in the Yeshiva, where he would certainly become a man of fame and the glory of the family.

When little Isaac of Sirintch was brought by R. Leib Soreh's before R. Shmelkeh, the boy was asked to sing some of the shepherds' songs he knew. When in time Isaacle himself became the shepherd of great flocks of Hassidim, and known as the famous R. Yitzkhak Isaac of Kaaliv (1751–1821), one of the shepherd's songs, to which he added lines of his own, was on the lips of young and old:

Forest, O forest, how big you are!
Rose, O rose, how far you are!
If the forest were small,
The rose would be near.
If I were taken from the forest,
Together we should be.

Exile, O exile, how big you are!
O Divine Presence, how far you are!
If exile were smaller,
Divine Presence would be nearer.
If I were taken from exile,
Together we would be.

R. Elimelekh of Lizhensk, whom many considered as the successor of the Maggid of Mezritch and the third in line after R. Israel Baal Shem Tov in Hassidic leadership and importance, once came for a visit to Nicholsburg. There he conversed with some of the young men who studied at the Yeshiva and were among R. Shmelkeh's most cherished pupils. R. Elimelekh became so impressed while chatting with Isaacle, that he took him, with R. Shmelkeh's permission, for three years to Lizhensk there to be a source of inspiration to others as well as to R. Elimelekh himself.

R. Yitzkhak Isaac's humility and modesty were without bounds, and when he was offered the position of Rabbi in Kaaliv, he first refused, out of conviction that he was not fit for the role and task. Among the representatives of the Kaaliv Jewish community who had come to offer Isaacle the Rabbinic chair of the town, was a very old man, R. Yaakov Fisch, who in his youth had been blessed by R. Israel Baal Shem Tov, the Besht. It was a blessing by R. Yaakov that influenced Isaacle to give in and become the Rabbi of Kaaliv.

Every human being was of equal importance to R. Yitzkhak Isaac of Kaaliv; any difficulty, even the most minor, that a person complained of, was considered by him to be of the greatest urgency to be dealt with and eliminated with the utmost speed. Every one who had come with a troubled heart to the sweet-singing and sweet-talking Hassidic master to unburden himself emotionally, left him with a heart full of joy and hope.

R. Moshe Leib of Sassov was six years older than R. Yitzkhak Isaac of Kaaliv. Just as among R. Shmelkeh's disciples, the Sassover became the personification of Hassidic humility, so became the Kaaliver the symbol of Hassidic joy, longing and love of God, expressed by means of song and dance. Even when already the spiritual shepherd of numerous Hassidim, the soul within the Kaaliver remained as it was in the days when he tended a flock of geese at the outskirts of his birthplace. Whenever the occasion permitted, R. Yitzkhak Isaac slipped out of Kaaliv and betook himself to the green pastures. He inhaled the aroma of the woods, of the fields, and of the meadows. His ears and his heart were open to the shepherd tunes he heard from near and far. Many such tunes were "cleansed" by R. Yitzkhak Isaac "with the sparks of sanctity," by re-arranging them as tunes for the congregational Synagogue Prayers and for the "Zemirot," the mealtime hymnals of the Sabbath Day. Not only did R. Yitzkhak Isaac lay the foundation of a Hassidic fortress in Hungary, but thanks to his talent as a composer and singer, tune, song, and dance became embedded in the sociability and comradeship of Hassidic life.

The Kaaliver had made it a custom that no more than one wedding per day should take place in the city, because he wished to be present at every marriage, making sure that young men and women did not dance together. He also used his personal charm and influence to bring back into the traditional fold many who had strayed away in their youth, either because of heresy or just to be free of religious discipline. Some of those who repented later became well-known personalities in the ranks of traditional Jewry on Hungarian soil. Notwithstanding his large number of followers, Yitzkhak Isaac actually supported himself and his family from the meager salary paid him by the local Jewish community for being its Rabbi. His spoken teachings actually consisted of repeating the teachings of other Hassidic leaders and of recalling their deeds. He believed in music and song as the best forms of creating human brotherhood. He personally forged kinship between Hungarian shepherd tunes and age-old Jewish prayers and hymns. R. Yitzkhak Isaac's last wish was that none of his sons succeed him. As his life was ebbing, after forty years of being the Rabbi of the local community and the first leading Hassidic teacher on Hungarian soil, his Hassidim began to cry when he told them that after his death, everyone could pick a new master for himself, choosing from among the then living Hassidic leaders. "And who can be considered a real Tzadik?" asked R. Yitzkhak Isaac, and immediately answered his own question: "It is he who fulfills his duty by taking out the Hassid's soul, washing it in the way one does with laundry, and then returning to the Hassid a cleansed soul."

Some of the songs written by R. Yitzkhak Isaac were not in Hebrew or Yiddish words, but in the Hungarian language, as if he wished to create bonds of understanding between the Jews and the non-Jews within the population.

One of those songs created in Hungarian by R. Yitzkhak Isaac Taub of Kaaliv is known under the name *The Cock Crows:*

The cock crows:
Morning is alight;
In a green forest,
On a white field,
A bird is strolling.
How beautiful you are,
O how beautiful you are!

Gleam-legged, gleam-beaked
Looks at me the bird.

Wait a bit, bird!
Wait a bit, bird!
If God will espouse you unto me,
I will live with you in joy.

The cock crows;
Morning is alight!
Let the Temple be built,
Let Zion become inhabited!
When will the generation be redeemed?
There we will sing a new song in a lofty voice:
The time has come!

Today, all the Hassidim, all who long for personal and national redemption, all Jewish universalists, as well as all idealistic universalists of other beliefs, are waiting for the day when it will be possible to sing, in the unison of lofty voices, the final lines of such poems as *The Cock Crows:*

The day is alight,
The time has come!

VII

R. Shneur Zalman of Ladi:
Wisdom, Understanding, Knowledge

WHEN A YOUNG Talmudic giant named Shneur Zalman (1747–1813) came from White Russia to join the inner circle of the disciples of R. Ber, the Maggid of Mezritch, it turned out to be historically one of the major events in the development of Hassidut.

R. Shneur Zalman was born in the town of Liozhni, and in his early youth he had already become famous for his Talmudic knowledge and his great intellectual capacity.

> In his old age, R' Shneur Zalman was once driving through the country with his grandson. Birds were hopping about and twittering everywhere. The rabbi put his head out of the carriage for a while. "How fast they chatter," he said to the child. "They have their own alphabet. All you need do is listen and grasp well, and you will understand their language."

> Once he interrupted his prayers and said: "I do not want Your paradise. I do not want Your coming world. I want You, and You only."
>
> *(Buber: Tales of the Hasidim, Early Masters, pp. 266–267.)*

After the passing of R. Ber, the Maggid, R. Shneur Zalman joined the circle of the disciples of R. Mendel of Vitebsk. When the latter emigrated to the Holy Land, R. Shneur Zalman became leader in his place, and later he was famous as the Rav of Ladi,

the town where he later settled and established his own center of
teaching and activity.

Said the Ladier: "I have labored twenty-one years on truth;
seven years to learn what truth is; seven years, to drive out falsehood; and seven years to acquire the habit of truthfulness."

The Rav asked a disciple who had just entered his room:
"Moshe, what do we mean when we say 'God'?" The disciple
was silent. The Rav asked him a second and third time. Then he
said: "Why are you silent?"
"Because I do not know."
"Do you think I know?" said the Rav. "But I must say it,
for it is so, and therefore I must say it: He is definitely there,
and except for Him nothing is definitely there—and this is He."
(Emet Kneh, p. 74; Newman: Hassidic Anthology, p. 491; Buber:
Tales of the Hasidim, Early Masters, p. 269.)

In Vilna, known as the "Jerusalem of Lithuania," because of
its Jewish scholarship, resided R. Eliyahu the Gaon, the exalted
Talmudic authority of his age and simultaneously the spiritual
leader of the Mitnagdim, opponents of the Hassidim. The opponents were adamant in their decision to uproot the Hassidic
movement in Lithuania and White Russia, and the extremists
among them went even so far as to denounce R. Shneur Zalman
to the Russian authorities for disloyalty to the government. He
was twice incarcerated in St. Petersburg, in 1796 and in 1800.
During the Napoleonic invasion, R. Shneur Zalman sided with
Russia. As the invaders progressed, R. Shneur Zalman and the
closest of his disciples sought refuge in the region of the Ural
Mountains. He died in a village near Kursk and was buried in
Hadick, in the Poltava Region.

R. Shneur Zalman was a prolific writer of commentaries on

the Jewish Code of Laws, of commentaries to biblical books and to the *Zohar,* the latter being the main source of Jewish mysticism. For twenty years, he labored on his main work known as the *Tanyah* or *Liqqutei Amarim.* This work is a philosophical and theological interpretation of Judaism and is the source book of the special school of Hassidut known as *Khabad,* being the Hebrew abbreviation of the terms Wisdom *(Khokhmah),* Understanding *(Binah),* and Knowledge *(Daat).* It is related that when the great Hassidic leader, R. Levi Yitzkhak of Berdichev, studied R. Shneur Zalman's *Tanyah* for the first time, he exclaimed: "How great is the wisdom of the author that he could compress the greatness of God into so small a book."

R. Shneur Zalman's successor was his son, R. Dov Ber (1773–1827), and since he had established his residence in the town of Lubavitch, the followers of the Khabad school became known as Lubavitcher Hassidim. His heir to leadership was his nephew and son-in-law R. Menkahem Mendel (1789–1866), who is still popular as the author of the book *Tzemakh Tzedek.* He, in turn, was succeeded by the youngest of his five sons, R. Shmuel (1834–1882), known as the "Moharash," the Hebrew abbreviation of his title and name. The fifth in line was R. Sholem Dovber (1860–1920), who was especially active in the founding of Yeshivot. To help needy Jewish workers, R. Sholem Dovber established a textile factory. During World War I, he setttled in Rostov. It fell to his heir, R. Yoseph Yitzkhak Shneurson (1880–1950), to be the last Lubavitcher Rabbi in Russia. He was threatened by the Communist regime with execution for his activities in behalf of Jewish religious education. He was arrested but later permitted to leave the Soviet Union. After residing for a time in Riga, Latvia, R. Yoseph Yitzkhak emigrated to the

United States and settled in Brooklyn, where he established the great Lubavitcher Hassidic center on Eastern Parkway; it being also the headquarters of the Lubavicher Yeshivot and publishing house. He was succeeded by his son-in-law, the present leader of the Khabad Hassidim, R. Menahem Shneurson, who has successfully widened Lubavicher activities among native-born American Jews and sponsored the publication of *Tanyah* in English by Dr. Nissan Mindel (New York, 1965, 369 pages). Among the English books published by the Kehot Publication Society of the Lubavitcher, is a biography of R. Shneur Zalman, founder of the dynasty, written by Dr. Gershon Kantzler.

R. Shneur Zalman's successors and many sharp minds among various generations of Lubavicher Hassidim, have illuminated the Khabad-teachings of the Rav. The foundation of these teachings is the *a priori* belief that "The Holy One, blessed be He! Nothing is outside of Him and there is no place devoid of Him."

> God is totally distinct from both the upper and lower worlds and can in no way be compared to the soul of man.
>
> All that man sees—sky, earth, and its fullness—are God's outer garments, manifesting an inner spirit, the divine vital elan which permeates them.
>
> When man completes a product, his relation to it ends; but God's power continues to permeate His creatures.
> *(Tanyah 1796, Yihud, ch. 2, p. 42; Iggeret Ha Kodesh, III, 1805; A Treasury of Jewish Quotations, ed. by J.L. Baron, New York, 1956.)*

The Holy One, blessed be He, knows all that befalls all created beings, both higher and lower, because they all receive their influence from Him, may He be blessed, as is written: "For all things come of Thee." (I Chron.. 29:14). And this is the meaning of what we say: "Verily also nothing that is formed is withheld from Thee." (Liturgy, Musaf for the New Year). And as Maimonides has said (and this has been accepted by the scholars of the Quabbalah, as Rabbi Moses Cordovero writes in Pardess), that "knowing Himself, as it were, He knows all created things that exist by virtue of His true existence," etc.

(Liqqutei Amarim [Tanya] translated by Nissan Mindel p. 271.)

The Holy One, blessed be He, however, is not, Heaven forbid, affected by the accidents of the world and its changes, nor by the world itself, for they do not affect any change in Him, G-d forbid. In order to help us perceive this well with our intelligence, the Scholars of Truth have already treated of it at length in their books. But all Jews are "believers descended from believers," (Shabbat 92a) who, without human intellectual speculation whatever, say:

"Thou wast the same ere the world was created," and so forth.
(Liturgy. Cf. Yalqut, Wa-ethanan 836, quoting a Talm. Yer. source; Liqqutei Amarim [Tanya], p. 272.)

According to R. Shneur Zalman's teachings, the brain rules the heart, and reason in the human spirit has a greater mission than being just a vessel. Man has the power of choice to make his mind rule over his heart, and he can say to himself that he does not wish to commit acts that will estrange him from God. He insisted:

Virtue arising from Reason is higher than virtue which is not founded on Reason.
(Tanya, 1796. S. A. Horodetzky: Leaders of the Hassidism, London, 1928, p. 60.)

The essence of knowledge is not the knowing alone, that people should know the greatness of G-d from authors and books; but

the essential thing is to immerse one's mind deeply into the greatness of G-d and fix one's thought on G-d with all the strength and
vigor of the heart and mind, until his thought shall be bound to
G-d with a strong and vivid bond, as it is bound to a material
thing that he sees with his physical eyes and concentrates his
thought on it.
(Liqqutei Amarim [Tanya], p. 267.)

Concerning the observance of the Torah commands dealing
with prohibitions, R. Shneur Zalman was of the opinion that,
"What is prohibited, is prohibited; and what is permitted, is
unnecessary." Seeing Creation in everything, he expressed the
conviction that every month is a renewal of life from naught to
substance. Concerning the necessities of life, he stressed the
following:

> It is true the law teaches that one's own life comes first, but
> this applies only to things on which life depends . . . But if it
> is a question of bread and clothes and wood on one side, and
> dinners with fish and meat and fruit on the other side, the latter
> have to be given up as superfluities . . . This is the real meaning
> of the law, but it is not worthy of a man to insist upon the law
> in such cases. He ought not to think of his life.
> *(Tanya, [1796] 1896, 52a; Solomon Schechter: Studies in Judaism,
> Vol. II, p. 172.)*

Behold, when a person fortifies his divine soul and wages war
against his animal soul to such an extent that he expels and
eradicates its evil from the left part—as is written, "And thou
shalt root out the evil from within you" (Deut. 21:21)—yet the
evil is not actually converted to goodness, he is called "incompletely
righteous," or "a righteous man who suffers (evil)." That is to
say, there still lingers in him a fragment of wickedness in the
left part, except that it is subjugated and nullified by the good,

because of the former's minuteness. Hence he imagines that he has driven it out and it has quite disappeared. In truth, however, had all the evil in him entirely departed and disappeared, it would have been converted into actual goodness.

The explanation of the matter is that "a completely righteous man," in whom the evil has been converted to goodness, and who is consequently called "a righteous man who prospers," has completely divested himself of the filthy garments of evil. That is to say, he utterly despises the pleasures of this world, finding no enjoyment in human pleasures or merely gratifying the physical appetites.
(*Liqqutei Amarim* [*Tanya*], *pp. 68–69.*)

The problem of how to overpower evil inclinations is dealt with extensively in the writings of the Rav, and he came to the conclusion that the beastly body and spirit within man tend and clothe the divine soul and do not permit it to leave its casement. The two souls, the animalistic and the divine, are in constant battle to win rulership over the body. In the divine soul of the human being, shines the infinite light of the Blessed One, clothed and concealed in its light of Wisdom to radiate life. The human being can learn from it to understand something of the upper spheres that are shining in his soul which is composed of them. Evil itself, he insisted, can be transformed into outright goodness if you remove from it the soiled garments, the base pleasures of this world:

The very fire of sin must be sublimated into a sacred flame, and the very fire of the Evil Inclination must be employed in the service of God.

Don't attempt to drive folly out of your mind by force. Rather ignore evil thoughts, and concentrate on God.
(*Liqqutei Amarim* [*Tanya*], [*1796*] *1912, p. 70, Liqqutei Toray,*

Deut. 1848 [1928]; A Treasury of Jewish Quotations, New York, 1956.)

It has been said: "Better is one hour of repentance and good works in this world than the whole life of the world to come." (Abot 4:17) For the world to come is that state where one enjoys the splendor of the Divine Presence, (Berakhot 16b) which is the pleasure of comprehension, yet no created being—even celestial—can comprehend more than some reflection of the Divine Light; that is why the reference is to "Splendor of the Divine Presence" (Ziv ha-Shekhinah i.e., the "glow" of the Shekhinah, not the Shekhinah itself).

(Liqqutei Amarim [Tanya], p. 39.)

Even in the mind alone, in so far as sinful thoughts are concerned, evil has no power to compel the mind's volition to entertain willingly, G-d forbid, any wicked thought rising of its own accord from the heart to the brain, as discussed above. (Beg. ch. 9). But no sooner does it reach there than he thrusts it out with both hands and averts his mind from it the instant he reminds himself that it is an evil thought, refusing to accept it willingly, even to let his thoughts play on it willingly; how much more so to entertain any idea of putting it into effect, G-d forbid, or even to put it into words. For he who wilfully indulges in such thoughts is deemed wicked at such time, whereas the "intermediate" person is never wicked for a single moment.

So, too, in matters affecting a person's relations with his neighbor, as soon as there rises from his heart to his mind some animosity or hatred, G-d forbid, or jealousy or anger, or a grudge and suchlike, he gives them no entrance into his mind and will. On the contrary, his mind exercises its authority and power over the spirit in his heart, to do the very opposite and to conduct himself towards his neighbor with the quality of kindness and a display of overly love, to the extent of suffering at his hands to the extreme limits without becoming provoked into anger, G-d forbid, or to revenge

in kind, G-d forbid; but rather to repay the offenders with favors, as taught in the Zohar, (I, 201a f.) that one should learn from the example of Joseph towards his brothers.
(Liqqutei Amarim [Tanya], pp. 82–83.)

In his writings, R. Shneur Zalman devoted many pages to human brotherhood, compassion and charity. He interpreted a biblical passage: "As in water, face answereth to face, so the heart of man to man" (Proverbs 27:19), as meaning that true love inspires the return of love and thus true brotherhood is created. God's Divine Presence rests upon the body of a human being only because of his meritorious deeds.

In various writings, R. Shneur Zalman advanced specific teachings about charity:

> Charity is one of the remedies against alien thoughts. It is a magnet with more power to attract the Divine influence than any other precept.
>
> Charity removes the stain of sin, and the hand that does charity becomes a limb in the Chariot of the Holy One.
>
> As lightning springs out of its concealment in dark clouds to flash through the world, so the Divine light, imbedded in matter, emerges through charitable deeds . . . Thus through charity, a sort of Divine revelation occurs in the soul.
> *('Seder Tefillot, 1816; Liqqutei Torah: Ro-eh, 1858; Tanya, [1796] 1896, 23; Teitelbaum, HaRav MeLadi, II 225; A Treasury of Jewish Quotations, ed. by J. L. Baron, New York 1956.)*

"Joy has proven to be the most potent of all medicines," said R. Shneur Zalman, and he stressed that in the high temples there are spheres whose gates are opened only to the sound of song.

In the teachings of R. Shneur Zalman about the End of Days, is emphasized the belief that in the Messianic era, the world will rise out of its corporeality and the splendor of God will be revealed; and that the World-to-Come means that those who merit it will enjoy Divine Glory.

It is well known that the Messianic Era and especially the time of the Resurrection of the dead, is the fulfillment and culmination of the creation of the world, for which purpose it was originally created. (The receiving of the reward is essentially in the seventh millenium, as is stated in Liqqutei Torah of Rabbi Isaac Luria, of blessed memory).
(Liqqutei Amarim [Tanya] translated by Nissan Mindel, p. 210.)

R. Menakhem Mendel, the grandson of R. Shneur Zalman added his own illumination: "In this world people can feel God, but in the Heavenly World, God is actually seen."

VIII

The Karleener:
Hassidism Comes to Lithuania

R. AARON of Karlin (1735–1772) was only thirty-seven years
old when he died. He had been one of the youngest among the
disciples of R. Dov Ber of Mezritch, the Besht's successor; but
in the history of Hassidism, he is immortal as R. Aaron the
Great. And great he was, indeed, in learning, as was befitting
an illustrious son of Lithuanian Jewry; in piety, as was befitting
a great scholar who had become an inspired Hassid; and as a
leader, for it was thanks to his fervor that Lithuanian Jewry, the
fortress of anti-Hassidism, was stormed by the adherents of Hassidism, who established further conquests in Lithuania and in
neighboring White Russia. His seat was in Karlin, a suburb of
Pinsk; and since the spiritual concentration of the Hassidic forces
were in Karlin, all Hassidim in Lithuania were nicknamed
"Karleener" by their opponents, the Mitnagdim.

R. Aaron visited the Maggid of Mezritch quite often, and the
successor of the Besht was proud that a young scholar from the
anti-Hassidic environment had joined the ranks of the Hassidim.
When R. Aaron returned home from his first visit to Mezritch,
he was asked derisively what he had learned from R. Dov Ber.
He replied: "Absolutely nothing." "If so, why have you become a
Hassid?" "Because I have been learning all the time that I am
nothing."

R. Aaron added to the teachings of the Besht and of the Maggid the fruits of his own inspired scholarship. And just as he was a courageous leader in battle for the Hassidic movement, so he was a courageous teacher who dared to show new ways and forms in belief and behavior. His teachings are recorded in the work called *Bayt Aharon*, meaning *The House of Aaron,* collected and recorded by his grandson, known as R. Aaron of Karlin the Second.

R. Aaron the Great placed emphasis on the following credos:

"The most important knowledge is the knowledge of God.

"It is meritorious to judge all people favorably. (Ethic of the Fathers 1:6). How more so should we judge favorably Almighty God Himself and not question his ways and actions.

"Sadness leads to dullness of the heart.

"Even the minutest bitterness is a result of sadness, and even the coarsest joy is rooted in sanctity.

"A human being who does not become gradually better becomes gradually worse.

"Egoism is evil because the egotist believes that the world owes him material and spiritual well-being. He would enjoy life if he came to the conclusion that others owe him nothing, but he owes much to his fellow-humans."

R. Aaron was a talented singer and an author of verse. He wrote religious poetry, and his song on the Sabbath is actually the introduction to the great work *Bayt Aaron.*

The Karleener Hassidim used to sing a Yiddish song dealing with repentance:

> Why should we worry about what could happen tomorrow?
> Let's rather think of what occurred yesterday,
> Perhaps we will be able to correct our wrongs today.

In his last will and testament, R. Aaron wrote down the following words: "I doubt whether there is anyone who is worse than me," and he forbade the use of praise when talking about him.

Why did R. Aaron the Great die at so early an age? His devotees had their answer: "He was consumed by flaming Fear of God."

After R. Aaron's passing, it was said among the Hassidim that when he had been alive, the gates of all pleasures and joys were open to him, but he refused to take anything that he could get without trying very hard.

When R. Aaron the Great died, the leadership of the Karleener was taken over by his closest associate and disciple, R. Shlomo (1737–1792), who was only two or three years younger. The Lithuanian-White Russian Mitnagdim, on their part, started a furious counter-offensive against the Hassidim. In R. Shlomo's home was reared R. Aaron the Great's orphaned son Asher, later to be known as R. Asher of Stolin. The two were like father and son. The devotion of teacher and disciple to each other was so great that R. Shlomo once declared that he had been born for one purpose only: to remove the doubts of beloved Asher.

R. Shlomo was a man of concentrated prayer and thought, and he was not made to be a central figure in battle. As the counterattacks of the Mitnagdim became more intense, R. Shlomo left Karlin in 1781 and settled in the Vohlynian city of Ludmir, where he soon won a number of close disciples and many adherents. Thanks to his role as a teacher, some of his disciples had the proper training and vision to conquer new positions for Hassidut all over Eastern Europe.

R. Aaron emphasized in his teachings that everyone should

remember that he is a prince, the child of the Almighty King of the Universe. Nevertheless, one should not act in a detached princely manner when it is the occasion to help a fellow-man. He also stressed the importance of careful education of one's own children, because one is rewarded in Heaven according to the way one treats his children on earth. He stressed that it was not enough to fulfill the precepts of God—the non-Hassidim were also fulfilling them daily—but there must be a feeling of joy in the deeds; precepts must be observed because of love, and not because of ordinary obligation or fear. "Those who fulfill precepts without joy, are even driven from Paradise by those who cannot stand the morose forms of piety," said R. Shlomo.

His teachings, as related and recorded by his disciples, comprise the collection *Shemah Shlomo,* meaning *The Fame of Solomon,* the title being taken from a biblical passage: "And when the Queen of Sheba heard of the fame of Solomon because of the name of the Lord, she came to prove him with hard questions" (First Kings, 10:1). The collection was published posthumously. The essence of R. Shlomo's teachings is found in the following paragraphs:

I. I wish that I could love even the pious in the great manner that the Almighty loves the wicked.

II. If you desire to raise one from the mire, you must get into the mud, and bring him from there to light. From above, this cannot be done.

III. The essence of repentance is thought, and one must cleanse his thoughts from all things that are materialistic, unclean and prohibited and attach his thoughts only to good things. Thought rules every deed and expression. When one guards his mouth, his eyes and his ears, passion will not rule over him. He who is governed by passion is a fool, because the wise man rules over his passion even in the midst of a passionate act.

The early leaders of the Karleener Hassidim were not blessed with longevity. R. Aaron died at the age of thirty-seven and his successor R. Shlomo passed away at the age of fifty-five, in a most tragic manner. A Cossack shot him in the leg while he was saying the Sabbath Prayers. His disciple, R. Asher, wanted the bullet removed on the very same day, but R. Shlomo refused to give in, arguing: "Because of so small a thing, should we forget the Creator of all worlds?" The leg became infected, the infection spread to other parts of his body, and five days after he had been wounded, R. Shlomo died. Before he was called to the Heavenly Yeshiva, R. Shlomo advised his Hassidim to recognize R. Mordecai of Neshkhiz as their master. The greatest among his disciples later became Hassidic masters themselves, among them R. Uri of Strelisk (? –1826).

R. Asher of Stolin (1765–1826) was only seven years old at the death of his father, R. Aaron the Great. His father's successor, R. Shlomo, took upon himself the task of preparing little Asher for the leadership his father had begun. R. Asher and R. Mordecai of Lekhovitch, similarly a disciple of R. Shlomo, carried on the battle of Hassidut in Lithuania; both tasted the bitterness of languishing in prison, and both tasted the fruits of victory, their dynasties continuing to teach on the soil of Lithuania and White Russia.

Like his teacher R. Shlomo before him, R. Asher was forced by his opponents to leave Karlin, and he settled in Stolin, giving that town a place in the historic development of Hassidism. Since R. Asher grew to maturity in Ludmir, his brand of Hassidut had both the poetic softness of the Hassidic environment of Vohlynia and the scholarly ingredients of Lithuanian Talmudism, joined together by the traditional ethics and morals expressed in Hassidic terminology. The sum total of Lithuanian Hassidut is found in the statement by R. Mordecai of Lekhovitch at the circumcision ceremony of R. Asher's son. He bent over the crib of the eight-day-old child and said to him: "Don't try to fool God! Never fool human beings, and don't fool yourself."

It is related that one day a man came to R. Asher, crying bitterly, and told him that according to the various books on human behavior, there was no forgiveness for his sins. R. Asher consoled him: "Why should you care what the authors of books write about? Your task is to repent. You fear that it would be of no value and that you will never inherit a share in the World-to-Come. So what of it? Our Sages of old thought that one hour of repentance and good deeds in this world is of greater value than the entire life in the future world."

R. Asher taught his Hassidim never to hide the negative aspects of their deeds and behavior. He called their attention to the important principle that when Hassidim came to their master, they should not boast of their piety, but on the contrary, they should uncover their shortcomings. "When I visited my master, R. Shlomo, I always covered up the favorable things about my behavior and instead I showed him all my sores and shortcomings.'"

In connection with this principle, R. Asher interpreted the passage from the *Song of Songs* (A lily of the valley 2:1) as meaning a lily that blooms from the valley-depths of the heart.

R. Asher spoke to his Hassidim very often on problems of faith, goodness, truth, suffering, evil inclination and repentance:

I. He who takes upon himself fully the Yoke of Heaven, enters into the world of liberty.

II. Everything that is good is called simple, because it contains nothing else in addition to the good. Good has no other attribute except the fact that it is simply good.

III. "The Lip of truth shall be established forever" (Proverbs 12:19), means that just a lip-size of the truth, even a bit of truth, exists into eternity.

IV. The greatest of all afflictions is that one has passed his fortieth birthday without ever having experienced any afflictions.

V. "Why are there some people who cannot overpower evil inclination, while we accomplish this? Because the others shout at the evil inclination with the help of the evil inclination itself, so it does not fear them; but we threaten inclination with the help of God, so it escapes immediately."

R. Asher said once to his son Aaron, later famous as the Second R. Aaron: "God should protect you from the need of repentance. It is woe and bitter when one has to resort to repentance."

R. Aaron the Second (1808–1873) made an effort to transform Karlin once more into the main center of Hassidut in Lithuania, after it had gained so many adherents all over Eastern Europe, with the loftiness of its prayers and depths of its teachings. R. Aaron, who was given that name to perpetuate among the living the name of his grandfather, R. Aaron the Great, devoted his energies to collecting the teachings of his grandfather, of his father and of his father's teacher. Old animosities had not died down in Karlin, and R. Aaron had to return to Stolin. Thanks to his collection *Bayt Aaron*, the main teachings of the Karleener have been recorded for posterity.

R. Aaron was asked why Hassidim loved to dance. He replied: "Because dancing enables them to rise above the ground."

In addition to collecting the teachings of his predecessors and repeating them to his devotees, R. Aaron the Second stressed his own views on matters of faith and behavior.

His teachings include the following:

I.   Fear of God but without love of God, is a damaged fear; and love without fear is altogether worthless. Where there is fear of God, it is wonderful; and when one possesses no fear, he certainly has good reasons to be very fearful.

II.   Wisdom without feeling is worthless.

III.   He who feels humble is in an elevated position, and he who considers himself very high, is actually very low.

IV.   When one does a good deed and everybody knows about it, then he should consider the publicity as God's punishment.

V.   One should fear the poor as one fears the sword, and simultaneously one's heart should be tied to the heart of the needy as if to something very precious.

VI.   One should remember, that although this is the lowest of all worlds, it is also the highest among all worlds.

Among the young men who joined R. Shlomo when he left Karlin and settled in the Vohlynian city of Ludmir, was a young disciple named Mordecai. He was born in Neshkhiz, but years later he became famous as the Hassidic master R. Mordecai of Lekhovitch (? –1811).

After a long stay in Ludmir, he left for home. One day he received a letter from R. Shlomo, asking him to return to Ludmir because he wanted to authorize him to become his successor. In the meantime, R. Shlomo died from a Cossack's bullet. The brokenhearted Mordecai and the fellow-disciple Asher, son of R. Aaron the Great, stayed for a short time in the Hassidic Court of R. Barukh of Medzibozh, grandson of the Besht. He later settled in Lekhovitch, and became a Hassidic master as his teacher R. Shlomo had planned.

The die-hard opponents of the Hassidim went so far as to denounce R. Mordecai and R. Asher of Stolin to the Czarist authorities accusing them of disloyal acts. Both faced the threat of being exiled to Siberia, but on the fourth day of the Feast of Lights (Hanukah), 1798, the two were freed after the charges against them had been proven untrue.

His way of Hassidut was the way of serving the Almighty with joy and trust. Nothing could lessen his optimism, not even the death of a daughter in the prime of her life: "God hath given, God hath taken, the name of God be blessed."

Speaking of worry, he said: "Melancholy is a worthless merchandise both in this world and in the World-to-Come. Only one kind of worry is permitted: the worry why one is worried."

R. Mordecai drew so much pleasure from prayer that he doubted whether he would merit a Heavenly Reward for praying. He always saw to it that no coin remained in his possession at night; before sundown he would distribute among the poor all the money given to him by devotees during that particular day. He explained to the closest among his disciples: "Whenever a coin remained in my pocket after the day had gone, it used to rub my flesh and I had a sleepless night. Now I make sure that I have no coin when I get into bed, so that I can sleep peacefully, and when I get up the next morning, I am again dependent upon the mercy of God."

Emphasizing constantly the utmost devotion to principles of morals and ethics, R. Mordecai asked his Hassidim that they be constantly on guard to become neither influenced by outer forms of value, nor by words of those who always wish to avoid responsibility. Speaking of the worthless character of things that seem valuable to the naked eye, he quoted a Biblical passage: "Deceitful is grace; vain is beauty" (Proverbs 31:30). Why so? Because deceit they call grace, and vanity they call beauty.

R. Mordecai once happened to be present at a meeting of the Community Council, and he criticized its leaders for dealing constantly with ordinary problems. He demanded: "Why don't you ever call a meeting to take steps against the evil spirit? He runs over all the places and murders people, but you ignore it as if nothing happened."

When a man asked R. Mordecai for a remedy to become humble, he pointed at the clock and said: "Whenever the clock sounds, it announces that another hour of our life has passed, and the sound reminds us to think back in order to find out what wrong or what good one has done during that specific hour."

R. Mordecai's successor was his son R. Noakh (1774–1834). Like his father, he was a man of great optimism, and this optimism gave him a feeling of certainty that the Hassidic dynasty of Lekhovitch would overcome the last forces of opposition to Hassidut in Lithuania.

In addition to re-emphasizing the teachings of his father, R. Noah expressed his own views on human behavior and on human weaknesses in epigramatic sentences: "Man has been called a 'small world.' This means that he is a world when humble, and small when conceited."

In this manner he reformulated an often-quoted saying by his father, giving it greater clarity: "The Almighty it is impossible to fool; human beings it is forbidden to fool. Consequently,

the deceivers fool only themselves, and it is they who remain the
fools."

R. Moshe of Kobrin (1783–1858) was a devoted disciple of
R. Mordecai and later of R. Noah of Lekhovitch. A man of
pious simplicity, he was forced into becoming a Hassidic teacher
by his fellow-Hassidim who felt orphaned after the demise of
the father and the son. He refused to be called "Rabbi" and
would have wanted to continue his life as a fellow-Hassid who
visited his master during specific times of each year. Only out
of humility did he give in to the wishes of his devotees who
were ever growing in numbers.

R. Moshe joined the Hassidim in his early youth, but he
married into a non-Hassidic family. His father-in-law was a
Mitnaged, an opponent of the Hassidim, and so were the other
family members, and young Moshe suffered many abuses at their
hands.

The fear that he was a Hassidic master under false pretenses
troubled him constantly. On one occasion while in the midst of
studying, he suddenly stopped and cried out: "Lord of the
Universe. Have pity on my soul; show compassion because of my
white beard and enable me to repent in my old age."

Once he was told that a Hassid of his, a man over seventy
years old, was walking from his home town to Kobrin, a stretch
of sixty miles, in order to be with his master on the High
Holidays. Many Hassidim were present when R. Moshe was
told about the old Hassid's devotion to him. When hearing about
it, R. Moshe exclaimed: "Let everybody see how strong is the
power of my fraudulence, that I can deceive a man of over
seventy to walk for weeks so as to be with me on Rosh Hashonah.

I am destined to give an account in the World-to-Come for every single step of that old man. I do not desire any other Heavenly rewards but the pleasure of sitting there together with my masters."

R. Moshe said of his masters:

"They left no books, but their teachings are inscribed in the hearts of their disciples. As for me, whenever I heard from one of my teachers a specific instruction about behavior, I refused to hear anything else until I had practiced that instruction, and only then did I listen to other behavioral instructions."

The Master of the Kobrin Hassidim emphasized brotherhood in connection with faith. He interpreted a biblical command: "From thy brethren shalt thou set king over thee" (Deut. 17:15), as meaning that as a result of brotherhood, one can really come to the acceptance of the Kingship of God.

A Hassid complained that he had no strength to fast so many days as he desired during each week. R. Moshe said to him: "There is one fast that needs no physical strength—that is fasting from telling lies and spreading rumors."

R. Moshe repeated a saying by his own masters, but strengthened it with a biblical passage:

"Ye shall not lie one to another" (Lev. 19:11): The Almighty you cannot fool; others you are not permitted to fool; and if you fool yourself, you are a fool.

R. Moshe of Kobrin was the shepherd of a Hassidic flock for over a quarter of a century. His teachings are recorded in the collection *Amorot Tehorot,* meaning *Pure Words,* a title based on a biblical passage: "The words of the Lord are pure words" (Ps. 12:7). His basic teachings about God, man and behavior can be summarized as follows:

The greatness of God cannot be comprehended by means of

philosophic speculation or ordinary research, for "His greatness is unsearchable" (Ps. 145:3). On the other hand, God is to be found everywhere, even in a crumb of bread. The sufferings visited upon us by God, are not bad but bitter, as are all medicines. Many poor people would be happy if they realized how lucky they are by not possessing any wealth. A truly pious man is he who practices piety less publicly and more privately; that is, when he is alone and only the Creator sees his deeds and actions."

One should never say that the days of the past were better than are the days of the present. He who says so is a fool. Has he tried to emulate the great personalities of bygone days and not succeeded? Everyone should try, and it stands to reason that the endeavor will end in success.

R. Moshe understood well that daily life, with its difficulties and heartbreaks, makes it impossible for humans to practice all rules of ethics and morals. In defense of human beings, he used to sing a song of his own directed to an angel in Heaven:

> Angel, my angel,
> You're an angel,
> Be it so.
> But is it really remarkable
> To be an angel?
>
> You're in heavenly heights.
> You don't have to eat,
> You don't have to drink.
> Children you don't have,
> Income doesn't worry you.
>
> Contrawise, angel my angel,
> Come down on earth to us,

> Be also in need of food,
> Be also in need of drink,
> And be a parent of children,
> Then we will see
> Whether you're really an angel.

But R. Moshe of Kobrin was truly an angel in human disguise.

Soon after R. Uri's marriage, his wife hired herself out as a servant in rabbinic homes, and this enabled him to stay away from home for long periods, and he utilized the time to be with his beloved master, R. Shlomo.

When already the leader of the poorest among Hassidim, R. Uri prayed with greater fire than before. He prayed with such fervor that at times he thought that he might die in the midst of praying. So every morning, before leaving his house for the Synagogue, he parted with every member of his household, since he was uncertain whether he would see them again. At taking leave, he also reminded the family that the writings in his possession were not his own, but the teachings of his master R. Shlomo.

He avoided, as much as possible, the search for blemishes in others.

He used all means in order to instill in his devotees the attribute of humility. Whoever came to him, rich man or poor man, scholar or illiterate, rabbi or artisan, had to go first to the well and return with two cansful of water and do other chores usually attended to by servants.

It was related among the Hassidim, that on every Friday afternoon, the keys of hell were entrusted to R. Uri, with the assurance that as long as the keys were in his hands, the sinners would not be punished. But every Saturday night, when the Sabbath came to an end, the keys were taken from him, and until the next Friday afternoon he had no control over the fate of the sinners whom he wished to save permanently from the tortures at the hands of demons.

R. Uri Strelisker's thoughts are found in the collections, *Imray Kadosh (The Words of a Saintly Man),* in which are stressed faith and ethical behavior. Some of his teachings are epigramatic in form, while others are more explanatory, but even the latter are brief and to the point:

I. The truthful thing needs no help since it comes by its own power without external assistance.

II. The human being is like a tree. If one stands constantly near the tree to watch it grow, he does not notice anything. It is better to watch the tree at intervals and remove what can harm its growth. In the same manner, a human being should attend to his own spiritual growth and development.

III. One should guard his ears against things which one should not hear. But since such watchfulness is humanly impossible, one should pray to God to protect him from the harm of unnecessary and unworthy things one hears.

IV. When one is ill, he should not rely on the physician alone. The physician uses things of nature as remedies, but God and Nature are a unity. One should therefore rely on God for the healing of both his body and his soul.

V. God uses two ways to provide for human beings. To some, He gives with His own hands; to others, he helps by using wealthy people as His messengers. Some prove themselves to be unworthy messengers.

VI. When one has the chance to do good things for others, and avoids doing them, he wrongs himself more than somebody else.

In the tradition of the earlier Hassidic leaders, R. Uri's son was not his spiritual heir. When the Seraph was called to join the other Seraphim in Heaven, his most beloved disciple, R. Tzvi Yehudah of Stretin, became the master of the poorest among the poor in the Hassidic masses of Galicia.

IX

R. Nakhman of Bratzlav:
Genius of Hassidism

May it be Thy will, O Lord our God, God of our fathers, to abolish wars and the shedding of blood. Bring a wonderful peace upon earth so that nation shall not lift up sword upon nation, neither shall they learn war anymore; and all inhabitants of the world shall realize and know that we have come into this world, not for the purpose of warfare, and not for reasons of jealousy, instigation or the shedding of blood; but that we have come into this world to recognize Thee and to know Thee. Let Thou be blessed from this time forth and for evermore.

(A Prayer for Peace, by R. Nakhman of Bratzlav.)

R. NAKHMAN (1772–1810) died at the age of thirty-seven and a half, but during the short span of his activities, his deeds and his writings gained him immortality as a genius whose personal influence is felt even down to our very own day.

R. Nakhman was a great-grandson of the Besht, founder of Hassidut, and of R. Nakhman of Horodenka, who had belonged to the Besht's circle before settling in the Holy Land. His mother, Feigeh, a woman known for her "Divine Inspiration," was a daughter of Odell, the Besht's only female child, and his father, R. Simkha, of a rabbinic family, was cantor in the Besht's synagogue of Medzibozh, the city where R. Nakhman was born. He was not a very good pupil in the traditional one-room "Kheder" or school, but what he lacked in formal studies he made up for by the practice of extreme piety, fasting and other forms of self-mortification. Strongly influenced by his two maternal uncles, the Hassidic leaders, R. Moshe Khaim Ephrayim of Sudilkov and R. Barukh of Medzibozh, R. Nakhman proved in time that he possessed the great humility and piety of the former, and the spirit of self-assurance and self-importance of the latter.

R. Nakhman married at a very early age, and while living in the village home of his father-in-law had enough spare time to study, devoting himself also to the intricacies of Jewish mysticism; and to become in time a great scholar in his own right. He often communed with nature, and the landscapes, the fields, the forests, and the brooks touched the springs of his poetic soul. He also became acquainted with the life and sorrows of the non-Jewish peasants in the surrounding areas. His love of nature and the universalism inspired by it later found expression in his teachings:

Each thing has a heart, and the world as a whole has a heart.

All the greatness and the good that the peoples of the world enjoy, is also for their own good and for the greatness of the Jews.

Nothing in this world occurs in vain. Everything certainly has root and reason above. This world possesses such wonders and great sciences that people could actually sustain themselves without food or drink.

Our world is full of great wonders and supreme knowledge, and one should strive to know all that it is possible to know. Every human being can reach the loftiest heights. It all depends on personal choice. The essence of the human being is knowledge. He who has no knowledge, is a primitive being.

In the winter, the earth is pregnant. It bears within itself a great secret. In the summer, the secret is disclosed.

If a man kills a tree before its time, it is as though he had murdered a soul.

The character of a country is revealed by the sorts of hilarity and sport its people engage in.

Gauge a country's prosperity by its treatment of the aged.

If there were peace, the entire world could be drawn into the united service of God. When there is peace, people talk one to the other. They are unified in search of answers about the world and its nature, and they explain one to another the truth that nothing remains of the human being except what he has prepared for himself to take after death to the Eternal World.
(Tale of the Seven Beggars; Liqqutey Eitzot; Liqqutei Moharan; Seffer HaMiddot; Hillel Zeitlin: R' Nakhman Bratzlaver, p. 60; Treasury of Jewish Quotations, New York, 1956.)

After the death of his father-in-law, R. Nakhman settled in the town of Medvedivka, where he soon found himself at the head of a circle of Hassidim who felt very honored that their young teacher was a great-grandson of the Besht and the nephew of two other prominent Hassidic leaders.

It was in these days that R. Nakhman started to formulate his ideas about the role of the *Tzadik,* the pious Hassidic leader, in the life of his followers, as recorded in his works *Liqqutei Moharan* and *Liqqutei Eitzot:*

The *Tzadik* is the central point. With the *Hassidim* who are bound to him as his followers, he converses on matters of faith; and they, in turn, inspire him, each with the Holy spark within himself. Each *Hassid* should carry on conversations with the other *Hassidim,* so that everyone receives something from the good within the others. There is a vast difference between learning from a book and listening to the words from the *Tzadik's* mouth, since he personally perfects the spirituality within each of his followers. He who hears the words of the *Tzadik*, his soul becomes attached to the *Tzadik's* soul. The *Tzadik* hears the sighs of all who are attached to him and he gives spiritual vitality to each of his *Hassidim*.

The *Tzadik* eats in order to beautify his own soul, and thus he becomes a person of understanding. When someone eats more than is necessary for him, the superfluous part of the meal becomes cattle food. Excessive eating and drinking dull and confuse one's mind and thought.

It was an act of great courage at the time, when R. Nakhman decided in 1798, in the era of the Napoleonic wars, to visit the Holy Land. Neither the pleas of his wife nor the tears of his children could persuade him to change his plan. He spent less than a year in the Holy Land, mostly in the city of Tiberias. After his return, he settled in the city of Zlotopol.

R. Nakhman felt the urge to bring about a renewal in Hassidic teaching because he had become convinced that the Hassidut of his great-grandfather's time had to be revitalized. He stated openly: "I am beginning a new way which has not been trodden by anyone before me." By his statements and his derisive remarks about other Hassidic leaders of his generation, he aroused in them much resentment and opposition. The leader of his opponents was R. Aryeh Leib, who had been a disciple of R. Pinkhas of Koretz with whom he had visited the Besht, and the founder of Hassidut encouraged R. Aryeh Leib to prepare himself for Hassidic leadership. R. Aryeh Leib became famous as a Tzadik under the name of "Grandfather of Shpolah."

The opposition to R. Nakhman grew in intensity when other

Hassidic leaders heard that he had assumed the role of the last of the Hassidic tradition before the advent of the Messianic era. His uncle, R. Barukh of Medzibezh, who years before had occupied the position of Maggid (Preacher) in Bratzlav (often pronounced Brasslav), used his influence at the local Jewish community to give his nephew the same post. So in 1802 R. Nakhman settled in Bratzlav. Because of his stay there for eight years, he became known as R. Nakhman Bratzlaver. But fame has its disadvantages, as R. Nakhman came to know well from personal experience. He explained, "Fame causes many difficulties because he who has become famous must often suffer for the sake of others. But sometimes one is forced by God to become famous" (*Liqqutei Eitzot*). R. Nakhman often felt the urge to shake off some of the burdens of Hassidic leadership in order to have wider opportunities to observe human beings in their daily tasks, and many such opportunities were given him during his travels to various communities, particularly in his native Ukraine.

It was R. Nakhman's good fortune that young R. Nathan of Nemirov, who had been brought up in a scholarly anti-Hassidic environment, and later became a carefree Hassidic Bohemian, joined R. Nakhman's inner circle of disciples. The searching R. Nathan found in R. Nakhman the ideal teacher, and R. Nakhman found in R. Nathan the ideal copyist, the "scribe," to whom he dictated, from notes, his thoughts, commentaries and tales. The latter were told exclusively in Yiddish. After recording the tales in the original tongue, R. Nathan recast them also in Hebrew. It is because of these tales that R. Nakhman is considered one of the early creators of Yiddish literature in the new era. Modern Yiddish writers have used some of the tales as material for their own creativity. Shmuel Niger, the foremost critic in Yiddish literature, wrote a special study on R. Nakhman's artistry as a story-teller. The martyred Hebrew-Yiddish writer and thinker, Hillel Zeitlin, wrote a whole book (with additions by his son, the poet Aaron Zeitlin), on the life, times and activities of R. Nakhman with special attention to the activities of R. Nathan, the scribe, and his associate R. Naphtali. Samuel Setzer, biographer of the Besht, published a revised edition of R. Nakhman's tales and of the story of his travels to the Holy Land. Eliezer Steinman, the Hebrew-Yiddish novelist, essayist and anthologist of Hassidut, devoted a special volume to R. Nakhman in his series of books dealing with Hassidism in general. The *Biographical Dictionary of Modern Yiddish Literature* (in the original: *Leksikon Fun Der Nayer Yiddisher Literatur*), now in its seventh of eight volumes, begins the new year with R. Nakhman's tales. English versions of R. Nakhman's stories are included in Meyer Levin's book *Classic Hassidic Tales* (The Citadel Press, New York, 1966); in *A Treasury of Yiddish Stories* by Irving Howe and Eliezer Greenberg; in *Great Jewish Stories,* edited by Saul Bellow, and in a number of other anthologies.

Explaining his way of teaching by means of telling stories, R. Nakhman stressed the opposite of the common belief: "Others think that tales are a good remedy to put one to sleep, and I maintain that stories are useful to awaken people." As a creator of fiction and of works on morals, ethics, faith and piety, R. Nakhman was naturally interested in the literary technique of writing as a form of expression, and in the characteristics of authors and of their works. He voiced the thought that "every original book contains the image of the author whose mind produced the contents of the book."

R. Nakhman's dictum was: "Good Heavens! Don't lose hope."

He asked of his Hassidim joy, song, and dance, and simultaneously to engage in reflection and self-criticism. There was often no visible line of demarcation between R. Nakhman's pietistic teachings and his poetic discourses on nature, music and song. He explained:

A good shepherd has a special tune, according to the grass and according to the place where he tends his flock. There is a special grass for every different kind among the animals. Every blade of grass has its special tunes, and from the tunes of the different grasses is composed the shepherd's tune.

Each science, religion, philosophy, even atheism, has its particular song. The loftier the religion or science, the more exalted is its music.

When someone hears a beautiful tune, he attaches himself to the Almighty, because all melodies come from the source of sanctity. But impurity does not sing, for it knows no joy. It is the source of melancholy.

Song and music clothe God's Divine Presence in radiant garments; prayer through song mollifies Divine Judgment. It is of importance that every one cause joy to his own soul by means of an inspiring tune.

Common sense is strengthened by joy, but melancholy is a symptom of oncoming sickness. All sadness is very damaging, because it gives strength to the evil inclinations.

Peace is also the result of joy. The ascent to holiness is through joy, because joy is the world of freedom.
(Liqqutei Moharan; Kitzur Liqqutei Moharan; Sefer Hamidot; S.A.; Horodetzky: Leaders of Hassidism, London, 1928, p. 96; A Treasury of Jewish Quotations, New York, 1956.)

Whenever possible R. Nakhman loved to inject irony and humor into his teachings—but rather in passing than directly. The following are several of his humorous and satiric remarks:

One of the reasons why a vessel of clay is broken after the successful arranging of a wedding, is to remind the male that if the woman turns out to be a shrew, he should not betray her, nor divorce her, because thanks to her he will not be sentenced to hell after death.

It was hard for Satan alone to mislead the world, so he appointed prominent rabbis in different localities.

It was difficult for the Angel of Death to kill everybody in the whole world, so he appointed doctors to assist him.

The dead must be amused when people bewail him, as if to say: "It were better if you lived longer and suffered more!"

It is the way of philosophic works to ask questions which seem very difficult, and to offer answers which are very weak. *(Liqqutei Moharan; Maggid Sikhot; Liqqutei Moharan Tanianah; Liqqutei Eitzot; A Treasury of Jewish Quotations, New York 1956.)*

On one occasion, he spoke ironically of the various schools of philosophy and science: "In every generation philosophic knowledge is enlarged and new sciences appear; thus every generation suffers from new illnesses." Speaking in a serious mood, he emphasized: "Mysticism begins where philosophic science ends."

This is similar to the statement of Albert Einstein that faith and religion begin where science ends.

While there are certain similarities between the opinions of R. Nakhman and those of his forerunners and some of his contemporaries, he did "pave a new way" through original thinking and teaching, as can be seen from the opinions expressed in *Liqqutei Moharan,* the only book that appeared during his lifetime, and in the works of his which were published posthumously.

R. Nakhman, like other Hassidic leaders, devoted his chats,

biblical commentaries and ethical works to such subjects as God, faith, piety, behavior, love, charity, evil inclinations and similar themes.

R. Nakhman emphasized God's timelessness, and he added that the human brain is unable to comprehend the full meaning of the term "timeless." Nonetheless, the essence of the human being is reason. He who does not possess reason is a primitive creature who does not deserve the name "human being" because he is an animal in human disguise. The essence of all reason is the knowledge that there is a God who rules the world and each human being has to fulfill His commands. Without reason there can be no love. Hatred abounds when the mind becomes polluted. Even in the lowest places of this world, shines forth the Infinite Light of the Almighty but it is covered by many wrappings. Even in the lowest depths, one can attach himself to God. All existing things cry out the glory of the Creator because the whole earth is full of His glory.

In regard to faith, R. Nakhman stressed that faith itself has its own vitality and roots. There exists a special "World of Faith," and from it human faith derives its Faith, the foundation and the root of all sanctity; and he who has no faith, disdains reproof and instruction.

According to R. Nakhman, faith is renewed every day within the believer, and when he possesses real faith, he is afraid of no human being and nothing harms him. Faith itself needs no reasonable explanation to the believing person. Nevertheless, to the believing person his faith is revealed as if he saw with his own eyes the things he believes in. This in itself is a result of his great faith. Faith is the foundation and root of all sanctity and the tube through which flow all of the Lord's emanations and blessings. He who has no faith usually refuses to be guided by moral and ethical disciplines. Perfect faith means that one believes in God without reasoning about it, without search. He is in no need of signs and miracles. The renewal of the world can be understood only by faith, not by means of pure reason. In essence, faith means the Messianic Era. But how can one attain this? R. Nakhman answered: "The main attachment to Holy thinking is by means of simplicity. Integrity and simplicity are higher than everything else. When one prays in the field, all blades of grass and each of the plants enter into his prayer and assist him so that it possesses the proper strength, and when a person prays in this kind of environment, all grasses and all shrubs become part of his prayers."

R. Nakhman encouraged his Hassidim to pray in Yiddish, in addition to their regular prayers in Hebrew, and to devote time to solitude:

> It would be better for every man to pray when he feels inspired, to pray his own prayer and in a language familiar to him.
> (S.A. Horodetzky: Leaders of Hassidism, London, 1928, p. 94.)

He stressed that, "It is best to practice solitude at night, when interests of the material world can no longer interfere. One should also have a special place for solitude where others will not disturb him. In one hour of solitude, one easily can enumerate his own transgressions and, through prayer, cancel one evil act after another. Then he can begin to consider himself as naught. When he no longer has any feelings of haughtiness and pride, and his heart becomes filled with humility, his soul can be included in its Heavenly Source."

> Solitude is the highest stage. Only in solitude can man attain . . . union with the eternal God. Therefore, a man must seek to be alone, at least for an hour each day, especially at night, when

everyone is asleep and all things are quiet. Solitude in the open air, in the forest or in the desert, is of the utmost importance. *(Liqqutei Moharan; Liqqutei Eitzot; S.A. Horodetzky: Leaders of Hassidism, London, 1928.)*

Concerning piety, truthful repentance and reward, R. Nakhman stressed the necessity of a broken heart, but he was against rigidity in observance. He emphasized that all repentance depends upon the heart, and that a broken heart is a very precious thing. He reminded his followers that a broken heart and sadness are not the same thing, because grief is often an expression of anger and wrath; but someone with a broken heart is like a son who pleads with his father, or like a child that cries and complains when the father is too far away. Such an atttitude is very precious and dear before the Almighty. Those who are very rigid in their religious observances draw no vitality from their acts because they are constantly in a melancholy frame of mind. But when a man feels that he is right in his way of fulfilling his obligations, he should not fear the scoffers and the opponents, even if he believes them to be more pious and better than himself, so long as his aim is to serve the Almighty.

It is improper for you to expect rewards for your piety, since all your good deeds and all your prayers come from the Lord.

Only then is a man's service of God sincere when he wants no publicity for it.
(Liqqutei Eitzot; Kitzur Liqqutei Moharan; Sefer HaMiddot; Newman: Hassidic Anthology, p. 397; A Treasury of Jewish Quotations, New York, 1956.)

R. Nakhman devoted many teachings to the problems of harmony and disharmony between body and soul, belief and practice; to acts of cruelty, humility and compassion; to human frailities in general, and to distinctions between the positive and the negative in the day-to-day activities of human beings.

In his teachings on the above mentioned and similar problems, R. Nakhman stated the following:

I.   In this world every human being has to cross a very narrow bridge, and it is important that he should have no fear of crossing.

II.   The essence of the human being's individuality is the "I," and this is the soul, the essence of which is eternal.

III.   Every human being should lengthen the days of his life by lengthening every future day and every future hour in such a form that they become longer and wider by additional sanctity.

IV.   Every human being goes through various sufferings in every stage or activity in his life. It is therefore necessary that everyone fortify himself with patience so that the realities of life do not break his spirit.

V.   Sometimes one has a setback and falls to a very low position for his own good, so that he can strengthen himself and become renewed in vitality and in mind.

VI.   One should do his work quickly and diligently as if it were the last day in his life and it must be finished before death comes; only when engaging in spiritual matters one should not be hasty, but believe that he still has a hundred years to live.

VII.   All falsehood derives from fear. One should never permit external fear to overpower him. If he has a sudden feeling of fear, let him recognize that it is the fear of God and make use of this fear to serve the Almighty with great love and joy.

VIII.   A person should never lose confidence. Even if one thinks that because of being preoccupied with personal ordinary matters, his positive deeds are of minor values, particularly if he has committed a number of transgressions, nevertheless he should not become despondent but have the certainty that he will be rewarded by Divine Providence for his devotion.

R. Nakhman emphasized the above cited opinions by stressing also the following points:

Everyone can raise himself, but only by his own actions.

Hindrances are given to man on the path of goodness, in order to increase his desire to achieve the good deed. It is man's nature to desire more, that which is hard to attain.

There is no hindrance or obstacle that a man may not overcome if he intensely desires to do so.

The man of understanding will discover God even in the hindrance to a Holy act.

The battle against obstacles moulds a man into a vessel ready to receive Holiness.

Hindrances are merely imaginary obstacles. God sends no hindrances which man cannot overcome.

The greatest hindrance arises when our reason and heart do not agree on the worth of the Holiness we seek to achieve.

When a man's heart is in his service to the Lord, every place in the world is the proper place for it.
(*Liqqutei Eitzot HaSholem, pp. 62–64; Newman: Hassidic Anthology, p. 454; S.A. Horodetzky: Leaders of Hassidism, London, 1928, p. 80.*)

Accentuating that life in this world and in the hereafter are not separated, R. Nakhman reiterated in his writings the necessity of equilibrium between ordinary matters and things of the spirit. Following are some of the ideas he expressed concerning physical health, dress, body and soul, word, and thought, wisdom and knowledge, resurrection reward, and similar matters:

A person should have pity upon his body and cleanse it thoroughly so that his soul may have a proper abode and be able to tell him constantly of his own accomplishments in spiritual elevation. When the body is pure, it is not the captive of ordinary pleasures, and this enables the soul to engage in pleasures of its own. But he who possesses too great physical strength, usually does not possess so much reason. It is important that brain and Holy reason should lead the body, so that the body may turn into part of the Holy soul, which is brains and reason. As compared to the soul, the body is matter, beast, folly and darkness, which are characteristics of death. The essence of the soul consists of form, human being, radiance, wisdom and life. The words that are spoken are the expression of the brain and of its power of imagination; they are the essence of the brain itself. If the brain is pure, the words are likewise. As expressions of the pure brain, the words are Holy. Sin blemishes the soul, and since the soul expresses itself in words, confession of sins must also be in words. When one blemishes the days of his life, even if he grows old, he cannot be considered an elderly person. On the contrary, he is considered short-lived.

By means of an honest sigh, one can actually become a new person in body and soul.

A person should eat only the quantity he needs. The lust for more food and drink than the body really needs weakens his soul's spiritual strength. When a person lives modestly, his thoughts are exceptionally clear and pure. People should live frugally and only make use of what is really necessary in daily life. Of those who act otherwise, it is written: "The belly of the wicked shall want" (Prov. 13:25) because they always need too much. But the pious person who subdues his inclinations even towards those things which are permissible, he is always alive spiritually.

The clothes of a man testify to his general behavior. One should take great care of his clothes and avoid abusing them, because the clothes judge a man if he does not take care of them properly. A prominent person must be more careful than others in such matters because people expect higher standards from such individuals. He who abuses his clothes belongs to the category of those who rebel against law and order.

Human thought is like the clock's pendulum which never stops. Just as there are great distances between heaven and earth, so there are the distances between thinking and talking, between the human mouth and the human heart.

Pure thoughts are like clean animals, and evil thoughts are like unclean animals. The struggle in a person's mind between the two different categories of thought, is an actual war between the clean and the unclean animals. God has purposely put such thoughts in the human's head because He enjoys the struggle between them, seeing someone choosing to fight the unclean animals until he is victorious.

It is actually impossible to simultaneously have two different thoughts. It is therefore not difficult to drive out from the mind evil thoughts by means of other thoughts, even thoughts about buying or selling merchandise.

"Better is the seeing of the eyes than the wanderings of the heart" (Eccles. 6:9), because seeing makes possible the heart going forth and this is the borderline.

According to the growth of wisdom, are the chances of peace.

Quarrel, anger and cruelty are the result of ignorance. The more the knowledge, the greater the compassion, the kindness and the peace. The wisdom of all wisdom is to realize that one is not so wise.

Every human being should practice to accustom himself to life in the World-to-Come. He should, for example, abstain as much as possible from physical passions that are absent in the Future World. Excessive eating and drinking, as well as bestial desires, damage and destroy this world that we live in. Everyone's rewards in the World-to-Come are already painted upon his face. The Eternal Life of the Future will be the result of the perfection of the knowledge of God. When people will possess perfect knowledge, they will be included in God's Oneness and they will be as eternal as He is.

R. Nakhman was a student of human character and psychology, and in his teachings he juxtaposed the negative and the positive in humans. Realizing that every human being is born with some wickedness within him, he explained that the evil instinct walks around with a closed fist. When the fist is opened, then comes the realization that it was empty. The evil inclination in most people is crude and lowly. But it is good when a person has some evil desires, so he can curb them and make use of their enthusiasm and fervor in the service of God.

In regard to such human frailties as pride, thirst for honor and wealth, rivalry and the like, R. Nakhman expounded the idea that everyone should seek fewer honors for himself and enlarge the honor of the Almighty. If one does not run after honors, others will not engage in discussion as to whether he is worthy or not to receive them. But of him who runs after honors, people ask: "Who is he, anyway, that he believes himself worthy

enough of such honors?" And they who ask usually agree that
he is not worthy. R. Nakhman reminded his followers and
readers that the Sages of the Talmud emphasized that an arrogant person is a cripple. The Sages probably meant to say that
because the haughty are aware of their own spiritual and educa-
tional shortcomings, so they compensate themselves by a show of
pride. In reality, he who seeks honor is a fool, but the modest
people have clear minds. The Messsiah will come only when
pride disappears from the world.

R. Nakhman, in his early youth, was often overpowered by
fits of anger but he learned how to subdue them. As if speaking
from personal experience, he stressed that one should avoid anger
because nothing blemishes the soul to so great an extent as do
resentment and fury. He who utters a lie, pollutes his own
blood. Actually, all mental illness has the character of a quarrel.
Body and soul cannot harmonize, so there is no peace in the
person's body. Through evil talk, a human being falls altogether
into a beastly state.

Where wealth is concerned, R. Nakhman insisted that almost
all wealthy men are somewhat crazy because love of money
drives them to insanity. Those who have a passionate desire to
earn lots of money, usually die in debt with nothing in their
possession. The greater the desire for riches, the stronger becomes
the mania. Charity is the only way to break the lust for money,
for charity transforms cruelty into humility. Compassion is at
the root of all Creation.

To become a friend's rival in a trade or profession, warned
R. Nakhman, is just as sinful as having sexual relations with
someone else's wife. But anyone who can curb his adulterous
desires, can easily curb his other passions. Tears of the aggrieved

make all passions seem repugnant. On the other hand, it is good when a man retains some evil inclinations. He can thus serve the Almighty by taking the fire of his evil desires and using them in Divine Service. When there is no evil inclination present in a person, he has neither enthusiasm nor inspiration.

Implanting ideas of brotherly love, R. Nakhman advanced the teaching that he who does not pray that his generation be granted Divine Compassion, is in the end himself punished. He who does not possess reason also lacks compassion. Real peace and true compassion develop simultaneously with reason.

R. Nakhman interpreted the biblical passage "And yet a little while and the wicked is no more" (Ps. 37:10), as a verse which teaches us to judge everyone favorably. Even when someone's behavior makes him look wicked in your eyes, you should search in him the bit of good where evil is not present. One should have the same favorable attitude toward himself. He should draw joy and encouragement from the bit of good within him. But sadness and melancholy are very damaging because in the end they give strength to the evil inclination.

Dwelling on the subject of brotherly love, R. Nakhman underlined that one should always try to judge other people favorably, even those who oppose or abuse him, for thus he will be saved from controversy and quarrel. If one judges his fellow favorably, although he is evil, it is possible to find in the evil person some good, and by means of this good, the evil man can be influenced to repentance. When two are quarreling, each should judge his opponent on the scale of merit, because every controversy has two sides: either it is because the other person is greater, and so the one is angry for not having reached the other's position—and he should rather make an effort to be on the same scale with the other one—or he is personally more important than the other and the opponent quarrels with him because of envy for not having reached the same position that he has. If so, he should certainly judge his opponent on the scale of merit, for thus he will elevate his opponent; and they will be on the same level and the quarrel will most certainly cease. Thanks to peaceful relations among human beings, they search for truth and explain the truth one to another. Because of this everyone throws away his golden idol and comes nearer to approach the truth.

A human being, insisted R. Nakhman, is called human only by virtue of his acts of charity and loving kindness. But the attribute of compassion is also in need of great compassion. It lies in a hidden corner and there is no one compassionate enough to show compassion for compassion. The misers and all those who are constantly motivated by the lust for money, die in debt since nothing remains in their hands. Therefore, by giving more charity, one conquers the passion for money and thus he is rewarded as if he had offered incense in the Sanctuary.

Truth is the interior, the inside of the entire countenance of Holiness. In the absence of truth, kindness, humility and charity cannot exist. Humility leads to repentance. The main basis of repentance is the recognition of one's own insignificance, and this leads one to understanding that it is proper to suffer in order to reach the goal of truth. This is true repentance. The more humble and compassionate one becomes, the greater his ability to draw to earth the Divine Presence. This is also God's will since the time of Creation.

Before a man attains greatness, he must descend to lowliness.

Seek the good in everyone, and reveal it, bring it forth.

Even a criminal has his good side.

God commanded the ravens, symbols of cruelty, to feed Elijah (I Kings 17:4) to show that cruelty may be turned to kindness.

A small coin before the eye will hide the biggest mountain.

Humility for the sake of approval is the worst arrogance.

When the rays of the sun enter a house through a dusty window, they form illumined pillars. But if one tries to feel them, he discovers there is nothing there. Worldly desires are comparable to these seeming pillars fashioned by the sun.

1. When envy will cease, Redemption will come.
2. Envy is oftentimes the cause of destruction and murder.
3. Envy of another man's property may cause derangement of mind.

Declare at all times: "The world was created for my sake." Do not declare: "Of what concern is this to me?" But do your share to add some improvement, to supply something that is missing, and to leave the world a little better for your sojourn in it.
(Liqqutei Moharan; Kitzur Liqqutei Moharan; Sefer HaMiddot; S.A. Horodetzky: Leaders of Hassidism, London, 1928, p. 98; S. Dubnov: Toldot HaHassidut, p. 513; A Treasury of Jewish Quotations, New York 1956; Newman: Hassidic Anthology, p. 62; 513.)

Destiny was unkind to the young genius of Hassidism. R. Nakhman evidently contracted tuberculosis at an early age. His stay in the Holy Land, in times of a ravaging epidemic, and in the days of the Napoleonic siege, as well as the other trials and tribulations he experienced during and after his pilgrimage, taxed the strength of his frail body. The attacks of leading figures within the Hassidic fold added to his personal woes. He went to Lvov (Lemberg) to consult physicians in the hope that they might find a cure for him, or at least to arrest his illness. His only consolation was the printing of his work *Liqqutei Moharan,* meaning *Extracts by Our Teacher Rabbi Nakhman.*

A fire destroyed many homes in Bratzlav, and the house where R. Nakhman held his Hassidic "Court" also went up in flames. So, in 1800, he transferred his seat to the city of Uman, one of the towns whose Jewish communities had been martyred during the massacres by the Cossacks in Vohlynia, Podolyah and the Ukraine in the years 1648–1649. From the windows of his home, R. Nakhman could see the cemetery that contained the bodies of those who had been butchered a century and a half before by the Cossack hordes under the leadership of the "Hetman," Bogdan Chmielnitzky. R. Nakhman realized that the very same sanctified ground would soon also contain his body. As he had done on numerous previous occasions, he told his adherents during the last days of his life: "Good Heavens! don't lose hope!" In Uman he had contacts with the local *Maskilim,* adherents of the anti-Hassidic Jewish Enlightenment (Haskalah) movement. He eased the fears of his disciples: "Don't worry! All that the Maskilim say, they have read in books, and when they finish the books, they will have nothing to say."

Meanwhile his body became weaker and weaker. On his death-bed he spoke softly to those who surrounded him, using words similar to those which his great-grandfather, the Besht, had uttered to his own disciples before his soul departed from his body. Said R. Nakhman to his Hassidim: "I'm simply going from one room to another . . . I will certainly hear if I am called . . . I wish to remain among you . . . You should visit my grave . . . My flame will not be extinguished before the arrival of the Messiah."

On the fourth day of the Succoth Tabernacles Festival in 1810, the soul of R. Nakhman "returned to the Academy on High, at the Throne of the Almighty."

Since R. Nakhman considered himself to be the last in the line of four great teachers—the Sage R. Shimon Bar Yokhai, R. Isaac Luria (the Ari, leader of the Kabbalah-Mystics in Safed) and R. Israel Baal Shem Tov, the Besht, R. Nakhman's great-grandfather, having been the first three before him—no one was chosen to be R. Nakhman's successor. Because the Bratzlaver-Umaner Hassidim had no living leader, and their activities consisted of studying R. Nakhman's writings, singing his songs and dancing his dances, they were nicknamed "Death Hassidim." But they cared very little what their opponents said. They were not discouraged even when the Hassidic opposition destroyed their meeting houses, the *shtiblekh,* and burned their teacher's works. The faithful scribe, R. Nathan Shternhartz of Nemirov turned his own home into a printing shop and published both his teacher's books and his own. He visited the Holy Land for the purpose of acquainting the Sephardim (descendants of the Jews who had escaped from Spain in the era of the Inquisition in the Middle Ages) with the teachings of his master. In his own work *Allim LeTrufah (Leaves for Healing),* Nathan stated: "He whose heart is after the truth, finds that all good books are a call to people to turn towards truth . . . When someone feels like crying, he should know that it is a sign for him to rejoice." R. Nathan's *Life of Moharan,* the biography of R. Nakhman, belongs to the classics of Hassidic literature.

Thanks to R. Nathan's endeavors as scribe, printer and author,

Bratzlaver-Umaner Hassidim continue their group existence to this very day. They established a Yeshivah of their own in Jerusalem, and have *Shtiblech* in various countries. A new edition of *Liqqutei Moharan,* with comments and additions, was issued not so long ago in New York, on the initiative of the Bratzlaver Hassidim in the United States and Canada.

During the Ghetto Revolt of the Warsaw Jews in the Passover days of 1943, the Bratzlaver Hassidim painted in large letters the dictum of their teacher R. Nakhman: "Jews! Don't lose hope!" R. Nakhman's words became a motto of the Ghetto Rebels. When the State of Israel proclaimed its independence in 1948, in the 150th year after R. Nakhman's visit to the Holy Land, and five years after the Ghetto Revolt of the Jews in Warsaw, it was verified that if human beings do not lose hope, their dreams can become inspiring reality.

X

The Worlds
Of Six Hassidic Masters

THE CONQUESTS of Hassidut in different parts of Eastern Europe must be attributed not only to the needs of the Jewish masses, but also to the great and gifted Hassidic masters who spread its teachings, both in oral and written form.

Symbolic of such masters, each of whom made his appearance at the proper time and at the proper place, are six men whose teachings in the realm of faith, human behavior, ethics and morality, will be reviewed in this chapter.

R. LEVI YITZKHAK OF BERDICHEV

R. Levi Yitzkhak of Berdichev (1740–1809) occupies a unique place among the great masters of Hassidut. He is immortal in Hassidic history as the Defender of the People and as the Public Prosecutor who protested to God for His dealing often harshly instead of compassionately towards His children.

R. Levi Yitzkhak was born in the town of Huskov, near Jaroslaw, in the Pszemysl region of Galicia.

According to Hassidic lore, R. Israel Baal Shem Tov, the Besht, once called together his disciples and distributed refreshments among them, explaining that the celebration was in honor of a great soul that had come down to earth. The child born on that day was to become famous as "The Great Defender," R. Levi

Yitzkhak of Berdichev, who was to take notice of the most noble merits even among the greatest of sinners.

A second Hassidic tradition relates:

> When Levi Yitzkhak was about to be born, Satan complained that if that soul were to descend on earth, it would reform the world, and his own power would come to an end. Then the Holy One comforted Satan, and said: "But he will be a rabbi, and he will be too occupied with communal affairs."
> (*A. Kahana, Sefer HaHasidut, 1922, p. 250; A Treasury of Jewish Quotations, ed. by J.L. Baron, New York 1956.*)

After marrying the daughter of a very wealthy man, R. Levi Yitzkhak settled in Lubartow, then a center of Jewish learning to which the young Talmudic "Genius of Jaroslaw," as he was called after the city where he had studied, gave additional lustre. R. Levi Yitzkhak was an admirer of the Rabbi of Ritchevol, later to become famous as R. Shmelkeh of Nicholsburg. On the advice of R. Shmelkeh, he traveled to Mezritch in order to visit the leading Hassidic master of the time, R. Dov Ber, the Maggid, successor to the Besht. When Levi Yitzkhak returned from his first visit to the Maggid of Mezritch, his father-in-law asked whether there was something special that he had learned from R. Dov Ber.

"I have found out that there is God in the world," replied Levi Yitzkhak.

"But this is known to everybody," retorted the father-in-law, and he called over the maid, asking whether there is God in the world.

"Yes," said the maid.

"She says, but I know," shot back the inspired Levi Yitzkhak.

His specific Hassidic knowledge of God later resulted in many painful incidents in his life, but also gained him one of the exalted positions in the history of Hassidut. When R. Shmelkeh moved to Nicholsburg, R. Levi Yitzkhak became his successor as Rabbi of Ritchevol. From there, he was later called to occupy the rabbinic seat at Zhelikhov, Poland. Zhelikhov was, in those days, a fortress of Mitnagdim, opponents of the Hassidim, and their opposition made life so difficult for him that he left Zelikhov in haste, and later became the spiritual head of the Jewish community in Pinsk. Because of his Hassidic ways, he fared much worse in Pinsk than in Zhelikhov, but after many wanderings and great difficulties, he was accepted as Rabbi in the Ukrainian city of Berdichev where he resided until his death, twenty-five years later. The man who had suffered so much from human beings, before occupying the honored position in Berdichev, became famous as the Hassidic master who saw no blemish in others and interpreted their misdeeds as expressions of high personal qualities. Although a man of great piety, he often spoke out against God, symbolically rather than actually, in defense of human beings. This was in harmony with his conviction that the Tzadik, the master, should show more love for the wicked person than for the believer. For if the wicked person is rejected, he will sink altogether in his wickedness; and if the believing person is shown special favor, he will become proud, and this is also a wickedness.

Characteristic of R. Levi Yitzkhak's attitude and actions, are the following incidents:

1. Once a thief got into his house and stole the candlesticks, The Code of Laws and a clock. R. Levi Yitzkhak defended the

thief by saying: "It was all because of his piety. He wished to know when it was time to get up in the darkness, light the candles and study the Code of Laws."

II. On a certain morning, when R. Levi Yitzkhak was on his way to the synagogue, the wife of one of his opponents ran out into the street and threw at him a canful of water. When he came into the synagogue, R. Levi Yitzkhak began to pray that God should not punish the woman because she was a dutiful wife and had done what her husband ordered her to do.

III. A wealthy miser once came to pay his respects to R. Levi Yitzkhak. He led the miser to a window facing the main street and said to him: "When one looks through the ordinary glass of the pane, one sees other people, but when one looks into a mirror, he sees only himself. Why so? Because the glass of the mirror has gold-dust on the other side."

> The Berdichever insisted upon serving his guests himself. He would bring them food and prepare their beds for them. When asked why he did not leave these duties to his servant, he responded: "Hospitality is an excellent deed when performed without payment. The servant would do it for pay, and the intrinsic kindness of the good deed would be lost."

> Said R. Levi Yitzkhak: "I have learned to welcome even the ignorant and untutored to my home. Does not the Lord do likewise? When the time of the Resurrection comes, and the Lord prepares a banquet for the righteous, I shall be privileged to mingle with the guests. If it is asked: 'How did this uncultured person find entrance among us?', I shall reply: 'I deserve to be here because I also gave hospitality at my banquets to men more ignorant than myself.'"

> He once remarked: "There is a saying to the effect that King Solomon was wiser than any one, even than an idiot. This may be

explained as follows: 'Every idiot sincerely believes he is wiser than everybody else, and it is almost impossible to convince him of his fallacy. Solomon, however was so wise, he could persuade even the idiot to acknowledge himself a fool.' "

Rabbi Levi Yitzkhak said: "Whether a man really loves God—that can be determined by the love he bears his fellow-men. I shall give you a parable.

" 'Once upon a time, a country was suffering from the ravages of war. The general who headed the army which was sent against the foe was vanquished. The king discharged him and put in his place another man who succeeded in driving out the invader. The first general was suspected of betraying his country. The king wondered whether there was any way to find out whether he really loved or hated him. He realized that there was one un-erring sign which would discover the truth for him: if the man, about whom he was in doubt, showed friendship for his rival and expressed unalloyed joy at his success, he might be regarded as trustworthy; but if he plotted against his rival, this would prove his guilt.' "

"God created man to strive against the evil in his soul. Now there is many a man who does, indeed, love God, but is defeated in that bitter struggle. He can be recognized by his ability to share whole-heartedly and without reservations in the happiness of his victorious fellow-man." (*Niflaot Bet Levi, p. 14; Siakh Sarfey Kodesh, IV, p. 136; Esser Orot, p. 61; Newman: Hassidic Anthology, pp. 14, 122; Buber: Tales of the Hassidim, Early Masters, p. 227.*)

He once called in the beadle and said to him: "Run immediately to the main synagogue and notify all those present, young and old, that the universe has an Almighty!"

R. Levi Yitzkhak danced at the funeral procession of his son, R. Meir. He explained: "I was presented from Heaven with a pure soul, and now I am returning it as pure as it was given to me."

A Hassid once boasted to R. Aaron of Karlin that he knew well R. Levi Yitzkhak of Berdichev.

"You are badly mistaken," said R. Aaron, "when you believe that you know R. Levi Yitzkhak. You only know his suit of clothes, his overcoat, but of R. Levi Yitzkhak, the great Tzadik, you have no conception at all. You are like Potiphar's wife of whom it is written in regard to Joseph: 'She caught him by his garment.' " (Gen. 39:12)

The teachings of R. Levi Yitzkhak are included in the book *Kedushot Levi,* meaning *Sanctity of the Levite.* It is one of the chief classics in Hassidic literature.

He emphasized: "A person who serves God because of fear loves his own self; but a person who serves God because of love forgets his own self. There is no greater pleasure than the pleasure of devoutness with fear in purity. Pure faith in the Almighty inspires one to sing praise."

His Yiddish prayer *God of Abraham* is recited to this very day by pious Jewish women on Saturdays at Twilight, before the Sabbath is concluded. He composed, in honor of God, a special song, the *Thou-Thou* song, popularly known as the *Dudehleh,* which to this very day is one of the most popular numbers in Jewish concert programs.

Rabbi Levi Yitzkhak used say: I shall sing Thee, Master of the Universe, the "Thou" song. Wherever I go, there art Thou, and wherever I stand there art Thou. Only Thou and again Thou and forever Thou, Thou, Thou, Thou. If I feel good, Thou hast caused it; and if, Heaven forbid, I feel bad, again it is Thou. Only Thou and again Thou and forever Thou, Thou, Thou, Thou.

In Heaven Thou art, and on earth Thou art. Above and below
only Thou and again Thou and forever Thou, Thou, Thou, Thou.

Part of another English version of the same song reads as
follows:

> Where I wander—You!
> Where I ponder—You!
> Only You, You again, always You!
> You! You! You!
> When I am gladdened—You!
> When I am saddened—You!
> Only You, You again, always You!
> You! You! You!
> Sky is You! Earth is You!
> You above! You below!
> In every trend, at every end,
> Only You! You again, always You!
> You! You! You!
> *(Eliezer Steinman: The Garden*
> *of Hassidim, p. 190; Buber:*
> *Tales of the Hasidim, Early*
> *Masters, p. 212.)*

In the book *Kedushat Levi,* are transmitted his opinions, directly and indirectly connected with interpretations of biblical
passages and comments on them. The book contains R. Levi
Yitzkhak's opinions on the spiritual make-up of the human being
in general and his thoughts on faith in God, piety, prayer, love of
husband and wife; thoughts on sin and repentance, hate and
anger, pride and humility; on truth, charity, peace and related
themes:

God renews constantly the work of Creation and every day He
blesses with a new clearness and lucidity and bestows new loving

kindness. He who serves God, receives every day new brightness and wisdom that he did not possess the day before.

All pleasures in the world are worthless compared to the pleasure of worship of the heart by means of prayers to the Creator.

The essence of joy is within the heart, but joy would soon cease if it were not replenished by means of words and song.

Although the human being is on this earth, as a result of his good deeds he is worthy to walk all his life in the worlds above. Wherever one goes, he goes towards his own root and source.

There are two forms of matrimonial relations: one is physical love which is gratification of the man's passion, and this means that he does not love his wife at all, but he loves only himself; the other form is loving the wife because she is the means by which he fulfills the commands of the Almighty, and this is true love.

The chief attributes of the evil inclination are anger and hate.

There is a difference between the sinner because of passion and the sinner who is motivated just by spite. The spiteful are lost forever, but one who was beguiled by passion can easily repent.

If it were not confirmed in books, it would be difficult to believe that a human being, made of dust and ashes, today alive, tomorrow in the grave, could have the audacity to become proud.

The misers who think only of accumulating more wealth and refuse to give charity, do not realize that "shrouds have no pockets," and one cannot take his money to the grave.

Truth is very high and to reach it is a very difficult task.

If the world could actually exist without the necessity of truth, human beings would never strive on their own to find the truth. The truth is too high a thing and cannot be gotten easily.

Following are some gleanings from R. Levi Yitzkhak's comments on biblical passages:

"In the beginning God created the heaven and the earth" (Gen. 1:1): God created everything and He is everything, and every moment since Creation, He benevolently influences the world and all that is within it.

"And thou, (Joseph) saidst unto thy servants: 'Except your youngest brother come down with you, ye shall see my face no more'" (Gen. 44:23): There are great individuals who keep only to themselves and think only of themselves. Scripture hints that the Almighty rejects such behavior. "Except your youngest brother come down with you," means that if you do not take with you the younger and less important than you to teach them and show them the proper way, then "ye shall see my face no more"; the Holy one, blessed be He, does not want such men of self-importance.

"And let them make Me a sanctuary that I may dwell among them" (Exod. 25:8): The human brain is the Holy of Holies, therefore one should refrain from thinking unholy thoughts. If one does think unholy thoughts, it is as if he had placed an abomination in the Sanctuary.

"If any man shall sin through error, in any of the things which the Lord hath commanded not to be done, and shall do any of them" (Lev. 4:2): Even "one of them" is also in the category of sin. When someone commits any transgression and is aware of it, his heart is broken and he turns to repentance. But he who fulfils a precept and takes pride in it, and says "I have made God richer," this is not a good deed but a transgression.

"This is a statute of the law which the Lord hath commanded" (Num. 19:2): The Lord commanded us to obey laws which are inexplicable to reason, in order to prove that we obey such laws, not because of our conviction that they are logical, but because the Lord commanded them.

"To execute the Lord's vengeance on Midian" (Num. 31:3):
When people go to war for a just cause, not for aggrandizement
but for Divine justice, they are certain to succeed.

"And thou shalt not bring an abomination into thy house"
(Deut. 7:26): If you permit a haughty person into your house,
you are transgressing the command not to bring an abomination
into your home, as is verified by another passage: "Every one
that is proud in heart, is an abomination to the Lord" (Prov.
16:5).

"Truth springeth out of the earth" (Ps. 85:12): In earthly
matters it is impossible to exist without the truth.

Whenever R. Levi Yitzkhak mentioned the Almighty—and he
did so when saying something—he used the Yiddish synonym,
Derbarimdiger, meaning "Compassionate."

When the Russian government decreed that every Czarist
subject adopt a family name, two government officials visited
him to register the name he had chosen. When they entered, he
cried out "Derbarimdiger," and the officials thought he was
telling them the name under which he wished his family to be
known, so they registered him as "Levi Yitzkhak Derbarimdiger."
Today, the family name Derbarimdiger can be found in the
telephone books of the boroughs of Manhattan and Brooklyn.

A Hassidic story-teller, possessing both imagination and humor,
has left for posterity the following tale:

R. Levi Yitzkhak died and his soul reached the Heavenly
World. He said that before being taken to Paradise, he would
like to visit Hell. The Heavenly Court could not refuse him,
and two angels escorted him through all the seven compartments
of Purgatory. Upon seeing the tortures experienced by the sinners,
R. Levi Yitzkhak declared that he would not leave Hell unless it

was immediately emptied of all sinners. The Heavenly Court was in a quandary and it was ready to accept a compromise whereby all sinners should be freed, except those who committed such unpardonable sins as idol worship, incest and the shedding of innocent blood. But R. Levi Yitzkhak refused to agree. "All sinners without exception, must be freed from Hell," he continued to argue, "otherwise I'll stay here with them." Suddenly an announcement was heard that a great man had died and all souls in Paradise were asked to gather and observe from Heaven his funeral on earth. Since escorting a funeral procession is a great precept, the soul of R. Levi Yitzkhak was also sent to observe the funeral of the great man. He did not realize that it was his own funeral that was taking place, and while his soul was on the way to fulfillment of the funeral precept, the gates of Hell were tightly closed, and the protesting R. Levi Yitzkhak was forced into Paradise to stay there forever.

R. ISRAEL OF KOZHENITZ

The influence of the Hassidic movement among the Jews of Eastern Europe affected also some of their non-Jewish neighbors. In towns that had Hassidic masters, local patriotism often motivated the Christians to consider the master of their town the most important of all. Other non-Jews even went so far as to become devotees of certain Hassidic leaders, believing in the effectiveness of the blessings of such saintly individuals.

One of the first Hassidic leaders to have a non-Jewish following, was R. Israel, the Maggid (Preacher) of Kozhenitz (? –1814. He was born in the Polish city of Apta, the son of a pious bookbinder whom R. Israel Baal Shem Tov *blessed* to become the father of a son after many years of childlessness.

Young Israel, inspired by the books he saw in his father's bindery, devoted himself to traditional Jewish studies and several great Talmudists were his teachers.

In his early youth, Israel was the teacher of a small group of Jewish children in a Polish village. He never permitted anyone to make his bed. By accident someone touched his bed, and it was discovered that instead of sleeping on straw, he slept on bricks. When he realized what had been found out—the inhabitants began to regard him as a holy man—he disappeared from the village.

After his marriage, R. Israel settled in the town of Pshyskha, and the local Maggid, who taught him the art of preaching, influenced him to become a Hassid. When Israel visited R. Shmelke Hurwitz, Rabbi in Ritchevol, later to become Rabbi of Nicholsburg, he advised him to travel to Mezritch, to see the Maggid R. Dov Ber, R. Israel Baal Shem Tov's spiritual heir. After that visit, R. Israel declared: "I had studied eight hundred books of Kabbalah—Jewish mysticism—but I became convinced that I had as yet not started to learn anything." Later, R. Israel became a devotee of R. Elimelekh of Lizhensk. There he met R. Zusheh, R. Elimelekh's younger brother and R. Yaakov Yitzkhak, who in later years became famous as the "Seer of Lublin." He was also friendly with R. Levi Hitzkhak while he was still Rabbi of Zhelikhov, before becoming the Hassidic master of Berdichev.

When R. Elimelekh of Lizhensk had been "called to the Academy on High," many of his Hassidim became followers of R. Israel, the Maggid of Kozhenitz. In his preachings, he expressed thoughts of kindness and love, and the contributions given to him by those who had come to receive his advice and blessings, he distributed among the widows, orphans, and the needy of the town. Being a man of great wisdom, many non-Jews, among them members of the Polish nobility, sought his advice, in addition to his blessings. During the Napoleonic war, he sided with the French, hoping that their victory would be for the benefit of the oppressed, although other Hassidic masters were on the side of the Russian Czarist regime. Having in mind the welfare of the non-Jews as well as the Jews, the Maggid prayed: "Lord of the Universe! Redeem the people of Israel from Exile. If You do not wish to redeem the Jews, do not withhold the redemption of the Gentiles." An elderly Christian resident of Kozhenitz said many years after the passing of R. Israel:

"I once fulfilled, successfully, a very important mission he entrusted me with, so he blessed me so that no wrong should ever befall me or my home. It has been so ever since."

R. Israel prayed with great fervor, and he used to assert that nothing gives one such great pleasure as a hearty prayer. While reciting one of his personal prayers, he cried out: "Lord of the Universe! I stand before You like a messenger boy. Wherever You wish to send me, I am ready to go."

His form of praying was one of the expressions of his sanctity. R. Israel once confided to a circle of his closest disciples: "They probably know in Heaven that on earth I have no other pleasures than the pleasures of prayer, and I am being immediately rewarded. Thus I will have no reward in the World-to-Come."

R. Israel once visited Lublin to attend a circumcision ceremony. He stayed at the home of the "Seer," R. Yaakov Yitzkhak, and spent most of the time playing with the children. When the Seer entered and saw who was his guest, he welcomed him in the traditional manner, and then cried out: "Holy Maggid! I am being consumed by the flames of your sanctity."

During most of the latter years of his life, the Maggid of Kozhenitz was so weak that he could not stand on his legs, and he used to be carried on a stretcher to the synagogue. But once in the house of worship, his legs suddenly became strong and they served him the entire time of the devotions or preachings.

R. Israel was a great Talmudic scholar and a prolific writer. His descendants published posthumously more than ten collections of his commentaries on biblical books, on parts of the Talmud, on Jewish mysticism, on Hassidut and similar subjects, the title of each book containing also the name "Israel"; such as *Nezer Yisroel (Crown of Israel), Or Yisroel (The Light of Israel), Avodat Yisroel (The Service of Israel)*, and the like.

The Maggid received the Hassidim at his bedside, and he sometimes added a bit of humor to his statements and opinions. In this connection, it is related that a Hassid who was childless complained: "I have pleaded with the master that he intercede for me so that I may be blessed with fatherhood, but it was of no avail. Now I have heard that an opponent of the Hassidim, a man who had been childless for half a century, became a father recently." "This happened in order to teach you," said R. Israel, "that one should put his trust in God and not rely on human beings."

He used to say: "It is better not to fast and fool people by saying that you are fasting, rather than fast and fool yourself."

Commenting on such subjects as good manners, humility, eating and desires, he formulated the following ideas:

Don't permit your humility to go so far as to consider yourself an evil person.

When one does not like a specific food, he should not say that it is bad, but he should rather state that he is incapable of judging it, because just as it is forbidden to shame human beings, so it is prohibited to abuse food that means so much to others.

One should love food, not because of physical desire, but for its spiritual values, since in all things is to be found the Divine Presence.

He who throws garbage into the street, some of the refuse remains upon himself.

When one is overcome by passion, he should first penetrate into the unclean root of this physical desire; he should consider the holy spark within the lust; and finally he should think of the source of all this charm which motivated his lust, and after that, he should turn his desire to the Divine Presence.

R. Israel's biblical commentaries usually dealt with human behavior and faith, as did his teachings in general. Characteristic of his biblical interpretations are the following:

Every human being possesses the characteristics of his earliest ancestors: the jealously of Cain against Abel, the lust of the Generation of the Flood, and the conceit of the honor-thirsty generation that built the Tower of Babel. (Gen. 4: 6, 7, 11).

"And he [Abraham], believed in the Lord, and he counted it to him for righteousness" (Gen. 15:6): Abraham recognized the righteousness of God for having granted him a heart to understand and reach the most complete form of faith.

"And the Lord said unto Moses: 'Lo, I come to thee in a thick cloud, that the people may hear when I speak with thee'" (Exod. 19:9): God decided to speak with Moses in simple terms, to stress the importance of speaking on important matters in a way that the most simple people can understand.

"Can any hide himself in secret places and I shall not see him? saith the Lord" (Jer. 23:24): A man may secretly and in hiding do acts of charity and fulfill all the precepts, but if he will say in his heart *and I,* I am a scholar, I am a good and pious man, then the Lord says, "And I shall not see him."

A number of R. Israel's disciples became prominent Hassidic leaders. In fact the Hassidic dynasty that was started with the Maggid of Kozhenitz has its continuation at the present time in the United States, in the Holy Land, and in other countries.

R. AVROHOM YEHOSHUAH HESHEL OF APTA

R. Avrohom Yehoshuah Heshel (? –1825) is known in Hassidic tradition as *Ohev Yisroel,* meaning "Lover of Israel." This is the title he asked to adorn his tombstone, and such is also the name of one of the two books containing his teachings, the other being *Torat Emmet,* translatable as *True Law* and *Law of Truth.* Both books were published posthumously. Because of his love of the truth and his courageous acts in the face of hypocrisy and falsehood, R. Avrohom Yehoshuah made many enemies.

He was born in Nowomiasty where his father was the local Rabbi. At the age of seventeen, he first visited R. Elimelekh of Lizhensk who had been told that even in early childhood the young man had already shown a sharp perception of knowledge and understanding. Becoming a scholar of renown, he was given a rabbinic position in Kolbashow. Later, he became Rabbi in the Roumanian city of Jassy. The opposition to him grew because of his Hassidic ways and as a result of his refusal to abide by the wishes of the community heads. He later moved to Apta where his Hassidic leadership gained him a large following in the entire region. He became known as the "Apter."

While his opponents saw in him a man adamant and demanding, his Hassidim basked in the sunshine of his humor and the exaggerations that made him a great story teller.

One of his closest disciples was R. Khayim Yekhiel Meir, the "Seraph" of Mogelnitza, grandson of R. Israel, the Maggid of Kozhenitz. The master once turned to the Seraph and said to him: "Why do you remain in hiding? It's high time that you became the leader of a Hassidic community." "How can a fraud like me take upon himself such a role?" asked R. Khayim Yekhiel Meir, out of his great humility. "We are both of the same sort," assured the Apter laughingly. "If I can be a Hassidic master, so can you."

The Hassidim of R. Avrohom Yehoshuah Heshel loved to listen to his extravagant stories—stories that testified that, in addition to humor, he also had a great imagination. He once told his devotees: "For my son's wedding, the cooks prepared such long noodles that they had to hang them from the rooftop to dry, and from the roof they reached to the ground. So many guests came to the wedding, that two wagons of straw had to be brought so that the guests could clean their teeth after the meal. From the shells of the eggs and from the peelings of the onions used in preparing the wedding feast, it was possible to build two bridges over the largest river in town."

Commenting on human characteristics in general, the Apter made the following observations: "A human being should be like a vessel, and accept what the Creator pours into it, either good or bad, either wine or vinegar."

"We are always wondering why people who possess great wealth are constantly engaged in accumulating more money. The answer is that they have eyes that see not. Because they are blind, they imagine that they have no riches, and that is why they dissipate their energies in search of wealth."

Emphasizing the importance of the moral obligations of the individual, the Apter referred to the style of the Ten Commandments:

"The Ten Commandments begin with the words, 'I am the Lord, thy God.' (Exod. 20:2): 'Thy God' in the singular, not 'your God' in the plural, because the Lord spoke to everyone individually, according to his personal power to comprehend and act."

Speaking on such divergent subjects as tolerance and unquestioning faith, the Apter declared:

> We find that when Abraham spoke in defense of Sodom, he enumerated fifty just men, forty-five, and so forth. (Gen. 18:24–32). The Lord could have replied to him at once that Sodom did not contain a single just man, but He wished to teach a lesson, namely, that permission should be granted to one who argues, to bring out all his points. These should be answered one by one, with patience. It is not fitting that a man should give an abrupt answer immediately in order to silence his adversary.

> A man should not choose the form in which he wishes to perform the service of the Lord, but he should perform it in any manner the opportunity affords.
> (Midrash Ribash Tov II, 28; Menarah HaTehorah, p. 80; Newman: Hassidic Anthology, p. 154, p. 477.)

The Apter spent the last years of his life in Medzibozh, the town where Hassidut had been founded by R. Israel Baal Shem Tov. Before his death, he prayed:

"Lord of the Universe! I know that I have no merits that I be placed in Paradise among the pious, and You will place me in

Hell among the wicked. But You know that I hate those who transgress Your will. So how will I be able to tolerate such people? Therefore, I beseech You to take the wicked out of Hell in order that You be able to put me there to stay in Hell by myself."

It was a prayer in earnest, but mixed with humor, as were many serious statements of the Apter. Named after the Apter is one of the most prominent philosophers of Judaism in our time, his descendant, Abraham Joshua Heschel, professor at the Jewish Theological Seminary in New York.

R. ZVI ELIMELEKH OF DINOV

R. Zvi Hirsh Elimelekh of Dinov (1750–1841) was a nephew of the great Hassidic masters, R. Elimelekh of Lizhensk and R. Zusheh of Annipol. In time he became himself the founder of a Hassidic dynasty that has continued to our own day. R. Zvi Elimelekh was a disciple of the Seer of Lublin and of R. Mendel of Rimanov. Because of his great scholarship, he occupied rabbinic positions in a number of cities. Before returning to Dinov, where he established his Hassidic court, he had been the spiritual leader of the Jewish community in the Hungarian city of Munkacz. However, his opposition to the eating of the meat of stuffed geese, because of his belief that such meat was not meeting the requirements of the Jewish dietary laws, caused a great controversy and led him to return to the land of his birth where he soon became the master of many hundreds of Hassidim.

Although many Hassidim came daily to talk to him and receive his blessings, R. Elimelekh arranged his day in such a manner that he was able to find time for his own devotions and studies, and yet have spare time enough to write his books. His most popular work is a collection of comments on Jewish holidays and festive occasions called *Bnei Issakhar,* meaning *The Sons of Issakhar,* because the "Seer" of Lublin had told him that he was a descendant of Issakhar. Among his other works are: *Derekh Pekudaykha,* meaning *The Way of Thy Precepts* (Ps. 119:27); *Devorim Nekhmadim* or *Desirable Words; Brakha Meshuleshet,* meaning *The Three-Fold Blessing,* alluding to the priestly blessing recorded in the Bible (Num. 6:24–28); *M'Ayn Gannim,* meaning *Fountain of Gardens;* and *Rayakh Dohdahimm,* or *Fragrance of the Gardens;* the last two titles being based on passages in the Song of Songs (4:15; 7:14). The first two of the above-mentioned works have been studied among Hassidim since their publication, inspiring their readers to follow Jewish tradition and observe Jewish precepts as laws and ethics in synthesis.

R. Zvi Elimelekh was known as "Lover of the People of Israel," and this was the final sentence in most of his letters before the signature. Characteristic of his behavior in general is the following incident:

Once, on the Day of Atonement, when he was to lead the congregation in prayer, he looked for a while at the title page of the prayer book for the day, and then cried out: "Lord of the Universe! I don't know what to pray for and what to ask of Thee. Here, take the prayer book and choose the prayers you like best."

R. Zvi Elimelekh died at the age of 56. One of his three sons, R. David, because his successor.

Interpreting a biblical passage, he commented:

"This is the statute of the Law which the Lord hath commanded" (Num. 19:2): Even if the laws appeal to our reason, we must obey them not for their logic or usefulness, but because they are the commands of the Lord.

In his chats and books, R. Zvi Elimelekh stressed the following:

I. We do not recite a benediction before giving charity, because the needy person might die before we finish the benediction over the precept.

II. Fulfilling precepts is a means to raise ordinary acts to the loftiest spiritual heights. The same is true of the words one uses in daily conversation.

III. The Angel of Death is described as being full of eyes. If so, how many eyes must a human being possess in order to protect himself against the Angel of Death!

IV. One should practice humility, particularly when one has reason to feel self-important. When someone is poor or in need of something in general, such a person's humility is not so meritorious as the humility of one who may have feelings of pride because of his station or possessions.

R. MEIR OF PREMISHLAN

R. Meir of Premishlan (? –1852) was an extraordinary Hassidic teacher in many ways. Born in Premishlan, in the Eastern part of Galicia, his father R. Aryeh Leib named him after his own father, the first R. Meir of Premishlan, a disciple of R. Israel Baal Shem Tov, the Besht, founder of Hassidut.

R. Meir was the folksiest among the Hassidic masters of his day. He did not wait for the people to come to him, but, instead, made every endeavor to be among them. He drew to himself the most simple and unscholarly by his humor, his anecdotes and often by his deliberate mistranslations of biblical terms in order to apply passages in the Holy Scriptures to the life and the environment of his simple devotees. His teachings, as collected in the volumes *Or HaMeir* and *Margheneetah DeR' Meir,* meaning *Shining Light* and *Pearls of R. Meir,* prove him to have been a man of great scholarly attainments and human understanding. The stories he told about himself were, for the most part, pure inventions, in order to amuse his Hassidim at his own expense and show them that he was as simple and human as they were. His aim was to make use of anecdote and humor to elevate simple people to a higher level of spirituality.

He usually spoke of himself in the third person, mentioning his name without the addition of any title. His Hassidim called him R. Meir'el, the diminutive of his name. R. Meir'el related:

"When Meir was a little boy, his teacher criticized him for getting up late and coming late to his studies. 'Why don't you take the Evil Inclination as your example?' asked the teacher. 'God created it for the purpose of testing human beings' freedom of choice, and the Evil Inclination works diligently at the task of leading people away from the path of righteousness. How more so is your duty to get up in time to fulfill your tasks.' 'There is a vast difference between me and the Evil Inclination,' replied little Meir, 'for I possess an Evil Inclination, but the Evil Inclination has no Evil Inclination to interfere with its duties.' "

A preacher from out of town came to visit R. Meir and saw that the Hassidim were leaving large sums of money for their master. "Every one likes my preachings, but they give me miserly sums," said the preacher, "but your devotees give you large amounts."

"A Hassidic master has to influence his Hassidim," replied

R. Meir, "and since I disdain money, they do the same and give the money to me."

His Hassidim related: R. Meir'el was once walking downhill over a slippery road. While others slipped and bruised parts of their bodies, R. Meir walked erect and came downhill without difficulty. When asked how he did it, he replied: "When someone is tied to the Above, he cannot slip down."

Speaking to his devotees, he said: "The Patriarchs are called *Avot,* meaning 'Fathers,' because each of them did not rely on his own knowledge of God, but became a father-originator himself in the knowledge of the Almighty. God has given us two eyes: one eye to see the qualities of others, and the other eye to see everyone's own shortcomings."

Following are two examples of his biblical interpretations in a serious vein:

"Bind up the money in thy hand" (Deut. 14:25): Bind the money and rule over it, otherwise it will bind you and be your ruler.

"Thou lovest evil more than good; falsehood rather than speaking righteousness" (Ps. 52:5): Evil people are usually seeking something wrong in the good people, while seeing no blemish upon themselves. So King David reminded us to love the evil of the good person rather than the righteousness of the evil person.

Some of the anecdotes that R. Meir'el told of himself have become part of Yiddish folklore. His most quoted statement— in essays dealing with the question of fulfilling the tasks one is fit for, and not using one's shortcomings as a pretext for no endeavor altogether—is what he said once about his troubles in the World-to-Come.

Speaking of himself in the third person, he said:

"Before the Heavenly Court, Meir will have to give an accounting of his deeds. Meir will not have to defend himself against
the charge that his deeds did not match those of Moses, but Meir
will be held responsible for not having done what it was in Meir's
ability to do." (A similar thought is attributed to R. Zusheh.)

R. Meir'el's simple Hassidim understood the moral of the
story, and everyone did his best to fulfill his duties as a human
being according to his means and abilities.

R. SHOLEM OF BELZ

R. Sholem Rokeakh of Belz (? –1851) was perhaps the
only Hassidic master who became one as a result of his wife's
endeavors. He was born in the Galician city of Brody to a family
of a long line of great Talmudists. His father, R. Eliezer died
when Sholem was still very young, so his uncle, R. Issakhar
Dovber Rokeakh, Rabbi of Sokal, brought him to his house in
order to give him a proper home and the chance to continue the
traditional studies. The Rabbi of Sokal was an opponent of the
Hassidim, and did not countenance any poetic-symbolic interpretations of Biblical precepts introduced by R. Israel Baal Shem
Tov and his disciples. But R. Issakhar Dovber had a Hassidic rebel
in his own house, in the person of his daughter, Malkeh, meaning
Queen, who was known as Malkeleh, the diminutive of her name.
She favored the Hassidim, and was a great admirer of R. Shlomo
of Lutzk, a disciple of R. Dov Ber, the Maggid of Mezritch.
R. Shlomo of Lutzk was a resident of Sokal, and to Malkeleh he
seemed the personification of all that was beautiful and inspiring
in the Hassidic way of life.

After R. Sholem and Malkeleh were married, the young wife

succeeded in her efforts to make her husband enter the Hassidic fold. She knew his great potentialities. He once made a pact with two friends that they study together one thousand nights in succession. One of the friends could not continue after the one hundredth night; the second had to stop on the eight hundredth night, and Sholem alone finished the task as had been planned. He became a devotee of R. Shlomo of Lutzk and later he visited three of the most celebrated Hassidic leaders of the time: the "Seer" of Lublin, R. Uri of Strelisk, and R. Avrohom Yehoshuah Heshel of Apta, becoming a disciple of each. R. Sholem wished to remain a disciple, but the "Seer" of Lublin wanted him to become the leader of a Hassidic community. Contrary to the advice of his master, R. Sholem wished to become a businessman rather than a rabbi by profession and a teacher of Hassidim. In his first business venture, R. Sholem lost all his money. Only then did he realize that the "Seer" was right in insisting that if one is destined to engage in spiritual matters, he has a very small chance of becoming successful in material matters. After R. Sholem was given the rabbinical seat of Belz, at the recommendation of the "Seer," R. Sholem established there a Hassidic Court which existed until the early days of World War II. R. Sholem's wife became a Hassidic leader in her own right, some prominent men being among her spiritual devotees. Instead of influencing his followers by means of long discourses, R. Sholem created in Belz an atmosphere of piety. He had inborn architectural ability, and under his guidance the Great Synagogue of Belz was constructed. Synagogues in other cities were modeled after the Belz Synagogue wherever Belzer Hassidim built a house of worship. An exact copy of the Belz Synagogue now stands in the Israeli city of Benei Berak.

The Hassidic House of Belz became, in time, a tremendous spiritual and social force which flowed over the borders of eastern Galicia and reached the Jewish masses in the nearby Ukraine and far-off Hungary. R. Sholem was a powerful leader, and so were the first two of his successors: his youngest son, R. Yehoshuah and his grandson Issakhar Dov. The fourth in line, R. Aaron died in Tel Aviv, after having lost his entire family during the Nazi occupation in World War II. A nephew of R. Aaron, a young man in his teens, was chosen by the Belzer Hassidim in Israel as his successor, and Hassidim of the same dynasty, living in all parts of the world, concurred in the decision.

R. Sholem, founder of the Belzer dynasty, was known for his great powers in healing people who were victims of hysteria and schizophrenia. Many non-Jews were among those who turned to him when such illnesses occurred in their own families.

One of the opponents of the Hassidim reasoned with R. Sholem that his devotees were extremists, and it is better for human beings to use the middle of the road. "People walk on both sides of the street," replied R. Sholem, "only the horses walk in the middle of the road." (A similar reply to the same question is attributed to R. Mendel of Kotzk.)

A Hassid told R. Sholem that, according to medical diagnosis, he had but one *lung* and that the physicians had told him that there was no remedy for the defect. Consoling him, R. Sholem said: "First of all, I don't believe that the diagnosis of the physicians is correct; secondly, who ever issued an edict that a person must have two *lungs* in order to be well? thirdly, He who said that one must have *two lungs,* will also declare that one can live minus one lung."

R. Sholem often spoke of modesty, humility, love of fellow men and faith in the Almighty.

According to R. Sholem's observations, there are two kinds of modesty: the feeling that one is naught and so are others; and the feeling that one is naught when compared to others.

> "Now the man Moses was very meek" (Num. 12:3). There are two forms of humility. One is the humility of a person who believes that he is naught and so are all other human beings—this is hypocritical meekness. The second is the true humility of the person who believes that he is naught but other human beings are better and important.

> On the surface, it seems that it is quite difficult to fulfill the teaching, "Love thy neighbor as thyself" (Lev. 19:18); but if someone possesses real humility, he can accomplish this by realizing that his neighbor is more important a person than he and consequently more deserving; he will not begrudge him his necessities and he will love him as he loves himself.

> He interpreted a Biblical passage: "What aileth thee, O thou sea, that thou fleest? Thou Jordan that thou turnest backward?" (Ps. 114:5): Why is the present used and not the past? Just as it was a miracle in the past when Israel went out of Egypt, so it is a miracle also in the present, since the waves are always eager to flood the world, but God subdues them for the benefit of all livng.

R. Sholem became blind in the last years of his life, and his wife Malkeleh became the "seeing eyes," which brought him renewed spiritual vision and inspiration. He believed that being older, he would die first, but destiny willed it otherwise. When his wife died, a number of Hassidic masters and numerous disciples came to console the heartbroken Tzadik of Belz. But no words of consolation could penetrate his heart or mind. Burning tears streamed constantly from the blind eyes over the beard-covered cheeks. The tears ceased when R. Sholem was later re-united with his Malkeleh in the Heavenly World.

The teachings of R. Sholem and stories about him are recorded in the book *Doveyr Sholem,* meaning *Speaking Peace,* published posthumously.

XI

Leaders, Teachers, and Giants
Of Hassidut

EVERY GENERATION in Hassidut, from the days of its originator, R. Israel Baal Shem Tov, to the second half of the nineteenth century, produced giants of its own. Each of these great masters interpreted in his own way and manner the universalism of Jewish faith and ethics, often decorating them with poetic similes and inspiring parables.

At the communal Third Sabbath Meal, in the semi-darkness of twilight, the masters interpreted the prescribed Pentateuch portions of the week, often combining comments on current events with commentaries on biblical passages or on the sayings of the Sages as recorded in *Ethics of the Fathers,* the post-biblical Mishnah-Tractate dealing with proper behavior and philosophical observations. *Ethics of the Fathers* is usually studied on Saturday afternoons between the holidays of Passover and Rosh HaShanah, the last being the Universal New Year, according to Jewish tradition.

The teachings of a number of the Hassidic masters of various generations are dealt with in the present chapter.

R. MENAKHEM MENDEL OF RIMANOV AND
THE SERVANT R. ZVI HIRSH

After the passing of R. Elimelekh of Lizhensk, many of his

disciples and devotees became the followers of R. Mendel of Rimanov (? –1815). According to Hassidic lore, R. Elimelekh said of his beloved disciple that he prayed with such devotion that, when praying, sparks flew through his forehead. R. Elimelekh therefore left him, as an inheritance, "the soul of his own brains." Before settling in Rimanov, R. Mendel was the spiritual head of the Jewish community in the town of Pristyk.

When the future master of Rimanov was but eleven years old, his father took him for a visit to R. Dov Ber, the preacher of Mezritch, successor to R. Israel Baal Shem Tov, founder of Hassidut. In his youth, he studied first in the Yeshiva of R. Daniel Yaffe in Berlin, and then he became a student of R. Shmelkeh, later the Hassidic master and chief Rabbi of Nicholsburg, having as his fellow students two young men: Israel, who became in time the famous Hassidic master, R. Israel of Kozhenitz, and Yaakov Yitzkhak, who later influenced the development of Hassidut in Poland as the "Seer" of Lublin.

During the Napoleonic War, R. Mendel sided with the French against the Russians, hoping that Napoleon's victory would bring about the renewal of Poland's independence and consequently a better civil status for the Jewish population.

Opponents of the Hassidim caused the arrests of the three leading masters: the Seer of Lublin, R. Avrohom Yehushua Heshel of Apta and R. Mendel of Rimanov. The last acted as spokesman for all three. When the judge asked them what was their trade or profession, R. Mendel replied:

"We are servants of the king."

"What king?"

"The King of Kings, the Creator of Heaven and earth."

"Why do you dress yourselves in white?"

"These are priestly garments."

Stressing the importance of life in simplicity, R. Mendel forbade the womenfolk of his followers to wear fancy clothing or to bedeck themselves with jewelry. R. Mendel went himself or sent his representatives to examine the weights and measures of all storekeepers and of all who were doing business on the local market place. Before R. Mendel died, he ordered that a structure be built over his grave with a window facing the town so that he could continue to watch from his place of interment whether the townsmen transgressed the laws of honesty.

Non-Jews as well as Jews used to leave notes on his grave pleading for help when someone in the family was ill and in other times of woe and distress. A patriotic Polish nobleman left on R. Mendel's grave a note of a political nature: "Holy Teacher! Implore the God of Abraham, Isaac and Jacob to liberate two oppressed peoples: the Jews and the Poles." The father of the Cardinal of Lvov brought his son to R. Mendel's grave. The father, a man in the eighties, told the Cardinal: "When you were a child, you once became very ill, and your mother went to the Holy R. Mendel to ask him to pray that you remain alive and become well again. Your mother assured him that she had come to him not in the belief that a human being can perform miracles, but in the belief that the prayers of so devout a man would be acceptable to the Almighty. R. Mendel prayed for three hours, and then told your mother to go home cheerfully. Just when your mother entered the room where you were lying, you opened your eyes and asked for a drink. From that moment on, you began to feel better, and not long after that, you were a happy and healthy boy again."

The teachings, thoughts and biblical interpretations of R.

Mendel of Rimanov, as well as stories of his life and deeds, are recorded in four volumes, each of which has a title which includes his Hebrew name, Menakhem: *Menakhem Tziyon (Comforter of Zion), Divray Menakhem (The Words of Menakhem), Torat Menakhem (The Teaching of Menakhem),* and *Ateret Menakhem (The Crown of Menakhem).*

He spoke out against mockery and idle talk in general, and issued guide lines for proper behavior, stressing the spirituality that emanates from daily life and deeds, and the need to learn the proper lesson from whatever one sees and hears.

He once pointed at the sky and said: "How beautiful are the heavens! But scoffers can convince you that there are no skies. By means of mockery you can even abolish the reality of the world's existence. Had Pharaoh known the value of mockery, he would never have permitted the Israelites to leave Egypt but would have kept them there in eternal slavery amusing them by means of mockery."

R. Mendel considered idle talk as a criminal act:

"He who uses words that are superfluous, and when it is not necessary to use them, violates the commandment, 'Thou shalt not murder' Exod. 20:13. R. Mendel was in harmony with the general teaching of Hassidut, that silence is never tiresome, and if what one has to say in two words is sufficient, one should be careful not to use more words for the same purpose. "When someone stands with a friend behind a wall, and I hear his voice, I recognize by the tone, the face of the talker. The face of one who speaks is as if carved in his voice, and if he is engaged in idle talk, it is as if he murdered his own countenance."

Dealing with problems of self-esteem, modesty in eating, and brotherly love, he said: "When someone hears that he is praised for possessing a specific quality, then it is a sign that he has been notified from Heaven that he should really acquire that quality and use it to the utmost." Of eating, he said: "Every kind of food has two aspects, a physical and a spiritual. The pleasures from eating derive from the spiritual value of the food —from its taste, its looks and its aroma which are not perceptible. The body throws out the physical in the food because it cannot become assimilated."

Interpreting a biblical passage in a precise manner, R. Mendel declared: "Noah was in his generation a man righteous and wholehearted" (Gen. 6:9): He was a "man," he mixed with others, and helped them although they were sinners. At the root of all ethical behavior is love, and love enhances peace.

Among R. Mendel's disciples were the later famous Hassidic masters R. Moshe of Sambor, R. Naphtali of Ropshitz, R. Zvi Elimelekh of Dinov, and R. Zvi Hirsh of Zydichoiv.

Not a famous disciple of R. Mendel, nor a member of his immediate family, succeeded him as the master of Rimanov. His successor was the man who had come to him as a young man to be his servant, and in the history of Hassidut he is spoken of with reverence as "R. Hirsh the Servant."

R. ZVI HIRSH HAKOHEN KATZ

R. Zvi Hirsh HaKohen Katz (? –1846), successor of R. Mendel of Rimanov, and usually called "R. Hirsh Meshores" (R. Hirsh the Servant), was born in the town of Dombrova, near Tarnov, in the western region of Galicia. Before he reached the age of ten, both his parents died, and relatives apprenticed him to a tailor. He was a very pious boy, and when in his early teens he met R. Moshe of Psheversk, a scribe by profession, whose greatness as a Hassidic author was revealed only after his passing when the manuscript of his two-volume work *Or Pnay Moshe (The Radiance of Moshe's Face)* was found. Under R. Moshe's influence, young Hirsh became a Hassid. After he visited Pristyk, where R. Mendel then held Hassidic Court, Hirsh decided to remain in Pristyk, and with the assistance of scholars, whom he served as messenger boy, he gradually entered the world of Jewish learning. In time he became R. Mendel's personal servant, and when the master of Pristyk moved to Rimanov, he took Hirsh with him.

Under the guidance of the master, R. Hirsh advanced in his studies, and R. Mendel protected him against any abuse whatever because of his station. Before his passing, R. Mendel confided in his disciple, R. Naphtali of Ropshitz, his wish that not his own son but his servant become his successor. R. Hirsh was afraid to accept the leadership of the Rimanover Hassidim, and actually escaped to Ropshitz where he stayed for a number of years and where, under the guidance of R. Naphtali, he secretly prepared himself to fulfill R. Mendel's last wish. When he felt ready, R. Hirsh the Servant, as he was known, returned to Rimanov and gradually gained a large following.

Having had sad experiences as an orphan, and knowing the woes of those in need, he used to tax the rich among his Hassidim to provide him with large sums of money. It was rumored among both Hassidim and among those opposed to Hassidut in general, that R. Hirsh the Servant accumulated great wealth from his leadership, but in truth he always distributed the money among the needy, the orphans and the widows of his devotees. In time, some famous Hassidic masters became themselves Hassidim of the Servant, and R. Israel of Ruzhin, the great-grandson of the

Maggid of Mezritch, the Baal Shem Tov's successor, and himself one of the greatest Hassidic masters of the time, considered it a great honor that his own grandson married R. Hirsh the Servant's daughter.

R. Hirsh, although having attained one of the highest places in Hassidic leadership, never forgot that he himself was a descendant of simple folk, and just as he was specifically interested in the welfare of the masses, so the masses repaid him through joining by the thousands the ranks of his followers. R. Hirsh the Servant, the second master of Rimanov, left no books. But his thoughts and teachings were recorded in two volumes, *Mevasser Tov (Messenger of Good Tidings)*, based on Isa. 52:7, and *Beerot HaMayim (Wells of Water)* taken from a passage in Gen. 26:18.

Most of the thoughts and teachings of R. Hirsh the Servant were based on ethical interpretations of biblical passages, expressed orally at the Hassidic gatherings to the communal Third Sabbath Meal, during the short twilight time before the Sabbath was coming to an end.

Following are some of the biblical interpretations, as recorded later by the closest among his scholarly Hassidim:

"In the beginning God created the Heaven and the earth" (Gen. 1:1): The Jerusalemite Aramaic translation adds that God created the world with wisdom. What is wisdom? The fear of God, as it is written: "Behold, the fear of the Lord, that is wisdom" (Job 28:28). And this also referred to King David and Solomon his son: "How manifold are Thy works, O Lord! In wisdom hast Thou made them All" (Ps. 104:24); and "She opened her mouth with wisdom" (Prov. 31:26): Wisdom means the wisdom of truth, and this is explained by the conclusion of the same passage: "The law of kindness is on her tongue." Even one who is not learned but possesses the fear of God, is blessed with wisdom to interpret the Law; the law of kindness which is on his tongue. "These are the generations of Noah . . . And Noah begot three sons, Shem, Ham and Japhet" (Gen. 6:9–10). But a previous passage (Ibid., 5:32) has already told us that "Noah begot Shem, Ham and Japhet": then why the repetition? This is to teach us, by means of the Eternal Law, that every generation has at least one righteous and whole-hearted man to teach his contemporaries proper knowledge. It is mentioned twice that Noah begot three sons to remind us that there are three different forms in the deeds and behavior of a righteous leader. Sometimes the righteous and whole hearted leader is famous and it is possible to take him as an example. Often the righteous man of the generation is known only to the few but the flame of his whole-heartedness in the service of God is so strong that it brings inspirational warmth to others. Then there is the third form of righteousness. No one sees the great man's physical service of God, but he is inwardly so attached to the Almighty that he causes spiritual elevation to the masses in general. Each of Noah's three sons symbolized the three different kinds of teachers, one kind for a specific generation.

"I will put none of the diseases upon thee, which I have put on the Egyptians; for I am the Lord that healeth thee" (Exod. 15:26): This is similar to a king of flesh and blood who keeps a physician constantly in the palace, to visit him and his family daily, even though no one is ill. The Almighty, the Great Healer, does the same thing. He visits us daily and takes care of everyone's body and soul.

"And ye shall not wrong one another" (Lev. 25:17): The

other within a person is his truth. One should not do wrong, nor commit a falsehood against his own truth.

"But from thence you will seek the Lord, thy God; and thou shalt find Him if thou search after Him with all thy heart and all thy soul" (Deut. 4:29): If you search, from the searching itself, you will begin to understand how it is possible to seek the Lord.

"Judges and officers shalt thou make thee in all thy gates, which the Lord thy God giveth thee" (Deut. 16:18): God has given the human being seven "Gates." They are: two eyes, two ears, two nostrils and the mouth. One has to watch over his personal gates so as not to look at things the Creator has banned; not to talk and not to listen to what is forbidden to us by the Almighty, and not to inhale the aroma of things prohibited. We should always have over ourselves a superior who punishes until we accept his command. Every human being should himself be the judge and the officer in all the seven gates and keep watch over them.

Some present-day Hassidic leaders, who are descendants of the princely R. Israel of Ruzhin, are just as proud of their descent from the Servant R. Zvi Hirsh of Rimanov. They quote what the Rimanover said to the Ruzhiner during the arrangements of the marriage between the former's daughter to the latter's grandson: "For five years in my early youth I was a tailor's apprentice, and in those days I learned two important things: Not to damage the new and to fix properly the old."

R. NAPHTALI OF ROPSHITZ

Hassidic masters often added strands of humor to their teachings, biblical commentaries and parables; but only R. Naphtali

Horowitz of Ropshitz (1759–1826) was a humorist per se, and some of his anecdotes, and humorous tales about him, are still retold in Hassidic circles whenever there is occasion for pure, hearty laughter.

R. Naphtali was born in Linsk, Galicia, where his father occupied the seat of the local Rabbi. In his early youth, he became a disciple of three of the greatest masters of the time: R. Israel, the Maggid of Kozhenitz, R. Yaakov Yitzkhak, the "Seer of Lublin" and R. Menakhem Mendel of Rimanov.

R. Naphtali, possessing both great wisdom and talent, became very popular as a *Badkhan,* a jester or entertainer at wedding parties. After the passing of his teachers, he settled in Ropshitz, and he became the leader of many devotees. Several of his disciples later became Hassidic masters in their own right, among them R. Khayim Halberstam of Tzanz.

It is related that when R. Naphtali was a little boy, a man who frequented his father's house, said to him: "Naphtali, I'll give you a gold piece if you tell me where God lives." "I'll give you two gold pieces if you tell me where God does not live," replied Naphtali.

An epigram coined by R. Naphtali can be applied as a characterization of himself: "One has to possess great wisdom in order to be perfect in all its simplicity." R. Naphtali related:

> At first I did not want to be a Rabbi, for a Rabbi has to flatter his flock, and I thought of becoming a tailor. Then I saw that a tailor has to flatter his customers, and so has a shoemaker, and a bath-attendant; and I said to myself, "Where, then, is a Rabbi worse off?" And so I became a Rabbi.

He once proclaimed:

I'd rather be the partner of a wise man in Gehenna than the companion of a fool in Eden.

(M. Lipson, MiDor Dor, I, 109; HaDor, 1945, p. 673; A Treasury of Jewish Quotations, edited by J.L. Baron, New York, 1956.)

Poking fun at his own popularity, he once said: "In the far off places I am known as 'The Tzadik R. Naphtali'; in my city of residence, where people know me a little better, I am spoken of as 'Our Rabbi'; but my wife who knows me better than anyone else, calls me simply 'Naphtali.' "

Being constantly engaged in charitable activities, he was well aware of the feelings of the needy. He stated: "Asking sustenance from someone else is like getting honey from the bee—one is in danger of feeling the pain of the bee's sting."

Once, R. Naphtali came home very late and very tired from a meeting of the Community Council which dealt with assistance to the poor. When the wife asked him whether his appeal had any influence, he replied: "I was half successful; the poor are willing to take. Whether the rich will give, of this I am not sure yet."

A Hassidic master had come to Ropshitz incognito. But R. Naphtali recognized him, and said to him smilingly: "You can't fool me. You should know that it is quite difficult to steal from a thief."

An opponent of the Hassidim, once asked R. Naphtali: "Why do the Hassidim attach so much importance to drinking?" Replied R. Naphtali: "We have learned this from Noah, the Tzadik —the righteous man of his generation. He knew well the secret of imbibing: 'And he drank from the wine and was drunken' " (Gen. 9:21).

R. Naphtali was the author of two works: *Zerah Kodesh (Holy*

Seed) and *Ayalah Shelukha (A Hind Set Loose),* the title being taken from Jacob's blessing on his son Naphtali (Gen. 49:21). R. Naphtali's personality is depicted in the book *Ohel Naphtali (The Tent of Naphtali).*

R. Naphtali related: "Three things have I learned by observing a child: 1, It is always happy; 2, When it is in need of something, it cries; 3, When it is awake, it does not rest for a moment."

He interpreted a biblical passage in the following manner:

"And ye shall not wrong one another" (Lev. 25:17): This is according to strict justice. Beyond the line of strict justice, this means: Do not commit any wrongs against yourself.

Of music and prophecy, he said:

"By means of a tune, it is possible to open all the gates of Heaven but through sadness the gates are closed. All tunes have a Holy source, but defilement does not know how to sing, because it is the source of sadness."

"The difference between a prophet and a Hassidic master is this, that the prophet sees the future and the master sees the present. It is more difficult to look at the present than to gaze into the future."

R. ISRAEL OF RUZHIN

When R. Israel Baal Shem Tov, the Besht, felt that his end was near, he called over R. Dov Ber, the Mezritcher Maggid who was to be his successor, and whispered into his ear: "One of your descendants will bear my name, and he will find the true way to Hassidut."

R. Israel of Ruzhin (1797–1850) was R. Dov Ber's descendant whom the Besht had in mind, says Hassidic tradition. R. Israel, being the great-grandson of R. Dov Ber, on his father's side, and the grandson of R. Nakhum of Chernoble on his mother's side, was thus a scion of two Hassidic dynasties, and in addition he founded a dynasty of his own through his six sons, each of them establishing a Hassidic Court in a different town. Various Hassidic masters bearing the family name of Friedman trace their ancestry back to R. Israel of Ruzhin rather than to their earlier forbears.

R. Israel was born in the town of Prohibisch, in the Kiev region of the Ukraine, where his father, R. Sholem Shakhneh held Hassidic court. The master of Prohibisch died when Israel was very young, and the older brother, R. Abraham, the successor, took over the fatherly role, seeing to it that his younger brother had the proper spiritual preparation for Hassidic leadership. The older brother died when Israel was but sixteen years old, and the Hassidim of R. Sholem Shakhneh chose him to be their teacher and guide.

It is related that when R. Sholem Shakhneh was on his death bed, he called over his son Israel and told him that it was his destiny to become one of the great successors of the Besht himself, and he should therefore take care not to reveal this until the proper time.

"How will I know that the proper time has come?" asked the son.

"When you will hear a story about the Besht that you had never heard before," replied R. Sholem Shakhneh.

Israel visited many Hassidic masters and their disciples, but every story they told him about the founder of Hassidut he had already heard before. Israel also undertook a pilgrimage to Medzibozh, where the Besht had lived, and when there he mentioned the reason for his visit: to hear about the Besht something unknown to him. He was told that not far from Medzibozh lived a very old shepherd who had known the Besht when he, the shepherd, was still a young boy. Israel betook himself to the hut of the old Podolyan peasant, who related two incidents he had seen with his own eyes.

Once the Besht was in haste to fulfill an important mission, and as if an earthquake had caused it, two neighboring hills moved nearer to each other, and the Besht continued on his mission without the necessity of going down one mountain and climbing from the valley to the top of the other mountain.

At another time, continued the old shepherd, a vicious wolf appeared in the mountains. He attacked the herds and flocks of the region, escaping every time carrying a goat or a sheep, which he devoured in his lair. Since the shepherd boy had realized, after the incident with the hills, that the Besht was a miracle worker, he appealed to him for help. The Besht gave him a stick and said: "When you see the wolf coming nearer, raise the stick and shout at him, 'Run away, or you will be beaten by the Baal Shem Tov.'" "I did as I had been told by the Besht, the wolf escaped and was never seen again," finished the old shepherd, and he closed his eyes forever, as if he had lived that long only to relate something that Israel, the great-grandson of the Maggid, should hear about the Besht that he had not heard before, and thus realize that the time had come for him to be revealed as a master of Hassidut.

R. Israel later moved to the city of Ruzhin, and his numerous followers enabled him to build a palatial home, and in time the members of his family began to conduct themselves in the manner of ducal children. Perhaps this was what the Besht meant when he hinted to R. Dov Ber that a descendant bearing the name of "Israel" would find the true way to Hassidut, by giving its masters the status of spiritual princes. When asked why Hassidic masters of previous generations had lived in difficult circumstances, preferring to stay poor, although they had become famous and had many followers, while the Hassidic masters of later generations lived in beautiful homes and traveled in carriages fitting for the wealthy aristocracy, R. Israel replied:

"Three kinds of people come nowadays to the Hassidic leaders, giving them "Redemption" contributions. The three kinds are: real Hassidim; well-to-do home-owners; and sinners. The money is later separated according to the givers. With the "Redemption" sums of the Hassidim, religious articles are bought and the largest part is distributed for charitable purposes. With the sums given by well-to-do home owners, the Hassidic leaders sustain themselves; and the income from sinners they spend on luxuries."

Living in surroundings of wealth, R. Israel used very little for his personal needs. He once fasted from Saturday night to the next Sabbath eve. Later he explained: "I did not eat for reasons of fasting, I simply forgot to eat. Thank God, I was later reminded that the Sabbath had come, when fasting is forbidden, unless it happens to be the 'Day of Atonement.' "

The Ruzhiner applied to himself the biblical passage, "Return, O Israel, unto the Lord, thy God" (Hos., 14:2): Before I tell others to repent, I, Israel of Ruzhin, have to repent first, myself.

R. Israel wrote poetry in the form of prayers, expressing his great longings and hopes of Messianic redemption.

One of his Hassidim had told his little son that the master, R. Israel, had six golden wings. Some time later, the man traveled to Ruzhin and he also took along the boy to receive the master's blessing. When the boy entered R. Israel's reception room, he expressed loudly his disappointment because he saw no golden wings on the master. The father was terribly embarrassed, but R. Israel smiled radiantly and said to the man: "Go and show your child my six sons, for they are the golden wings that I possess."

Even the ideological opponents of R. Israel respected and loved him. When a disciple asked him how he had accomplished it, he replied: "I love my opponents so much that they have no choice but to repay me in kind."

But in addition to opponents, R. Israel also had enemies, and the Czarist Russian government made use of every pretext to oppress the Jewish population and subject its leaders to indignities and punishments. The aristocratic forms in R. Israel's Hassidic court were used as a pretext to accuse the master of Ruzhin that he was making preparations to become King of the Jews. He was arrested and for almost two years languished in the prisons of Kamenetz and Kiev. After being freed, he came to Keshinyev and from there went to Jassy. While staying in Rumania, he received permission from the Austrian government to settle in the province of Galicia. After twenty-five years of Hassidic leadership in the Ukraine, R. Israel bought the settlement of Potik, near Sadigorah, and there a palatial home was built for him to hold Hassidic court. Among the thousands who came to visit him and receive his blessings were men who were Hassidic masters in their own right.

Recalling his experiences in prison, R. Israel said to his disciples: "Before the arrest I could not fully understand why the evil inclination was called an 'old and foolish king' [Eccls. 4:13]. I did realize that it was called 'king' because the evil inclination rules over the human being; 'old' because it begins its rule at the moment of every human being's birth. But why 'fool'? After all, the evil inclination plays many clever tricks on everyone! But when I was in prison, this became clear to me. I was put in a prison cell because I was helpless against my accusers. But why did the evil inclination follow me into prison? Only a fool can do that."

The Ruzhiner impressed people with his noble bearing and great wisdom more than with his scholarship. His sayings, biblical interpretations and tales about him can be found in the collections *Tifferet Israel (Beauty of Israel)*, *Bet Israel (House of Israel)*, and in several others.

R. Israel was once standing near a horse and patted it fondly. He said to a Hassid who happened to pass by: "This horse is really worthy of honor. For forty years it has not wasted its time in idle talk."

When he heard that a certain Hassidic leader foretold when the coming of the Messiah would occur, R. Israel commented: "Those who foretell do not know, and those who know do not tell."

A young man came and complained that he did not know how to repent. So R. Israel asked: "How come that you knew how to sin?"

"First I had sinned and later I realized that I was a sinner."

"With repentance, it is the same," explained R. Israel. "First you repent, and then the repentance comes."

Once, when looking out through the window on a snowy day, he reminisced: "My father, of blessed memory, hated the snow, nor do I like it. Why? Its beginning is purity and whiteness, but its end is dirt and mire."

Speaking of such subjects as worship of God, spiritual cleanliness, and human behavior, he accentuated the following:

The best way to worship God, is to remember that what is prohibited is prohibited, and what is permissible, one should not rush to do.

The creations of artists are kept with great care in museums, but human beings, the creations of the Creator of the Universe, are often found rolling in dust.

To possess a pure spirit, one does not need a special spirit. He only has to take care that the spirit God gave him does not become defiled.

When a person is engaged in studies, he need not fear any darkness, because he carries the lantern within himself.

Following are examples of the Ruzhiner's interpretation of biblical passages:

"And ye shall serve the Lord your God, and He will bless thy bread and thy water; and I will take sickness away from the midst of you" (Ex. 23:25): So in the various herbs used for the preparation of medicines, their potency is derived from what the wind blows into them. When God wishes, he blows into bread the potency of medicine, and simple bread is also transformed into great medicinal value.

"An altar of earth shalt thou make unto Me" (Exod. 20:21): Just as the earth is silent, you be silent when talk is unnecessary.

"When any man of you bringeth an offering unto the Lord" (Lev. 1:2): The passage indicates that he who is really a man, brings himself as an offering to the Almighty.

"To be your God" (Num. 15:41): Even the things that are of importance to you materially in daily life, should be purified in order to transform them into Divine sanctity, fit to be placed in the Holy of Holies.

"He that formeth the mountains, and createth the winds"

(Amos 4:13): Those who speak evil of others, think that their words are innocent and do no harm to those spoken of. So God created the winds and the mountains to show that although the wind has no substance, it can desolate mountains and uproot things. So can words, although they have no substance; so can evil words and tale-bearing bring calamity and hatred.

"Strength and gladness are in His place" (I Chron. 16:27): He who wishes to attach himself to the Almighty, cannot be melancholy. He who forgets joyfulness, shows that he has forgotten the Lord of the Universe.

Of R. Israel's six sons, R. Sholem Yoseph died soon after his father. R. Avrohom Yaakov was his father's successor in Sadigorah; R. David Moshe established, in time, a Hassidic court in Chortkov; R. Dov Ber in Lyovah; R. Nakhum in Stephanesht and R. Mordecai Shragah in Husyatin.

R. AVROHOM YAAKOV OF SADIGORAH

The formal successor of R. Israel of Ruzhin was his son, R. Avrohom Yaakov of Sadigorah (1819–1882). In addition to his own inborn humility and consideration for all, he possessed most of his father's qualities for Hassidic leadership, and like his father before him, he was the target of accusations and bitter criticism. R. Khayim Halberstam of Tzanz, who had been a disciple of R. Israel of Ruzhin, led the opposition against R. Avrohom Yaakov, accusing him of contributing to the vulgarization and degeneration of Hassidut, using it as a means for self-aggrandizement and a life in wealth. The criticism and the attacks pained him, and he accepted the sufferings as a form of punishment on earth, which would lighten any punishments reserved for him in the Heavenly World-to-Come.

In the chats with his Hassidim and in his comments on passages of the Holy Scriptures, R. Avrohom Yaakov expressed thoughts and ideas similar to those of his forebears, but the similarity did not substract from their originality. He stated:

Our Sages have taught us that every person has his own place. If so, why do so many people feel as if they were crowded in? Because it is not enough for them to have each a place of his own, he also has an eye on the place of someone else.

When one lives a life of sanctity, he is considered an offering to the Almighty, and the food he digests, the meat animals, the agricultural products and the vegetables, become offerings to the Creator.

"The evil inclination constantly invents new transgressions. That is why in every generation, there are new illnesses unknown to previous generations. But the good inclination creates constantly new precepts, and God creates new medicines for every new sickness. This is why God is called "Creator of Healing."

Characteristic of his interpretations of biblical passages, are the following:

"Thou shalt love thy neighbor as thyself, I am the Lord" (Lev. 19:18): When a person helps his neighbor who is in need, he shows compassion; then "I am the Lord," God will look with compassion towards him who shows compassion for his fellowman. The passage means that God says to us: "According to your attitude towards others, I, the Lord, will act towards yourself."

"Give ear, ye heavens, and I will speak; and let the earth hear the words of my mouth" (Deut. 32:1): If someone is heard in Heaven, then his words will be accepted by the inhabitants of the earth.

"They that seek the Lord, want not any good thing" (Ps. 34:11): The seekers of the Lord accept lovingly whatever God provides for them.

In a time of accusations, attacks and criticism, R. Avrohom Yaakov lived according to his interpretation of the words of the Psalmist, and what God provided for him, he did accept with love and thanks.

R. ZVI HIRSH OF ZYDICHOIV

R. Zvi Hirsh Eichenstein (? –1831), known in Hassidic history as the master of Zydichoiv, was the brother of Hassidic teachers and the uncle of leading figures in Hassidut.

His mother gave birth to him while traveling through a forest. Many years later, when R. Zvi Hirsh was one of the distinguished disciples of R. Yaakov Yitzkhak, the *Khozeh* or "Seer" of Lublin, the latter made use of the name Zvi-Hirsh, meaning "deer," to compliment him by saying: "A deer of this kind is not born in every forest."

R. Zvi Hirsh was one of five sons born to the innkeeper Yitzkhak Isaac Eichenstein who lived in the village of Saphrin. Was it a village in Hungary or a village in the vicinity of Sambor, in Eastern Galicia? Place names were often changed, and this makes it difficult now to verify the exact location of certain settlements.

Why was the innkeeper Yitzkhak Isaac of Saphrin destined to become the ancestor of a great Hassidic dynasty? The lore of Hassidut relates: The nobleman who owned Saphrin and the entire region as well, wished to have someone prepare for him a full accounting of all his possessions, but no bookkeeper he hired could cope with the job, so immense was the aristocrat's wealth. The Jewish innkeeper of Saphrin was known among the village folk not only for his great piety, learning and kindness, but also for his extraordinary abilities concerning figures and mathematical problems. The owner sent for him, asking that he do him a favor and try his hand at preparing the financial report. The innkeeper agreed, and after several days work handed the aristocrat a full report of his possessions. The landlord was deeply moved when he realized how quickly Yitzkhak Isaac had finished his task, and knowing that the innkeeper would refuse to accept payment, since he, the owner had spoken of asking his help as a favor, he decided to outsmart the innkeeper by giving him a "friendly gift," which consisted of the inn itself, the mill, and the forest that surrounded the village. Yitzkhak Isaac made no personal use of this acquired wealth, but secretly used the income for charitable purposes and to help other innkeepers pay their rentals in time and thus be saved from being put in a dungeon.

Before R. Zvi Hirsh Eichenstein, son of the innkeeper of Saphrin, established a Hassidic court in Zydichoiv, he visited a number of Hassidic teachers of his time, among them R. Moshe Leib of Sassov, R. Israel, the Preacher of Kozhenitz, R. Barukh of Medzibozh, grandson of the Besht, founder of Hassidut, and R. Avrohom Yehoshuah Heshel of Apta. But he considered the "Seer" of Lublin as his master.

R. Zvi Hirsh of Zydichoiv was one of the great teachers of Jewish mysticism known as Kabbalah, and one of his four main books, entitled *Attereth Zvi,* meaning *The Crown of Zvi,* is really a crowning work in Kabbalistic interpretation. Simultaneously, he was one of the great Talmudists of his time, and his mastery of Jewish jurisprudence was phenomenal. He had an only son, who died at an early age after R. Zvi Hirsh himself passed away, and his many devotees became the devotees of his son-in-law, R. Zvi Yehudah of Rozdol, and others, in turn, became Hassidim of his two nephews, Yitzkhak Isaac of Zydichoiv and R. Yitzkhak Isaac of Komarna.

R. Zvi Hirsh's adherents knew that their master was a great scholar and mystic, whose teachings were far above their comprehension, and they were glad to receive his blessings. Actually, he did say many things of a general Hassidic nature, understandable to the most simple among his devotees:

I. Hassidim who say their master is the only one or the best, are guilty of a form of idolatry. They should rather believe that every master is good for his own Hassidim.

II. When I feel that I am about to become angry, I put it off for a later time, and then I forget all about it.

III. A normal human being must be like a fruitful tree. The tree is fruitful because it takes from the earth what it needs and it gives its products in return. Giving and taking is the normal behavior of a human being.

R. YITZKHAK ISAAC OF ZYDICHOIV

R. Yitzkhak Isaac of Zydichoiv (? –1873), son of R. Issakhar Berish Eichenstein, had been one of the closest disciples of his uncle R. Zvi Hirsh, and like the latter was also a man of great scholarly attainment. His field was the writing of commentaries on the *Midrash,* collections containing ethical, symbolic and legendary interpretations of biblical books, mostly of the Pentateuch. He became the Hassidic Master of Zydichoiv after the death of his father. The father, R. Issakhar Berish, who was the successor of R. Zvi Hirsh in Zydichoiv, followed him to the grave less than a year later.

R. Yitzkhak Isaac's devotees also contented themselves with their master's blessings, being sure of their effect.

R. Yitzkhak Isaac himself told of his attitude towards his followers:

"When someone comes to me as a Hassid for the first time, I give him a blessing and send him home. When he comes for the second time, I examine him closely as to his nature and spiritual level. When he comes for the third time, I take him and carry him on my shoulders."

R. Yitzkhak Isaac was on good terms with his name-sake and cousin, R. Yitzkhak Isaac of Komarna. The latter considered himself a devotee of the master of Zydichoiv, and sent him his manuscripts for examination until a scholarly dispute later led to their estrangement.

The master of Zydichoiv taught his Hassidim by means of his own exemplary behavior.

He never ate a meal without having a guest at the table; and when he had no guest, he skipped the meal or fasted throughout that particular day.

He confided about his work as an author:

"When I sit and write my manuscripts, I dip my pen first in the inkwell and then in the blood of my heart."

Warning his devotees against idle talk, he mentioned his own worries about having used words in vain:

"I spend my nights examining the words I have said during the day."

Most descendants of the innkeeper of Saphrin had ink in their blood, but none of them was as prolific a writer as the Hassidic master of Komarna, also named R. Yitzkhak Isaac.

R. KHAYIM OF TZANZ

Gigantic scholarship as a Talmudist; great humility; unbounded devotion to the widowed, the orphaned, the poor and the neglected; a fighting spirit which brought him in conflict with some of the greatest Hassidic leaders of his time—these were the main characteristics of R. Khayim Halberstam of Tzanz (1793– 1876). Although he had a crippled leg, which often caused him pain, he was always ready to fulfill difficult missions to lighten the pain of others and bring comfort to those who were in need of it. His work *Divrey Hayim,* meaning, *Words of Hayim* or *Living Words,* is considered a classic in the interpretation and application of Jewish law.

R. Khayim was born in the city of Tarnigrod, where his father was the local Rabbi. When he became a Hassid, he visited some of the great Hassidic masters of his time, but he considered himself a disciple of two: R. Israel of Rhuzin and R. Naphtali of Ropshitz. Becoming widowed several times, he always remarried and thus he became the founder of a dynasty whose spiritual territory included most of Western Galicia and some parts of Central Europe. Descendants of this dynasty have established Hassidic centers in the United States, in Israel, and in many other parts of the world.

For close to half a century, R. Khayim was the Rabbi of Tzanz, which became the center of thousands of Hassidim who came from near and far to hear their great master. Having been a disciple of R. Israel of Ruhzin, this did not stop him from declaring war against his master's son, R. Avrohom Yaakov of Sadigorah, because he had become convinced that the heirs of his master had made princely living a symbol of Hassidism, thus leading to its destruction. The battle of Tzanz against Sadigorah belongs to the saddest chapter in Hassidic history because it brought division not only within Hassidism, but it split many families, even leading to divorces and breach of marriage promises. R. Khayim was of the opinion that every new way loses its importance after a long span of time, and that Hassidism, as it was in the days of the Besht and his early disciples, must become revitalized in a manner that learning and good deeds should be the mark of a true Hassid.

He used to jot down in a notebook every minute he wasted not studying the Talmud. Once, before the Day of Atonement, he summed up the moments, and they amounted to three full hours, so R. Khayim sat down and cried for three hours straight as repentance for having wasted precious study-time.

R. Khayim often made humorous remarks mixed with irony: "When I say that my whole body hurts, no one believes me; when I say I am poor, no one believes me. But when I say that I am sinful—everyone believes me."

On another occasion, he stated: "I love the poor because God loves them. That is why He created so many of them."

His wife wanted to buy a turkey for the Sabbath meals, but the price was too high. Later she found that a poor man who received regular allowances from R. Khayim, had bought the turkey, paying the high price. She argued: "Your poor man can afford to pay high prices for turkeys, but I am unable to do so." R. Khayim replied: "I regret that up to now I had not realized that the poor man also needs turkey for the Sabbath meals. Henceforth, I will see to it that he gets a bigger sum for his household."

A bride gave a dance in Tzanz. R. Khayim's daughter asked him
for money with which to purchase new shoes, but the Rabbi refused
to give it. He noticed, however, that her companion, a daughter
of a Hebrew teacher, wore old shoes, and he asked her: "Are you
invited to the dance?" "Yes, Rabbi," she answered. "Here, then,
take this money and buy yourself stylish shoes," and the Rabbi
urged her to accept his gift. One of those present inquired from
R. Khayim why he treated a stranger better than his own daughter.
He answered: "I know that my daughter's friend comes from
excellent parents, yet should she wear old shoes to the dance, she
will be scorned. But my daughter will be treated with deference
even in old shoes."

*(M. Lipson: MiDor Dor, p. 283; Newman: Hassidic Anthology, p.
305.)*

R. Khayim was once standing at the window of his study, and
he called in, separately, three passers-by and asked each of them
the same question:

"If you found a large sum of money, knowing to whom it
belonged, would you return it?"

One man answered that he would return the money immediately. Rabbi Khayim commented: "You're a fool."

The second man replied: "Am I a fool to return so large a sum
of money?" Rabbi Khayim shouted at him: "You are wicked."

The third man said: "If I found the money, I would probably
know what to do. It is possible that I would be able to subdue
the desire for money, and it is possible that I would not. As
long as I have not been faced by such a dilemma, I really cannot
say how I would act in such a situation." Rabbi Khayim complimented him: "You gave the correct answer. It proves that you
are a man of reason."

A great scholar came for a visit with R. Khayim. He asked

him: "Who are you?" The scholar replied that he was the grandson of a famous Hassidic master. "I have asked you who you are," retorted R. Khayim, "not who was your grandfather!"

A poor woman who earned her livelihood by selling potatoes in a market place came in one day to complain that customers were not buying her new load of potatoes, claiming that they were bad, and thus she would lose all the money she had invested. R. Khayim immediately went to the market place, where he stood at the woman's potato stand and began to announce his product: "Good potatoes! Who wants to buy good potatoes?" The passersby, seeing that R. Khayim, the great scholar and leader, was in the potato business, rushed to buy. They did not bargain but paid more than the usual price, and within the hour the entire load was sold. Placing the income from the sale before the woman, R. Khayim said to her: "See, your potatoes were good, but our townspeople did not know it."

In his older years he used to say: "In my younger days, I wanted to bring all human beings to repentance; later, when I realized that this was impossible, I wished to bring my home town to piety, but I did not succeed; so I decided to try this on the members of my household; I soon realized that this was also impossible, so I decided to seek for myself alone a way to repentance, and even in this I have not been successful."

Commenting on such diverse subjects as egotism, humility, enjoyment, good food and good music, he made the following observations:

Everyone should correct his own character to the extent that he will become, in his own estimation, a person of no importance. He who loses the feeling of self-importance, does not miss anything. If one desires something, it is a sign that he still is not free from egotism.

One should repent when still young, when one has passions to conquer. When one waits for repentance until he reaches old age, his repentance is not acceptable.

The human soul also did not come down to earth so as to eat. Nevertheless, when it is not given any food, it escapes from the body.

The tunes of certain singers do not come from the heavenly Palace of Song, they are just an imitation of the music notes.

Characteristic of R. Khayim's interpretations of biblical passages, are the following commentaries from his pen:

"And he called his name Noah, saying: 'This same shall comfort us in our work, and in the toil of our hands'" (Gen. 5:29): It is written in the Midrash that before the generation of Noah, all human beings were born without separated fingers. But seeing how great is the lust of humans for money, the Almighty decided that with the generation of Noah, all humans would have separate fingers so that even unknown to the pos-sessors of money, some of it would slip through their fingers as help for the needy and the poor.

"Speak unto the Children of Israel that they take for Me an offering" (Exod. 25:2): God asks every human being, wherever he is, to offer a little corner of his heart for God Himself.

"When any man of you bringeth an offering unto the Lord" (Lev. 1:2): When you bring an offering, it should be "of your-self," with devotion and sincerity.

Several of R. Khayim's disciples in later years became leaders of Hassidic communities.

R. YEKHEZKEL SHRAGAH OF SHINYAVE

R. Yekhezkel Shragah Halberstam (1813–1899), the oldest son of R. Khayim of Tzanz, was born in Rudnik. Like his father, he was a great scholar, and like his father he was also devoted to the helpless and the needy; but, unlike his father he was opposed to many of the Hassidic lenient applications of certain Jewish precepts. He was a disciple of R. Naphtali of Ropshitz, of R. Sholem of Belz, of his father-in-law, R. Aryeh Leib of Wizhnitza, and his grandfather-in-law, R. Moshe Teitelbaum of Uhel. Most of his life he was the spiritual leader of the Jewish community of Shinyave, and for forty-four years he was Hassidic master with a very great following.

R. Yekhezkel managed to harmonize personal charm and understanding with rigorous interpretations of biblical and Talmudic Law. His attitude is best illustrated by the following story:

R. Yekhezkel once had a heated discussion with his father. During the discussion R. Khayim lost his patience and cried out: "Don't you dare step over the threshold of my door!" In order not to violate the command "Honor thy Father," R. Yekhezkel left the house through the window. Later R. Khayim regretted his outburst and pleaded with the son to come back through the door.

R. Yekhezkel visited, incognito, the centers of some of the most important Hassidic masters of his time in order to observe their ways and listen to their teachings. He recalled that he had occasionally seen disciples who were greater than the masters to whom each was devoted, but the disciples were unaware of their own greatness. On occasions, R. Yekhezkel was recognized but he defended himself with the truth that he had stopped over on the way to visit his son and his son's father-in-law, for he did not wish them to know that he had not come to them directly from Shinyave.

In connection with R. Yekhezkel's devotion to the truth, the following story used to be told by his devotees:

A tailor came to fit a new suit of clothes on one of his grandsons. The boy later refused to take the suit off. The tailor
promised the boy that if he took off the suit, he would make
beautiful pockets in the jacket. The boy agreed. Later R. Yekhezkel
said to the tailor: "Now I order you to make the pockets, because I don't want that child to become accustomed to lying."

R. Barukh of Gorlitz once drew a parallel between himself
and his brother R. Yekhezkel of Shinyave: "When my brother
sees a person who is full of lies and possesses only an iota of
truth, he honors and befriends him; but when I meet a man
who is ninety-nine percent truthful and possesses only one percent of untruth, I cannot stand near him within a radius of
four ells."

R. Yezhezkel's love of the needy did not call forth outright
hatred for those who refused to contribute to charity. R. Yekhezkel
emphasized: "How pitiful is the miser. He lives all his life like
a pauper in order to die in riches."

The teachings of the master of Shinyave are contained in the
collection *Divrey Yehezkel*, meaning *The Words of Ezekiel*.

R. YITZKHAK ISAAC OF KOMARNA

R. Yitzkhak Yehuda Yekhiel Isaac Saphrin of Komarna
(? –1874) was the grandson of a non-revealed Tzadik and
mystic, R. Yitzkhak Isaac Eichenstein, who had been a resident
of the village Saphrin, and for whom he was named. The son of
a Hassidic master and author, R. Alexander Saphrin, spiritual
leader of the Jewish communities of Zydichoiv and Zhuravna in
Eastern Galicia. Yitzkhak Isaac was also the nephew of four
Hassidic masters: R. Zvi Hirsh of Zydichoiv, R. Moshe of Sambor,
R. Leepah of Sambor and R. Issakhar Ber of Zydichoiv. R.
Yitzkhak Isaac later himself became a great Hassidic leader with

a tremendous following, leaving for posterity fifteen books in all fields of Jewish scholarship, mysticism, Bible commentary and Hassidut; each of his later works being either an addition to his previous works or a broader interpretation of previously expressed teachings, thoughts and comments. By the time Yitzkhak Isaac was nine years old, he had already been taken on visits to the great Hassidic masters of the day. After his father's early death, Yitzkhak Isaac sought solace at the Hassidic centers of his uncles, who were included among the eighteen masters of whom he considered himself to be a disciple. The last years of his life, R. Yitzkhak Isaac's father was Rabbi of the Jewish community in Komarna, a city in the region of Lvov (Lemberg). After the passing of his uncle, R. Zvi Hirsh of Zydichoiv, a number of his devotees selected the nephew to become their master. R. Yitzkhak Isaac settled permanently in Sambor, and shortly there-after he became one of the outstanding personalities in Hassidut, and many miraculous deeds were attributed to him by his de-votees. Most of his books require of the reader previous prepara-tion in the fields of Talmud and Kabbalah. His work *Netiv Mitzvotekha,* meaning *The Path of Thy Commandments,* (the title being based on a verse in Ps. 119:35), has held its popularity among the general Hassidic readers down to our own time.

When already nearing the end of his earthly life, R. Yitzkhak Isaac said to the closest among his Hassidim: "In my youth, I believed that it would be possible for me to rise up to Heaven in a storm like the Prophet Elijah. Now that I have grown older, I hope that I will be saved from the nethermost of Purgatory. If it were not for my pure youthful faith about ascending to Heavenly heights, who knows on how low a rung I would now find myself?"

R. Yitzkhak Isaac devoted many pages of his writings to the subjects of God and faith, the behavior of human beings, humility, sanctity, brotherly love and similar themes. He wrote:

I. The early Hassidim avoided a thousand gates of the things permissible, to guard themselves against one gate to the impermissible.

II. All things in the Universe have a life of their own. They all possess Divine Life which is unseen.

III. The most important thing is faith, because only by means of faith one can ascend the highest rungs. Although prayer is effective, faith itself is more effective. Any one who fulfills one precept faithfully, deserves that the Divine Spirit should rest upon him.

IV. When one has reliance in the Almighty, he does not need to humble himself to another human being. When a person merits punishment, then the feelings of trust, faith, reliance and confidence are taken away from him.

V. The soul of every human being possesses both good and bad powers. Even the most pious person has within himself the positive and the negative. The negative within him is his enemy, and even the negative hates the evil within him. A human being has no greater enemy than his own evil inclination. The joys of the evil inclination always end in sorrow. On the other hand, if a person has no evil inclination altogether, and he never sins, it proves that he is a human being without the power of choice. It is in the nature of the good to include the bad and transform it also into good.

VI. The roots of all bad traits are pride, anger and the seeking of honors. They are the fathers of spiritual uncleanliness. Just as joy inspired the Prophets and the Divine Spirit, so pride and conceit bring upon a person the unclean spirit. The good person and the evil person were created equal. Each has the same power of choice. Sanctity and piety are acquired after a struggle against their opposites. When someone conquers successfully the evil forces, he becomes peaceful, humble, joyous and acts with loving kindness to others. This teaches us that everyone and everything can be corrected.

VII. The surest proofs of a human being's sanctity, are humility and modesty. Pride is a form of idol-worship, and when someone obliterates all pride within himself, he is rewarded as if he had observed all the Law. Humility and modesty do not mean that a person should lower himself, because just as pride is idolatry, so also is self-degradation.

VIII. He who is not married, no matter how important he may be, lacks the truth and does not know what the service of God really means. An unmarried man is defective and blemished. The Divine Spirit does not rest upon an unmarried man, because Holy Inspiration is derived from one's wife.

IX. One should accustom himself to holy thoughts, because unholy thoughts are poison for the soul. A person's thoughts are what he actually is. Even an unbecoming thought has a Holy spark which can become a flame. The Almighty demands of every human being that he act according to the understanding granted to him, and not above his own comprehension. Understanding is the very life of all positive human behavior.

X. If you notice an act of transgression in someone else, it is a sign that you are being shown something of that sort within yourself. This is a call to your own repentance. He who wishes to correct others, should first correct his own misdeeds.

XI. Every sinful act has in it parts of idol-worship and

heresy. If one really believes in the Almighty, he has not the courage to commit even the minutest transgression. It does not mean that the transgressor is really a heretic, but that he sinned as a result of negligence or forgetfulness.

XII. He who engages in the lusts of the world, the pleasures of the World-to-Come are taken from him, while his existence in this world continues. Generally all the woes and sufferings of a person are the sentence he passes upon himself. Therefore, the main purpose of suffering is to bring one to repentance.

Characteristic of Yekhezkel Isaac's interpretations of the Holy Scriptures, are his following comments on specific verses:

"Thou shalt not make unto thee a graven image" (Exod. 20:4): Don't make an image of yourself, or consider yourself more important than others and resort to power over the poor and needy.

"Thou shalt not stand idly by the blood of thy brother" (Lev. 19:16): Don't stand idly while your brother is being insulted.

"Love thy neighbor as thyself; I am the Lord" (Lev. 19:18): Love thy neighbor as thyself, I am the Lord, who acts toward you also with love.

"Love thy neighbor" (Ibid.): How will thy love express itself? "As Thyself"—he will be in your eyes as important as yourself and you will not exalt yourself over him.

"This is the law, when a man dieth in a tent" (Num. 19:14): This is the law about man. The law was not given to animals but to human beings. He who does not behave ethically is like an unclean, vicious animal that devours its own soul. A person of this sort needs no law.

"When thou goest forth to battle against thine enemies" (Deut. 20:1): Meaning in the battle against the evil inclination, the struggle must be in thought, words and deeds, and the acceptance lovingly of all the tribulations connected with such a battle.

"When thou buildest a new house" (Deut. 22:8): Whenever a person corrects his deeds, he builds a new house for the good.

"To love the Lord thy God . . . and to cleave to Him" (Deut. 30:20): To cleave to Him is the main aim of service.

"Know thou the God of thy father and serve Him with a whole heart" (I Chron. 28:9): This is the essence of all knowledge.

XII

A Tale of Four Cities
In Poland

A NUMBER of Polish cities where great teachers resided played important roles in Hassidut's spiritual conquests in the communities of Eastern European Jewry. Four of these cities, Lublin, Pshyskha, Kotzk and Ger, played the most vital roles in these conquests—not only because of the great masters who had their courts there, but also because of the great disciples of those masters. A number of disciples became, in time, Hassidic masters themselves, establishing centers of their own in various regions within the boundaries of the historic territory of Poland. In addition, since Polish Jewry had long been a fortress of Jewish scholarship, aiming at "study for the sake of study itself," Hassidut in Poland attracted not only the broad masses, but became a movement to whose banner flocked many young Talmudic students, some of them later to become famous as authors of scholarly works or as heads of Talmudic academies and as communal leaders.

Contrary to the Hassidut in the Ukraine and in Galicia, where the masters aimed particularly at the spiritual elevation of the simple masses, Hassidut in Poland was transformed into a movement of both the learned and of those whose knowledge was on the Jewish elementary level. Since economic conditions in Poland made it possible for numerous Jews to accumulate wealth, the Hassidic masters saw to it that their rich devotees engaged in brotherly assistance to the poor Hassidim. The Hassidic brotherhood was strengthened, additionally, by the fact that the masters often acted as matchmakers so that young scholars of poor families married into families of wealth. Since most of the wealthy were merchants, the unification by marriage of poor scholarly families with the well-to-do, resulted in the establishment of new families which were a combination, according to an idiomatic phrase, of "Torah and merchandise."

THE "SEER" OF LUBLIN

Lublin, a city of commerce and trade, became the spiritual center of Polish Jews soon after they settled in the city at the beginning of the sixteenth century. Lublin was the seat of the Jewish "Council of the Four Lands," the autonomous legislative body of the Jewish communities in the four regions of Greater Poland. It was the city where resided some of the greatest Talmudic giants and commentators, and where academies produced scholars who later became the spiritual teachers of world Jewry.

Lublin developed into a center of the Hassidic movement, thanks to the activities of R. Yaakov Yitzkhak Halevy Horowitz (? –1815), immortal in Hassidic history as the *Khozeh* or "Seer" of Lublin. His first important contact with the Hassidic movement was during a visit at the court of R. Dov Ber, the Maggid of Mezritch, successor of R. Israel Baal Shem Tov, originator of Hassidut. Later he became a close disciple of R. Elimelekh of Lizhensk. In his early youth, R. Yaakov Yitzkhak realized that he possessed extraordinary visual faculties, and for years he walked around with closed eyes in order not to see the negative aspects of human beings and of worldly life in general.

R. Elimelekh, on noticing R. Yaakov Yitzkhak's greatness as a scholar, and being aware of his extraordinary gift of vision, prevailed upon him to become a Hassidic leader. R. Yaakov Yitzkhak stayed for a number of years in the city of Lantzut, and later he settled in Lublin, becoming the master of a great many devotees, among them young scholars who were intellectually and emotionally enriched by the Hassidic ethical-moral interpretations of Jewish ritual law, and by the spirit of comradeship within the Hassidic ranks. R. Yaakov Yitzkhak's devotees named their leader Seer although he was on the verge of total blindness, because they were, themselves, often witnesses of the power his weak eyes had to penetrate the depths of human beings and the essence of things. R. Israel, the Maggid of Kozhenitz, compared him to the *Urim Ve-Tumin,* the ornamental oracles worn by the High Priest in the Sanctuary (Ex. 28:30).

Although himself a very humble man, R. Yaakov Yitzkhak wished to raise Hassidic leadership to an exalted position, and it was actually the Seer who inaugurated in Hassidut the adoration of the master in a form usually accorded by subjects to their princely ruler.

In his great personal humility, the Seer declared: "If an angel descended from Heaven and told me that I possess the piety of a great Tzadik, I would not believe him; if God Himself would tell me this, I would believe it only during the moment of hearing it."

R. Azriel Horowitz, the Chief Rabbi of Lublin, was an opponent of the Hassidim, and whenever he met the Seer, he tried to provoke him in a manner that would cause him anguish. For his great Talmudic learning, the Chief Rabbi was known as the "Iron Head." He once asked the Seer:

"If you consider yourself so insignificant, why don't you announce in the synagogue that you are not a master and ask of the Hassidim not to come to you any more?"

The Seer did so announce and when the Hassidim saw their master's humility, they became more attached to him. When the Iron Head met the Seer again he said to him:

"Since the Hassidim remain attached to you because they admire your humility, my advice is that you announce in the Synagogue that you are a great scholar and very pious, so the Hassidim will leave you for being proud."

"I cannot take your advice to lie in public," replied the Seer.

At another occasion, the Chief Rabbi said to the Seer: "I cannot understand why you have so many followers. After all I am a greater scholar so I am entitled to a greater following."

"I am also wondering why it is so," replied R. Yaakov Yitzkhak, "because knowing myself as I do, I am puzzled why so many people come to me from near and far, yet they do not come to you. It is possible that so many are coming to me because I know who I really am, but they are not coming to you because you do not realize who you are."

Speaking of pride, the Seer told his devotees: "Those who are really great, are never proud. When someone shows pride, it is a sign that he is a very small person. Let us take a lesson from the proud and never lower ourselves to their level."

On the subjects of piety, repentance and peace, wickedness and humility, the Seer emphasized: "A truly pious man is not in love with himself, and a repentant sinner should not hate himself."

"An insincere peace is better than a sincere quarrel. One should act towards everyone in sincerity, but if one does not feel deep in his heart a true friendship for someone, it is still better to live superficially in peace rather than quarrel."

The Seer explained that in the *Zohar*, the source book of Jewish mysticism, repentance is called "mother," because when the sinner repents wholeheartedly he is like a newborn child, and the act of repentance is the mother who brought him into the world.

R. Yaakov Yitzkhak declared:

> I love more the wicked man, who knows he is wicked, than the righteous man who knows that he is righteous. The first one is truthful, and the Lord loves truth. The second one falsifies, since no human being is exempt from sin; and the Lord hates untruth.

> Once Rabbi Jacob Yitzkhak confidently expected salvation to come that very year. When the year was over, he said to his disciple the Yehudi: "The rank and file of people either have turned completely to God, or can, at any rate, do so. They present no obstacle. It is the superior people who constitute a hindrance. They cannot attain humility, and therefore they cannot achieve the turning."

(Niflaot HaKhozeh, p. 25; Buber: Tales of the Hassidim, Early Masters, pp. 308; 315; M. Lipson: MiDor Dor, p. 221; Newman: Hassidic Anthology, pp. 49; 487.)

The following commentaries of the Seer on biblical passages are characteristic of the majority of his commentaries:

"And let them judge the people at all seasons" (Ex. 18:22): Promulgation of laws and the issuance of judgments should be in accordance with the times.

"I am not worthy of all the mercies" (Gen. 32:11): When someone realizes how merciful God is to him, he also realizes how worthless he is himself.

'And the priest that is highest among his brethren" (Lev. 21:10): The high priest has to be of his brothers, a brother to and a friend of everyone, so that he understands what the people need, and takes part both in their joys and in their sorrows.

The teachings of the Seer are quoted to the present day, thanks to the collections of his teachings *Divray Emmeth (Truthful Words)* and *Zot Zikkaron (This in Remembrance)*.

A number of his closest disciples became, in time, Hassidic masters themselves, bringing into the fold of Hassidut many Jewish communities all over Poland.

THE HOLY "YOOD" OF PSHYSKHA

One of the closest disciples of the Seer of Lublin was his namesake R. Yaakov Yitzkhak of Pshedborzh (1765–1813) who later established an influential Hassidic court in the city of Pshyskha. Since it is an accepted rule in Judaism that a disciple should not be called by his teacher's name, the devotees of the second R. Yaakov Yitzkhak called him *Yood Hakadosh*, the "Holy Jew." According to another opinion, he was called the Holy Jew because of the sanctity he practiced in daily life. "Every day I am learning anew how to conduct myself Jewishly," he said and he demanded that his Hassidim do the same.

R. Yaakov Yitzkhak's father, R. Asher, was the Preacher of Pshedborzh. While the son was yet in his early teens, he began to show great capacity for learning, and he was enabled to pursue his studies under the guidance of some of the greatest Jewish scholars of the time. While studying in Apta, he came under the influence of the great Hassidic master R. Moshe Leib of Sassov who resided there at the time. He practiced

Hassidism secretly, but was discovered by the master of Apta, R. Avrohom Yehoshuah Heshel. Striving for a life of solitude and study, he accepted the position of teacher for groups of children in a small village. At the advice of R. David of Lelov, young Yaakov Yitzkhak became a Hassid of the Seer of Lublin.

There was rebellion in the heart of Yaakov Yitzkhak. After long periods of observation, he had become convinced that, because of its popularity, Hassidut was gradually losing its force and was sidetracking its original purpose to elevate spiritually the masses of its devotees. Among the young scholars at the court of the Seer, many accepted his viewpoint. R. Yaakov Yitzkhak left Lublin, settled in Pshyskha, and soon found himself to be the master of numerous young rebellious scholars who appreciated his desire to transform Hassidut into a fusion of study and piety, aiming at the spiritual self-elevation of the individual Hassid. Those who remained loyal to the Seer became bitter opponents of the adherents and of the ways of the master of Pshyskha. The controversies, while they disrupted the unity in the Hassidic movement, gave it new spiritual impetus, and the rebellion, initiated by R. Yaakov Yitzkhak, later to become known as the *Yood Hakodosh,* the Holy Jew, enabled Hassidut to storm the fortresses of anti-Hassidism among the scholars. Thus Hassidut went from conquest to conquest all over Poland, turning sons against their anti-Hassidic fathers, and in many cases leading many Mitnagdim (previously opponents of the Hassidim) to becoming founders of Hassidic dynasties.

The teachings of the *Yood Hakodosh* were gathered in several volumes, each of which has the word *HaYehudi (The Jew)* in its title: *Niflaot (Wonders Of) Ha Yehudi, Tifereth (Glory of)*

HaYehudi, Torat (Teachings of) Ha Yehudi, Ketter (The Crown of) Ha Yehudi.

The "Holy Jew" disliked publicity seekers who showed off their superficial piety. He did not think that human transgressions were altogether the work of the evil inclination. He stated:

"Just as publicity is often bad in worldly matters, so it is essentially unbecoming in heavenly matters. No one commits a sin unless he is motivated by a foolish inclination. This teaches us that every sinner is a fool."

Said the "Yood": "Accustom thyself to good-heartedness by degrees. At first refuse not a request for a pinch of tobacco, for the light of a match, or for other small gifts. Little kindnesses like these will broaden thy heart so that thou wilt thus habituate thyself to helping thy fellow-man in many ways."

Said the "Yood": "In the same way that a Surgeon sheds a man's blood in order to heal his body, a leader may shame a sinner even in public in order to cure his soul. And just as the surgeon may not operate when he knows it will not avail the sick patient, the leader may not shame a sinner when he knows that his rebuke will accomplish no good."

The "Yehudi" and Peretz his disciple, were crossing a meadow. Cattle put out to pasture there were lowing, and where it was watered by a stream a flock of geese rose from the water with a great cackling and beating of wings. "If only one could understand what all of them are saying!" cried Peretz. "When you get to the point of understanding the very core of what you yourself are saying," said the Rabbi, "you will understand the language of all creatures."

The "Yehudi" was asked: "In the Talmud it says that the stork is called *hasidah* in Hebrew, that is, the devout or the loving one, because he gives so much love to his mate and his young. Then why is he classed in the Scriptures with the unclean birds?" He answered: "Because he gives love only to his own."

Said the "Yood": "Display neither your material nor your spiritual wealth, lest those who lack it be led by you into envy and covetousness."
(Tiferet HaYehudi; p. 45; Niflaot Ha Yehudi, pp. 42, 58; Newman: Hassidic Anthology, pp. 224, 296, 319; Buber: Tales of the Hassidim, Later Masters, pp. 228, 231.)

The most-quoted of the commentaries by the Holy Jew on biblical passages, include the following:

"Love thy neighbor as thyself" (Lev. 19:18): How is it possible to love everyone alike? Just as you have a greater concern for some parts of your body than for others. You certainly consider your heart more important than your hands; the head more than your feet; in the same manner should you express love to others according to their importance.

"Know this day . . . that the Lord, He is God in Heaven above and upon the earth beneath; there is none else" (Deut. 4:39): This is the basic knowledge that a human being has to possess.

"After the Lord your God shall ye walk, and Him shall ye fear, and His commandments shall ye keep, and unto His voice shall ye hearken, and Him shall ye serve, and unto Him shall ye cleave" (Deut. 13:5): When one listens to and observes what the passage says, then he can reach the final: "And unto Him shall ye cleave."

"Behold, surely thus shall man be blessed that feareth the Lord" (Ps. 128:4). If one wishes to bless his friend, he should bless him to fear the Lord, so he will thus be blessed with everything.

R. SIMKHA BUNIM OF PSHYSHKA

Among those who had joined the rebellion of R. Yaakov Yitzkhak against the Seer of Lublin, was R. Simkha Bunim (1765–1827), later to become the successor of his master. Popularly known as R. Bunim of Pshyskha, he continued the task, and quite successfully, of saving Hassidut from spiritual stagnation by elevating it into a movement of non-conformist young scholars who detested pose and pride, superficiality and mechanical ritualism. It was this non-conformism that aroused the opposition of the other Hassidic leaders against the Pshyskha-way. The fact that the Hassidim of the Holy Jew and later of R. Bunim ignored the laws about prescribed hours for daily prayer, and rather waited, after preparation, for the proper mood of inward, intensive recitation of their pleas to the Almighty, resulted in their being accused of gross transgressions and even of heresy.

R. Yaakov Yitzkhak, the Holy Jew, died at the age of forty-eight. The man who was the oldest among his devotees, R. Bunim, was chosen by the Hassidim to be their new leader. After all, R. Bunim was the disciple whom the late master had always called "Center of My Heart" and "Our Man of Wisdom." R. Bunim did possess most of the qualities that R. Yaakov Yitzkhak wished to see in all those who considered themselves Hassidim.

R. Simkha Bunim was born in Voidislav, where his father, R. Zvi Hirsh, was the Preacher of the Jewish community. An author of scholarly books, the father was for several years a preacher in Berlin. R. Zvi Hirsh sent his son to the famous Yeshivot, the Talmudic Academies in the central European cities Matersdorf and Nicholsburg. Soon after returning home, the young man married the daughter of a prominent resident in the city of Bendin. While residing there, he became interested in Hassidut, and on occasion visited the Hassidic masters R. Moshe Leib of Sassov and R. Israel, the Maggid (Preacher) of Kozhenitz. R. Bunim did not wear the traditional garb of the Hassidic Eastern European Jews, and his Jewish knowledge was balanced by his general knowledge of the times. R. Israel of Kozhenitz became quite impressed with the manner, scholarship and wisdom of R. Bunim, and at the recommendation of R. Israel, he was given a managerial position in the lumber concern of Berko and Tamar Bergson, later to become the paternal ancestors of the famous French philosopher Henry Bergson. R. Bunim, like many Talmudic scholars and Rabbis of various eras and generations, was interested in medicine, and in time he became a licensed pharmacist. At the advice of R. David Lelov, R. Bunim became a devotee of the Seer of Lublin and a close friend of R. Yaakov Yitzkhak, the fellow Hassid who felt that Hassidut had lost its original force, and only a re-evaluation of ways and teachings could save it from spiritual degeneration. R. Bunim had seen the world outside the confines of Eastern Europe, and was familiar with the various accomplishments in the fields of science and art, including theatrical art. The new medicines on the shelves of his pharmacy in Pshyskha also bore witness that the world was progressing. Why should progress avoid so important a spiritual movement as Hassidut? So R. Bunim became a comrade-in-arms of the rebellious R. Yaakov Yitzkhak. They both detested the piety of "style" and various behavior forms which seemed to them nothing more than shallow imitations of personal convictions.

R. Bunim was once asked whether he had a good lodging in Pshyskha. He replied: "A person who does not take up too much room, has enough space everywhere."

It is related that during a visit to the city of Danzig, R. Bunim entered a store to buy something. The storekeeper recognized him and charged him a very low price. "Why do you sell me at so low a price?" asked R. Bunim. "Because I consider it an honor that so great a scholar and pious man should come into my store, so I am selling you at cost price."

"I did not come here to buy with scholarship or piety. I am like all regular customers: I am paying with money," insisted R. Bunim.

As the successor of the Holy Jew, R. Bunim explained that it was the duty of the Hassidic master to place a ladder before his Hassidim, but that they must climb on their own, and not rely on the master's shoulders.

R. Bunim himself wrote no books, but his sayings, incidents in his life, and his commentaries on biblical passages, are transmitted in the writings of others, particularly in the collections *Kol Simkha (The Voice of Gladness* based on Jer. 7:34) by R. Alexander of Plotzk; and *Ramatayim Tzofim* (I Sam. 1:1) by Samuel Shinyaver of Nashelsk, and in other Hassidic works.

A needy man came to R. Bunim for assistance, and he gave the man a certain sum. When the caller was already outside the door, R. Bunim ran after him and gave him an additional sum, explaining: "The Law uses twice the word 'Give' as it is written: 'Giving, thou shalt give him' (Deut. 15:10), so I handed you one sum for the word 'giving'; and for the other word 'give' I am adding another sum." He used to say:

I. A true secret is something that everybody hears but no one knows.

II. From the human heart to the mouth is the same distance as from Heaven to earth.

III. Money lost—nothing lost; courage lost—everything lost.

IV. A miser is so detestable that the Bible doesn't even have a prohibition of parsimony. Miserliness is so abominable that the Torah did not wish to deal with it at all.

V. The greatest wisdom is not to try to be too smart.

VI. When someone is only good, then he is an adulterer; if he is only pious, then he is a thief; if he is only wise, then he is a heretic. But one should be all things in unison: good, pious and wise.

VII. The modest person does not need too much space, that is why he finds a place everywhere.

VIII. Moses considered himself a small vessel which had been put upon a high place, but even then it continued to be a small vessel.

IX. The evil inclination should be imagined as if it were a murderer, always standing with an ax above your head, ready to chop it off at any moment. If one cannot imagine this, then it is a sign that one's head has already been chopped off by the evil desire.

X. Whenever I have nothing to be happy about, I walk into the hospital and ask: "Is Bunim lying here?" When they tell me "no," I realize with joy how thankful I should be for God's blessings to me.

Following are several incidents that are related in some Hassidic works:

While walking with a group of Hassidim, R. Bunim picked up a handful of sand and said to them: "He who does not believe that Providence decided that these grains of sand should lie in this exact place, is a heretic."

A man argued before him: "The Sages have taught us that he who runs away from honor, honor pursues him. All my life I have been running from honor but honor does not run after me."

R. Bunim replied: "The trouble with you is that when you run from honor, you turn your head backwards to see whether honor is pursuing you."

A Hassid complained that to keep up his household in a proper manner, he needed more money. The master comforted him: "Believe me, if it were possible to steal from Heaven a priceless object, I would steal it and give it to you, but I am helpless. How can I steal if God sees?"

A Hassid told R. Bunim that he had bought a very fine horse. "Before you bought the horse," commented the master, "your head was devoted to study, but now you are thinking only of the horse. Evidently your head has been turned into a stable."

Once he passed by the marketplace and heard how a peasant and a wheat merchant were bargaining over the price: "Do better," said the peasant. R. Bunim started to cry and said to the Hassidim who were with him: "Even a simple illiterate peasant calls upon us to do better and repent."

We read in Deut. 15:10: "Thou shalt surely give him and thine heart shall not be grieved when thou givest unto him." The Torah repeats several times the word "give," because in truth giving only once is of little, if any use. What we give the poor out of pity for him, is not accounted charity, just like a man who gives himself food when he is hungry, or medicine when he is sick, because he cannot bear the suffering of his body and so gives it food and medicine out of self-pity. Charity to the poor also comes within the category of self-pity. For that reason, one must give charity time and again, until "thine heart shall not be grieved." That is to say, until you no longer give out of pity for the poor. Nonetheless, you must continue to give. It is this additional giving that is considered an act of charity.

Who is accounted a Hassid? He who does more than the strict requirements of the law. It is written in the Torah: "And ye shall not wrong one another," whereas a Hassid interprets it: "Ye shall not wrong even every man himself."

Understanding is light while deeds are the inner secrets. Hence, understanding is greater than deeds.

Man should always have two pockets. In one of them shall lie the saying: "I am dust and ashes." In the other, the saying: "For me the world was created."

The injunction "Depart from evil and do good" means: depart from the thought of doing evil and annul it by doing good.

There is the story of the man who had made all the preparations for the wedding but had forgotten to provide himself with a wedding ring. Likewise, is the man who all his life engages in the affairs of this world and pays no heed to the needs of his soul.

When I look at the world, it sometimes seems to me that every man is a tree in a wilderness, and that God has no one in his world but him, and that he has no one to turn to, save only God.

The sins which man commits—those are not his great crimes. Temptation is powerful and his strength is slight! The great crime of man is that he can turn at every moment, and does not do so.

The Lord created the world in a state of beginning. The universe is always in an uncompleted state, in the form of its beginning. It is not like a vessel at which the master works and he finishes it; it requires continuous labor and unceasing renewal by creative forces. Were there a second's pause by these forces, the universe would return to primeval chaos.

It is said in the prayer: "At all times a man should have the fear of Heaven in secret." To the world you should appear as an ordinary man, and be secret in your piety.

The haughty and the arrogant fill their mind with selfishness, leaving no room for holiness. The lowly and the meek, however, have adequate room for holiness, and should strive to fill their mind with it. Of what use, otherwise, is their meekness?

Only the lowly are able to comprehend the highness of the Lord.
We read (Ps. 138:6): "The Lord is high, and the lowly see it."

When I look upon the world, it often seems to me as if the
universe were dead, and I had been left, the only living man.
From whom, then, can I ask help, outside of God?

Failure to repent is much worse than sin. A man may have
sinned for but a moment, but he may fail to repent of it moments
without number.

When a man's heart is heavy and full of anxiety, he may lighten
it through ardent prayer and a belief in God's mercies.

If by chance an opportunity comes to you to better yourself, do
not hesitate to seize hold of it. It is so decreed in Heaven. Cling
to it until another opportunity comes to you.

Life is good, for it may bring to a man the joys of the World-to-
Come. Hence, if one shows contempt for life by self-destruction, he
is deprived of his share in the World-to-Come.
*(Steinmann: The Garden of Hassidism, pp. 191–193; Buber: Tales
of the Hassidim, Later Masters, pp. 256–257; Siyakh Sarfay Kodesh,
vol. I, p. 11; Vol. 2, p. 17; Simkhat Israel, pp. 17, 37, 47, 65, 92;
Maasiyot Norahim, p. 37; Ramatayim Tzofim, p. 164; Newman:
Hassidic Anthology, pp. 62, 136, 143, 192, 278, 341, 386.)*

"In the beginning God created the Heaven and the earth"
(Gen. 1:1): During creation, God brought Himself into nature.

"In the beginning, God created" (Ibid): Even now, after
creation, the world is still in the beginning. It is not like something created by a craftsman, but at every moment the world is
in need of the renewal of its powers of Creation. Without this
power, the world would return to the state of being formless
and void.

"And God divided the light from the darkness" (Gen. 1:4):

Just as there is light and darkness in the whole world, so darkness and light are to be found in human life and in human thinking.

The serpent which beguiled Eve to eat the forbidden fruit and give it to Adam, was cursed by the Lord God: "Upon thy belly shalt thou go, and the dust shalt thou eat" (Gen. 3:14). It means that the serpent has its food wherever it reaches on its belly. So this is not a curse but a blessing. But while the serpent will always have something to eat and won't be in need of anything, it will never be able to work nor pray, and this in itself is the curse.

"And in the process of time, it came to pass, that Cain brought of the fruit of the ground an offering unto the Lord" (Gen. 4:3): Cain waited for the process of time, when he was already old, so the Lord did not respect his offering (Ibid., 4:5).

"And Jacob vowed . . . if God will . . . give me bread to eat, and raiment to put on" (Gen. 28:20): Man does not live on bread alone. But Jacob foresaw the critical times when the problems of bread and clothing would be of the utmost importance, so he prayed that human beings be granted bread and garments, that they might have the opportunity to devote themselves also to spiritual matters.

"Then Jacob said unto this household, and to all that were with him: 'put away the strange gods that are among you.' . . . And they gave unto Jacob all the foreign gods which were in their hands, and the rings which were in their ears" (Gen. 35:2–4): What connection is there between foreign gods and earrings? From this we learn that unnecessary jewelry and other luxuries are included in idolatry.

"And he, Jacob, said to him: 'Joseph, go now and see whether it is well with thy brethren'" (Gen. 37:14): Jacob taught

Joseph to see the positive side, not the negative side; to seek the virtues in human beings and not to search after unbecoming deeds.

When Jacob blessed his sons, he said of Issakhar: "He saw a resting place that was good . . . he bowed his shoulder to bear" (Gen. 49:15): When someone wishes to enjoy rest, he must become first accustomed to accept what life has in store for him.

"And these are the ordinances which thou shalt set before them" (Exod. 21:1): "Before them," means that the ordinances about everyone's behavior towards his fellowmen come before the ordinances about one's behavior toward God. Good manners precede religious laws.

"Ye shall do no unrighteousness in judgment" (Lev. 19:35): Don't make unrighteousness rightful by means of judging it to be right.

When the Ten Commandments were about to be handed down at Mount Sinai, "the mountain burned with fire unto the heart of heaven" (Deut. 4:11): The mountain burned itself into them until their hearts became heavenly.

"But from thence you will seek the Lord thy God and thou shalt find Him if thou search after Him with all thy heart and all thy soul" (Deut. 4:29): From there, from the depths of your heart, you can call to God and find Him, if only you search well within yourself.

After the handing down of the Ten Commandments, God said to Moses: "Go, say to them: 'Return ye to your tents' " (Deut. 5:27): Let us see how they will behave in their own homes.

"Justice, justice shalt thou follow" (Deut. 16:20): You should follow justice in a just manner, not by unjust means.

The foundation of all thinking should be a single biblical passage: "Lift up your eyes on high, and see: who hath created these?" (Isa. 40:26).

"Let the heart of them rejoice that seek the Lord" (Ps. 105:3): He who loses something, is worried and rejoices when he finds it. Likewise, those who seek the Lord, rejoice when they find Him.

"King David said: 'I am all prayer'" (Ps. 109:4): meaning to say that the prayer was within himself because he lacked words to clothe the prayer properly.

"He, the Lord, will fulfill the desire of them that fear Him" (Ps. 145:19): God created the desire, but man has to desire the desire.

Every moment of the day should be made use of for a worthy purpose, as one can see from the simple interpretation of the biblical passage: "And of the children of Issakhar, men that had understanding of the times" (I Chron. 12:33): The children of Issakhar knew the importance of time and that it is forbidden to waste it.

The Pshyskha form of Hassidut, while it attracted the younger generation of scholars, caused great concern among the more conservative masters and their followers.

One of the reasons, as mentioned before, that the Pshyskha form of Hassidut called forth such opposition on the part of other Hassidic masters, was that Pshyskha considered study and preparation for prayer as a means to pray properly, and thus they felt that the other Hassidim were transgressing the law of obligatory specific time for morning devotions.

R. Bunim's own doing away with some Hassidic traditions, his emphasis on learning and sharp-mindedness rather than on matter-of-fact piety, and his new ways of Hassidic teaching and behavior in general, aroused the opposition to drastic steps. An occasion presented itself for a final battle, called "The Wedding of Ustillah." It was the wedding of a grandchild of the venerable R. Avrohom Yehoshuah Heshel of Apta. Most Hassidic leaders of the time and their closest disciples were coming to the wedding, so it had been planned to make use of the gathering of such illustrious guests to place under a ban the Pshyskha trend in Hassidism. Instead of coming himself to the wedding at Ustillah, R. Bunim dispatched a delegation of three disciples, led by the great scholar R. Yitzkhak Meir, later to become the master of Ger. His arguments, and the intervention by the master of Apta, influenced the opposition to withdraw without a final battle against Pshyskha.

No one could dispute the fact that among R. Bunim's devotees, were some of the sharpest minds within the new generation of scholars produced by Polish Jewry.

R. Yitzkhak of Wurka and R. Mendel Kotzk were among the disciples of R. Bunim before they became Hassidic masters themselves. Once, when R. Yitzkhak returned from a visit to the court of R. Mordecai of Chernoble, R. Mendel asked him if he had seen something special there.

"I saw the table which had been used by R. Israel Baal Shem Tov," replied R. Yitzkhak.

"You saw there a table which is one hundred years old," commented R. Mendel, "but our master shows us much older things; he shows us the creation of the world."

R. Bunim became blind, and in the last years of his life he often spoke ironically of his situation, calling himself, "the old, blind Bunim." He used his physical handicaps to interpret, ironically, a Biblical passage: "And the Lord said to Moses: 'Speak unto the priests, the sons of Aaron, and say unto them' " (Lev. 21:1): According to the Midrash, God was then showing to Moses all future generations, their leaders and their community heads. If so, wouldn't it have been enough to show him only the leaders and community heads without showing him each generation in its entirety? The answer is: If Moses had been shown the blind Bunim as a leader, he would have been astounded and mortified. But when Moses saw the entire generation, he understood that such Hassidim do not deserve a better leader.

When R. Bunim was lying on his deathbed, his wife began to cry bitterly. He tried to soothe her, saying: "All my life I have been studying how to die."

"I want you to continue living," said the wife, "so that you can have some more time to study how to die."

R. MENAKHEM MENDEL OF KOTZK

After the death of R. Simkha Bunim, a number of his devotees became the Hassidim of his son, R. Avrohom Moshe, but the majority chose as their master one of the sharpest minds among R. Simkha Bunim's closest disciples, R. Menakhem Mendel Morgenstern (1788–1859), later to become one of the most outstanding figures in the history of Hassidut.

R. Mendel was born in Goray, in the region of Lublin. His father, R. Leibush, saw to it that his sons became scholars, and Mendel proved himself when still in his early teens, to be a great swimmer in "The Sea of the Talmud." The father, an uncompromising opponent of Hassidut, was certain that the "sect," as the opposition called the Hassidim, would never be able to "ensnare" his clever and sharp-minded Mendeleh, as he called the son in the diminutive of his name. After his marriage, R. Mendel settled in the town of Tomashov, and it was there that the Hassidim succeeded in bringing the young scholar into their fold. In the Hassidic courts of the Seer in Lublin, and of R. Bunim in Pshyakha, he became one of the outstanding disciples;

and many young scholars, who had rebelled against their anti-Hassidic fathers, sought his companionship and advice, enjoyed his puns and clever remarks, even at their own expense, because his statements were a mixture of wisdom, humor and satire. Even the master, R. Bunim, was once the recipient of a "gift" from R. Mendel's sharp tongue. It happened when R. Bunim said to R. Mendel:

"Talmudic law states that if a disciple is exiled, his master is exiled with him. If I am sent to hell, I will demand that they also bring to hell my master (The Seer of Lublin)."

R. Mendel assured him: "You, my teacher, will have no need to ask your master to join you in hell, but for me, the law will be of the great use."

R. Bunim understood the hint that he was being invited by his disciple to join him in hell!

After R. Bunim's passing, many Hassidim followed R. Mendel to Tomashov. Later he moved to Kotzk, and in the history of Hassidut, he is known as R. Mendel Kotzker.

R. Mendel wished to transform Hassidut from a mass movement into a kind of order of the spiritual elite. He felt that with a small group of Hassidic scholars, he would accomplish more if he shouted with them from the rooftops, "The Lord is God," than if he ministered to thousands. It was his aiming too high that later caused a rebellion and split in his own ranks; and this in turn brought him later to conclude his Hassidic leadership in a most tragic manner.

R. Mendel despised pose, seeing in it an expression of selfishness and a desire to deceive others. He cautioned his disciples that the selfish "I" is a thief and one should eliminate it from his heart. Similar to a thief, he said, is the person who makes a statement of which he himself is not convinced; also he whose sigh does not come from the heart-depths, and he who makes the slightest move that is not wholly honest.

He explained the meaning of humility: "According to the sages of the Talmud, the Ten commandments were handed down at Mount Sinai, the smallest of mountains in the desert, so that people should not become proud for knowing their teachings. If so, why were the Ten Commandments not given in a valley? Because to be low in a valley is no accomplishment; but it is very meritorious to feel humble while standing upon a mountain."

R. Mendel often spoke in epigramatic sentences:

"Silence is the strongest of all voices."

"The 'I' is the greatest thief."

"A false sigh is the same as stealing."

"Deception and imitation are equal vices."

"Everything can be imitated but the truth, because an imitated truth is a lie."

"The time of eating is when you are young: the time of sleeping is when one is in the grave."

"A false facial expression, like all hypocrisy, is a sin that belongs to the category of idol worship."

"Silence is often louder than the strongest scream, and it can make a greater impression than the biggest noise."

R. Mendel desired to have Hassidim whose quality would outweigh quantity. Almost every remark he made was aimed at the fulfillment of this hope. Thus he explained to his devotees the real meaning of prayer and warned them against the great dangers of being overpowered by reality:

"Prayer is like a bow and arrow. The more one draws the bow, the farther goes the arrow. The more one concentrates during prayers, the farther they penetrate the heavens."

"What you call 'sadness' I see as a form of casting off all responsibilities, since melancholy is the easiest way to escape responsibility for evil deeds."

Against the complaints of other Hassidic masters that in Kotzk prayers were not recited at the proper time, R. Mendel replied: "In Kotzk, we have a soul, not a clock."

Answering those who criticized his extremism, he said sarcastically: "Only horses go in the middle of the road."

Once, on observing his Hassidim dance with great enthusiasm, he encouraged them to continue, saying: "Set in motion the wheels of your souls!"

When asked how he could advise his Hassidim in business matters without having any personal experience in commerce, R. Mendel replied: "He who is outside has the proper perspective to see what is inside things."

A Hassid was praying fervently, and every few seconds he cried out "Father!" Another Hassid reprimanded him. Said R. Mendel: "Don't disturb him. He will cry 'Father' so long that in the end he will feel that God is really his father."

Another Hassid lost all his possessions in an unsuccessful business venture, and a group of fellow-Hassidim asked the master to wish the man better luck in a new undertaking. R. Mendel replied: "That man is a Hassid and very pious, so he has everything one needs."

A Hassid came to ask advice on how to develop a desire to study. The master was astonished: "I cannot understand how someone has no desire for so wonderful thing as study!"

In regard to evil inclinations, R. Mendel stated the following:

"One should always imagine that the evil desire looks like a murderer who stands with an axe ready to behead him at any moment. If one cannot imagine this, then it is a sign that one has already lost his head."

Two Hassidim chatted about their individual masters and the devotees of each. The follower of the master of Chernoble said:

"On Thursday we are up all night studying; on Fridays we distribute charity each according to his means; and on the Sabbath we recite the entire Book of Psalms."

The follower of R. Mendel Kotzker replied: "We stay up during all nights in the week for purposes of study; we distribute charity whenever a needy person comes around and whenever there is money in the pocket; but it is not according to our strength to recite in one day the entire Book of Psalms that took King David a lifetime of seventy years to compose."

A Hassid of R. Mendel said to a Hassid of R. Yitzkhak of Wurka, "Your master's teachings reach the heights of Heaven, but my master's teachings enter through the navel into the abdomen."

An opponent of the Hassidim once said sarcastically to R. Mendel: "You are so great that you reach to the seventh heaven."

"You are wrong," replied R. Mendel, "Actually I am so small that all the seven heavens have to be lowered for my sake."

The Hassidim of R. Mendel of Kotzk used to sing a special song on the virtue of modesty:

> Where does God live?
> There where He is admitted.
> Whereto is He admitted?
> Into a dwelling that is clean.
> Which dwelling is clean?
> A person who is modest.

Three characters can be found in a man about to perform a good deed: if he says: "I shall do it soon," his character is poor. If he says: "I am ready to do it now," his character is of average quality. If he says: "I am doing it," his character is praiseworthy.

Death is merely moving from one home to another. If we are wise, we will make the latter the more beautiful home.

The battle in a man's heart against evil impulses may be likened to warfare. Strategy must be employed in the inner battle exactly as in war. When the general succeeds in entrenching his position against the foe at one place, he does not rest content with this achievement lest the enemy assail him elsewhere.

Likewise if a man immunizes himself against a particular fault, he must guard himself against succumbing to another.

Take care of your own soul and of another man's body, but not of your own body, and of another man's soul.

R. Mendel of Kotzk once asked his disciple Yaakov of Radzimin: "Yaakov, to what purpose was man created?" He answered: "So that he might perfect his soul."

"Yaakov," said the Tzadik, "is that what we learned from our teacher, Rabbi Bunim? No, indeed! Man was created so that he might lift up the Heavens."

A Hassid told R. Mendel about his poverty and troubles. "Don't worry," advised the Rabbi. "Pray to God with all your heart, and the merciful Lord will have mercy upon you." "But I don't know how to pray," said the other. Pity surged up in the Master of Kotzk as he looked at him. "Then," he said, "you have indeed a great deal to worry about."

"Let the wicked forsake his way" (Isa. 55:7): Does the wicked man have a way? What he has is a mire, not a way. Now what is meant is this: Let the wicked man leave his "Way," that is, his illusion of having a way.

(Siakh Sarfey Kodesh, II, 94; IV, 20; M. Lipson: MiDor Dor,

p. 223; Fun Unzer Altn Oitzer, II, p. 82; Newman: Hassidic Anthology, pp. 29, 71, 432, 451; Buber: Tales of the Hassidim, Later Masters, pp. 276, 280, 281.)

Characteristic of R. Mendel are his interpretations of biblical passages:

"Gods of silver, or Gods of gold ye shall not make unto you" (Exod. 20:20): Don't make silver and gold your god.

"This is none other than the house of God, and this is the gate of heaven" (Gen. 28:17): One can find God everywhere, but it is important through which gate one goes to Him. Through the gate of heaven one finds Him immediately; through other gates one finds many distractions on the way.

"And Jacob sent (angelic) messengers before him to his brother Esau" (Gen. 32:4): He sent away the angels because he could get along without them, relying only on God.

"And a certain man found him, and behold, he was wandering in the field. And the man asked him saying: 'What seekest thou?' " (Gen. 37:15): The man who found Joseph wandering was actually an angel, and he taught Joseph that whenever one becomes lost in the difficulties of life, he should make clear to himself what he actually wishes to accomplish, since many difficulties are a result of one's own uncertainty about aims and wishes.

"And Judah said unto his brethren: 'What profit is it if we slay our brother (Joseph) and conceal his blood?' " (Gen. 37:26): If we have to conceal and keep something a secret, it is a sign that it is something bad. For every secret is a form of stealing.

"And the Lord said unto Moses: 'Come unto Pharaoh' " (Exod. 10:1): The passage does not mean "go to Pharaoh," because one cannot go away from God, since He is everywhere and the whole world is full of His glory. The passage says "come," because the Lord said: "Come with me, and I will be with your wherever you go."

"Ye shall be holy men unto me" (Exod. 22:30): Let your holiness be human and let your human deeds be holy. The holiness of human beings should be human. God has numberless angels and He is not in need of additional angels.

"And let them make Me a sanctuary, that I may dwell among them" (Exod. 25:8): It is not written "dwell in it" but "among them," to teach you that every person is obligated to build a sanctuary in his heart so that God may dwell among human beings. God dwells wherever He is permitted to enter.

"They shall give every man a ransom for his soul. . . . They shall give everyone . . . half a shekel" (Exod. 30:12–13): When someone gives charity with joy and enthusiasm, it is ransom for his soul, and it ceases to be just the giving of a coin that is cold. It is no longer without warmth.

"And the flesh that toucheth any unclean thing, shall not be eaten" (Lev. 7:19): When the unclean touches the clean, the clean also becomes unclean. Why couldn't it be in the reverse, that when the clean touches the unclean, the unclean should become clean? The answer is: What is unclean is certainly unclean, but the clean—who is going to vouch that the seemingly clean is really clean?

"For on this day shall atonement be made for you to cleanse you; from all your sins shall ye be clean before the Lord" (Lev. 16:30): On this day you shall atone, but it depends upon you to use your own endeavor to become clean.

"Ye shall therefore keep My statutes and Mine ordinances, which if a man do he shall live by them" (Lev. 18:5): Man should perform his duties and tasks with liveliness, not out of custom, but because it is the proper thing to do.

"And when a man shall sanctify his house to be holy unto the Lord" (Lev. 27:14): Holy is he whose home is holy.

The men whom Moses sent to spy out the Land of Canaan reported of the Nephilim giants they had seen: "And we were in our sight as grasshoppers; and so we were in their sight" (Num. 13:33): It stands to reason that they were in their own sight like grasshoppers, as compared to the giants; but "so we were in their sight"—why should one care how he looks in the sight of others?

"And Eliezer the priest said to the men of war that went to the battle" (Num. 31:21): But he spoke this time to them after they had returned from battle! He meant to tell them that after the battle against the Midianites, they would have a new war before them, the war with the evil inclinations.

R. Mendel emphasized that every individual must raise higher and higher his personal standards of deeds and behavior, until his fervor becomes like Mount Sinai at the time of the handing down of the Ten Commandments: ". . . And the mountain burned with fire unto the heart of heaven" (Deut. 4:11).

"And thou shall teach them diligently unto thy children" (Deut. 6:7): If you will first teach yourself properly, your children will be able to learn from you.

"Give ear, ye heavens" (Deut. 32:1): Give ear and perceive in a heavenly manner.

"The heavens are the heavens of the Lord, but the earth hath He given to the children of men" (Ps. 115:16): In order that men may transform material, earthly values into heavenly values of the spirit.

Said R. Mendel: "Some people are always preaching about

truth and they complain that the world is full of falsehood, but their actions in personal life are far from the spirit of truth. And this is actually what it meant by the Scriptural teaching: 'Buy the truth and sell it not' (Prov. 23:23): Buy the truth for personal usage, not for others."

A Hassid asked the master to give a proper interpretation of the biblical passage: "For in much wisdom, is much vexation" (Eccles. 1:18). For, he asked, "if wisdom causes vexation, who needs wisdom at all?"

R. Mendel replied: "Let it hurt, but we are compensated by knowing more."

"I said: 'I will get wisdom' but it is far from me" (Eccles. 7:23): If I try to talk myself into thinking that I am wise, then certainly 'it is far from me.' "

". . . Neither bread to the wise" (Eccles. 9:11): God says to those who consider themselves very wise: "If you are so clever, try to create food to sustain yourself."

R. Mendel once declared: "Before my death I would like to write the smallest book, consisting of only one page. The title of the book would be *MAN*."

R. Mendel's extraordinary demands upon the individual Hassid and his extremism in general often disturbed and saddened his devotees. Unlike the consoling words and inspirational deeds of other Hassidic masters, R. Mendel's statements and actions were of the kind that radiated neither inspiration nor hope to those in need of them. Only the very great scholars among his disciples enjoyed his tongue-lashings. Some of them even emulated the master in their behavior towards others. But the great majority of R. Mendel's Hassidim were dissatisfied, unhappy, and the rumbles of rebellion against R. Mendel's disdain of the masses were easily detected by those with ears sensitive to the inner voices of human beings. At the conclusion of the Succoth Festival, on the day of Rejoicing with the Law, known as *Simkhat Torah,* in the year 1838, the revolt broke out in the open. The leader of the revolt was R. Mordecai Yoseph Leiner, who had been a friend of R. Mendel since the days when both were young Hassidic scholars in Tomashov-Lubelsk. Later when R. Mendel was chosen master, after the passing of R. Simkha Bunim, R. Mordecai Yoseph became one of R. Mendel's most devoted disciples. The fact that R. Mordecai Yoseph had led the revolt, hurt R. Mendel perhaps more than the revolt itself. R. Mordecai Yoseph took with him to Tomashov some of the finest Hassidim, including R. Leibeleh Eiger and R. Tzadok HaKohen, both of whom later became Hassidic masters in Lublin. R. Mordecai Yoseph settled in Izhbitza, where he founded the Leiner dynasty which later had its center in the city of Radzin.

Although in time some of the rebellious Hassidim returned to Kotzk, the damages of the revolt could not be eradicated so far as R. Mendel was concerned. He was bitter, angry, morose, and for many years, until his death, he shut himself in his study in order to shut out the world from his life. Only two disciples were admitted into R. Mendel's self imposed prison-cell: the greatest scholar among his disciples, his brother-in-law R. Yitzkhak Meir, known as the Talmudic Giant of Warsaw, and R. Mendel's son-in-law, R. Abraham Bernstein, a great Talmudist in his own right and later a Hassidic master.

The tragic end of R. Mendel's leadership has been utilized by a number of Yiddish writers, both in novels and in dramatic works. The details of his life after the rebellion are mostly unknown in Hassidic history, since members of his family and his most loyal disciples wished to bury his past together with his remains. But the tragedy still lingers on in the minds of his descendants of the present generation.

R. Menakhem Mendel Morgenstern of Kotzk left no writings of his own, but the sayings, remarks and biblical commentaries are quoted in a number of works, chiefly in *Ohel Torah (The Tent of the Law), and Emmet VeEmunah (Truth and Faith).*

R. YITZKHAK MEIR OF GER

R. Yitzkhak Meir Ruthenberg-Alter (1799–1866), the "Talmudic Genius of Warsaw," was carried to Hassidic leadership on waves of admiration from many devotees of R. Mendel of Kotzk, after the end of their master's tragic life. R. Yitzkhak Meir had wished to be just a Hassidic disciple since the days when his father, R. Israel Ruthenberg, spiritual head of the Jewish communities in Magnishov and Ger (pronounced Gher, a Yiddish form of Gura Kalvariya) had taken him, when still a boy, to see R. Israel, the Maggid of Kozhenitz, who engaged him in scholarly disputes. Later, he visited occasionally the Seer of Lublin, and in time became one of the closest disciples of R. Bunim of Pshyskha. After R. Bunim died, many Hassidim expressed the wish that R. Yitzkhak Meir become their master, but he refused and advised them to choose the sharp-minded and sharp-tongued R. Mendel of Tomashov, later to be known as R. Mendel of Kotzk.

R. Yitzkhak Meir's father-in-law, R. Moshe Lifshitz, was one of the wealthiest men in Warsaw, and this enabled R. Yitzkhak Meir to refuse rabbinic positions offered him by various communities. He established courses for the training of young scholars. When R. Moshe Lifshitz lost his fortune, the son-in-law became a book dealer, thus avoiding the necessity of using his spiritual knowledge for material purposes, and he was happy in his role as a close disciple of R. Mendel Kotzker. After the passing of R. Mendel, some Hassidim chose his son, R. David to be their master, but the majority pressured the Talmudic Genius of Warsaw into the leadership. R. Yitzkhak Meir settled in Ger, and there he established a Hassidic dynasty which became the most influential in Poland. This dynasty now has its continuation in the Land of Israel.

It is related that when R. Yitzkhak Meir was a very young boy, he never slept longer than two hours, and the rest of the night he devoted to study. When his worried mother reproached him, he defended himself by saying:

"With sleeping it is the same as with studying. A diligent student can master in two hours what it takes an ordinary student a whole day. I am a diligent sleeper, and what it takes others to accomplish during a whole night's sleep, I accomplish within two hours."

After R. Yitzkhak Meir had been successful in his mission at the Hassidic wedding in Ustillah and had prevented a ban by other Hassidic masters because of the new ways of Hassidut instituted by R. Bunim of Pshyskha, the young Talmudic giant wrote a letter to the master, relating that he had been accorded great honor at Ustillah. R. Bunim read the letter to the closest among his disciples and then he commented: "This young man notifies us that he can even tolerate honors. It is like Joseph, who, after having made himself known to his brethren, said to them: 'And ye shall tell my father of all my glory in Egypt' " (Gen. 45:13).

R. Yitzkhak Meir himself characterized the differences in the Hassidic leadership of his two predecessors and his own:

"R. Bunim of Pshyskha led his Hassidim with love; R. Mendel of Kotzk led them with fear; but I am leading them with God's law."

Aware of his own accomplishments as a scholar, R. Yitzkhak Meir nevertheless spoke of them in a rather humorous manner. He once declared that if sentenced to hell, he would climb on the roof of hell and there begin to expound the laws and precepts of Moses according to Talmudic interpretation. Then all the pious in Paradise would climb on the roof of Hell to listen to his discourse, and thus Hell would become Paradise.

A Hassid complained that he lived in need, and existence was burdensome so he had decided to throw away the world altogether.

"The world is not your property," commented the master, "and what is not yours, you cannot throw away."

Another Hassid asked him whether he should become a Torah Scribe or a teacher. The master replied: "Take up teaching. You will learn a lot from your good pupils."

Traveling in the Carpathian mountains, he calmed the Hassidim who accompanied him and felt uneasy because of the up-and-down roads, fearing that they might meet catastrophe. He said to them:

"You should have become long accustomed to such dangers. During his lifetime, every individual travels through the world on roads that wind up the mountains and down the valleys."

R. Yitzhak Meir's greatness as a Talmudist is immortalized in his work *Khidushey HoRym,* the word *HoRym* being an abbreviation of *HORav Yitzkhak Meir,* and the full title meaning that the work contains his *Innovations or Horym* in interpreting Jewish law. The two volume work *Meir Aynay HaGolah (Light-*

giver to the Eyes of the Jews in Exile), contains his biography and excerpts from his Hassidic teachings.

R. Yitzkhak Meir's commentaries on Biblical passages and his interpretations of the sayings in *Ethics of the Fathers,* are studied diligently to this very day in Hassidic circles. Following are some of his characteristic comments:

The serpent was cursed for advising Eve to give Adam the forbidden fruit, and the curse was, "Dust shalt thou eat all the days of thy life" (Gen. 3:14). The Almighty told the serpent: "You can eat without a stop, as long as I do not have to hear your voice." And this is the true curse upon it.

"And the Lord said unto Cain: 'Why art thou wroth? And why is thy countenance fallen?' " (Gen. 4:6): The Almighty asked Cain to explain whether he was downcast because his own offering had not been accepted, or jealous because his brother Abel's offering had been accepted? Because of jealousy, people can often commit murder.

"Noah . . . was a man righteous" (Gen. 6:9): He was manly in his righteousness.

"And Judah sent the kid of the goats by the hand of his friend the Adullamite" (Gen. 38:20): Everyone should have a friend to whom he can reveal everything, even details of his most sinful acts, just as Judah acted in connection with his Adullamite friend.

"And they believed in the Lord" (Exod. 14:31): Although the Children of Israel had seen the miracles of God, they nevertheless had to have faith, because with faith one sees more than with the eyes.

"From thence you will seek the Lord thy God and there thou shalt find Him, if thou search after Him with all thy heart and with all thy soul" (Deut. 4:29): In your own heart you will seek God, and there you will find Him.

"Then thy heart be lifted up and thou forget the Lord thy God" (Deut. 8:14): This teaches us that forgetfulness is a result of haughtiness.

"Depart from evil and do good" (Ps. 34:15): Don't delve too much into the activities of the evil inclination because within the mire, you may become lowered and dirty. The good deed is cleansing and sanctification in unison.

"Hear, O my people, and I will speak" (Ps. 50:7): The Psalmist meant to say: "If you wish to hear, God will send me words to speak; but if your ears are closed to my words, then my mouth has nothing to say." And this is what Moses meant when he declared: "Give ear, ye heavens, and I will speak; and let the earth hear the words of my mouth" (Deut. 32:1): If you are ready to hear, I will have something to say.

"Truth springeth out of the earth" (Ps. 85:12): When falsehood is buried, then it is possible for truth to sprout.

"For I give you a good doctrine; forsake ye not my teaching" (Prov. 4:2): It means the power to choose the good was given to the human being.

" . . . an old and foolish king" (Eccles. 4:13) is interpreted to mean the evil inclination. As a matter of fact, the evil inclination is quite smart. If so, why the designation "old and foolish king"? For having dealings with fools.

"Judge all men charitably" *(Ethics of the Fathers* 1:6): Judge the human individual according to the characteristics of humanity in general, and you will realize that the individual has many shortcomings which are not his personal fault; then you will judge everyone charitably.

"Judge all the men charitably" (Ibid.): Judge in everyone the whole person, and you will find that everyone has some merits.

R. Yitzkhak Meir's only son, R. Avrohom Mordecai, who was to have been his successor, died during his father's lifetime. So the founder of the Hassidic dynasty of Ger was succeeded by his grandson, R. Yehudah Aryeh Leib, popularly known as the author of *Sefat Emmet (The Lip of Truth)*.

R. YEHUDAH ARYEH LEIB ALTER

R. Yehudah Aryeh Leib Alter (1847–1905), the second Hassidic master of Ger, was only nine years old when his father, R. Avrohom Mordecai Alter, died at any early age. His grandfather, the first master of Ger, found consolation in bringing up his bright grandson, who proved to be an excellent disciple in both Talmudic study and Hassidic lore. Ten years after the death of the father, the grandfather was "called to the Academy-on-High," and the Hassidim of R. Yitzkhak Meir wanted the nineteen year old Yehudah Aryeh Leib to become their new leader. But he refused and announced himself as a devotee of R. Khanokh Henikh HaKohen, a former disciple of his grandfather, who had his Hassidic court in the Polish city of Alexander. When R. Khanokh Henikh died, leaving no successor, because his only son had become a wealthy industrialist, R. Yehudah Aryeh Leib was prevailed upon by the previous devotees of his grandfather and of R. Khanokh Henikh to become their master. Later developments proved their choice to have been excellent in every respect.

The new master of Ger, famous for his great learning, was equally celebrated for his friendliness and personal charm. Of those who came to seek his advice and assistance, he treated equally the learned and the simple. Thanks to his personality,

Ger soon became the most important Hassidic center in all of Poland, and it remained so until shortly before the Nazi invasion of Polish territory at the beginning of World War II.

R. Yehudah Aryeh Leib was a lover of nature, and in the cold winter nights he loved to take long walks along the banks of the frozen Vistula River. During one such walk, he said to a prominent visting devotee: "If I were given the assurance that the Jews, now persecuted in so many places, would be permitted to live peacefully, I would like nothing better than to become a bird that thinks neither of this world nor of the World-to-Come and enjoys its flight in freedom."

He often spoke of nature in his chats with the Hassidim, emphasizing both the spiritual and the material in nature, in remarks such as the following:

"In nature we have the concentration of God's spirituality in material form. Nature contains all the wonders of the first six days of creation. Human sins have caused the mixture of good and bad life."

"Giving birth to a child is much easier than earning a livelihood. The soul of every human being is at birth still attached to a divine spirituality, and the material within are the parts of father and mother in the child. But in earning a livelihood, the material in nature predominates."

The master of Ger never made personal use of the "Redemption" contributions received from Hassidim for blessings and advice. The funds from such contributions were used for distribution among the needy, for the upkeep of young scholars, for dowries of poor brides, for the bailing out of those arrested when they could not pay their debts and for similar purposes. R. Yehudah Aryeh Leib's wife conducted a tobacco store in town and the master himself acted as bookkeeper to make sure that sales and profits were according to the strict specifications of Jewish law in regard to commerce.

While emphasizing the importance of Talmudic studies, R. Yehudah Aryeh Leib took care that his young scholarly devotees did not lose sight of the Hassidic ethic in the interpretation of Jewish law. Every day, after midnight, he conducted special courses in Hassidut, doing so during most of the thirty-five years of his leadership.

Because the master of Ger placed such importance on study, those among his Hassidim who were not scholars themselves were inspired to have scholarly sons and to acquire for their daughters scholarly husbands.

Following are some of his sayings, teachings, stories about his dealings with Hassidim, and his comments on biblical passages:

One should believe that God is the farthest of all and the nearest of all.

Whatever one needs is before him, but one has to have open eyes to see it.

In the daily prayers we praise God as the Maker of peace and Creator of all things, because peace is as important as all the wonders of creation put together.

A Hassid complained that the older he grew, the weaker became his memory. "It happens to everyone," the master of Ger comforted him, "and we should be thankful for not being able to remember all the troubles in the past years of our life."

Another Hassid complained to him that his hat had been stolen. "You should be happy that your head was not stolen," he comforted the complainant, "and take good care that it never happens."

"In the beginning God created the heaven and the earth. Now

the earth was unformed and void, and darkness was on the face of the deep. . . . And God said: 'Let there be light!' . . . and God divided the light from the darkness" (Gen. 1:1–4): Everyone who wishes to serve God should learn from this not to become disheartened for not being clear in his mind about his duties. The beginning of everything is unformed and void. But later, when light emerges, one should separate it from negative mixtures.

"And he [Noah] said: 'Cursed be Canaan; a servant of servants shall he be to his brethren' " (Gen. 9:25): The greatest curse is slavery; the greatest blessing is liberty.

"And he [Jacob] dreamed, and behold a ladder was set up on the earth, and the top of it reached to heaven" (Gen. 28:12): The human body is on the earth, but the top of it, the soul, reaches into heaven.

"They take for me an offering" (Exod. 25:2): The charity one gives is for his own benefit. That is why the giving of charity is also called a "taking" because by giving, one takes for himself.

"Thou shalt surely rebuke thy neighbor and not bear sin because of him" (Lev. 19:17): It means that when you rebuke your neighbor, you should also rebuke yourself, because you are a partner to his wrong deeds. Do not make him alone bear the entire responsibility for his sins.

To fulfill the precept, "Love thy neighbor as thyself" (Lev. 19:18) is very difficult. That is why the same passage ends with the words, "I am the Lord," which means that if you really wish to fulfill the precept, the Lord is ready to assist you in it.

R. Yehudah Aryeh Leib never permitted anyone to look at his manuscripts. Only after his passing, did the immediate male members of the family gather his writings for publication. It was found that the last words he wrote before his demise were a biblical quotation: "The lip of truth shall be established forever" (Prov. 12:19). So they decided to name the collection of his writings *The Lip of Truth, Sefat Emet* in the Hebrew original.

R. Yehudah Aryeh Leib was succeeded by his son, R. Avrohom Mordecai Alter, who later transferred the Hassidic court of Ger to Jerusalem. His son, R. Israel Alter, is now the master of the Gerer Hassidim, and his devotees come to him from all free lands where Polish Jews now reside. The Holy city is also the seat of a number of other Hassidic masters whose ancestors kept alive the hope of oppressed Jews in exile that Jerusalem would some day again be the capital of the People of Israel.

That hope has been transformed into reality in our days, before our very eyes!

XIII

On the Highways and Byways
Of Hassidut

R. Israel Baal Shem Tov, the Besht, his heir R. Ber, the Maggid (Preacher) of Mezritch, and their disciples and the disciples of their disciples, all found fertile ground for their teachings in the Jewish communities of Eastern Europe. The highways and byways which the inspired young Hassidim used in their wanderings to the centers of their beloved teachers, were also the highways and byways of Hassidic spiritual development and influence. Some of the early Hassidic universal and ethical teachings that at first had simply hinted at the new search for expression, were later clothed in clear sentences, formulations, and epigrams. After the days of the Besht and the Maggid, Hassidism began to gain followers also by means of a literature of its own, either in the form of commentaries on biblical portions of the week, or in works devoted to Hassidic lore in general.

In Eastern European towns and villages, the followers of specific *Tzaddikim* gathered in prayer houses of their own, usually called *shtiblekh,* which consisted of one or two room quarters. There they prayed together, studied together, helped one another in solving personal problems and organized special gatherings in connection with the anniversaries of the passing of great Hassidic leaders. At such gatherings, the special tunes of the deceased master were sung and his teachings and stories were retold by individuals who had the special talent necessary to lead the *Hillulahs,* as such Hassidic anniversary celebrations are called.

Of the three meals obligatory upon Jews during the Sabbath Day—Friday night, Saturday after the Morning Service, and Saturday between the Afternoon and the Evening Service—the Hassidim ate the last, not at home, but in their shtiblekh. In the shadows of twilight, they sang the Sabbath Hymns for the "Third Meal," and repeated the teachings of their favorite Hassidic leaders. Since each Hassidic leader utilized the Third Meal gatherings to comment on the biblical portion of the specific week, such comments were repeated during the gatherings in the shtiblekh.

The fact that some disciples of great Hassidic leaders became in time Hassidic masters themselves, played the most important part in turning Hassidut into a mass movement. Consequently, there was no region in Eastern Europe that had no Hassidic centers of its own. In later years, the sons or the sons-in-law, rather than the disciples, became the heirs of great Hassidic leaders, and thus entire Hassidic dynasties came into existence. Since everyone who teaches is called "Rabbi" by his pupils, it was natural that a new master's disciples, even those much older than himself, should accord him the utmost rabbinic respect and devotion.

The Hassidic leader was to his followers a "Tzadik," meaning a just, righteous and pious teacher. He hears the sighs of all who are attached to him and he gives spiritual vitality to each of his Hassidim. But, "to join with the common man, in order to lift him to a higher level, the Tzadik must himself have a particle of uncleanness." The biblical passage, "The righteous (Tzadik) shall live by his faith" (Hab. 2:4), means that his entire life is faith, and it is this faith which controls all his deeds.

Hassidic lore relates that the Besht once heard an evil man play on the violin. The sins that the man had committed were related by the strings as the bow touched them. If the Tzadik can understand what is contained in the tunes of a musical instrument, how much more can he understand what is contained in the world of human beings. The Besht used a biblical passage to explain the difference between two kinds of Tzaddikim: "The righteous shall flourish like a palm tree, he shall grow like a cedar in Lebanon" (Ps. 92:13): There is a kind of righteous man who is like a cedar, a mighty tree which bears no fruit. Such a Tzadik prays and studies, but he does nothing to enlarge the number of pious people. But there is another kind of Tzadik who is similar to a Palm Tree; he bears fruit by sustaining others and brings them to repentance. The Cedar of Lebanon grows for its own glory, but the Palm Tree flourishes. One of the later Hassidic teachers stated: "I used to pray that God grant me the ability to understand the sufferings of others. Now, when someone tells me of his afflictions, I feel them more than he who is troubled by them." While each of the Tzadikim descended from his special position in order to elevate the followers, his special position was not challenged and there was no desire to see him become one of the multitude.

R. Yaakov Yoseph, author of the first biography of the Besht, explained that the Tzadikkim are the soul and life of the world, and the other people are the body that clothes the soul. He also emphasized that just as the heart is inward and is the vitality of the body, so are the Tzadikkim the vitality of the world. The other inhabitants of the world are the bodies that cover the soul like a garment. *(Toledoth Yaakov Yoseph.)*

R. Nakhman of Bratzlav, the great-grandson of the Besht, emphasized the role of the individual Tzadik. According to him, the Tzadik is the central point. With the Hassidim, he converses on matters of faith, and they, in turn, inspire him, each with the holy spark within himself. R. Nakhman taught that there is a vast difference between learning from a book and listening to the words from the Tzadik's mouth, because the Tzadik perfects the spirituality within each of his followers. R. Nakhman compared the Tzadik to a tree. Just as the branches, the leaves and the bark draw their elements of vitality from the tree, so the Hassidim draw their spiritual vitality from the Tzadik. And there are grasses which are not near the tree, and it seems that they do not gain anything from the tree's presence, but actually they do, because the tree protects and saves them from the strong rays of the sun. So does the Tzadik to his Hassidim, even to those who are not near him. The transgressions of an individual are engraved on his bones. When he confesses in the presence of a great man, the engravings disappear and his sins are forgiven. *(Likutey Moharan, Likutey Eitzoth.)*

The relation between the Tzadik and the Hassid was explained in the following manner: The Tzadik places a ladder before the Hassid, who has to ascend alone, without relying on the master's assistance to help him climb to the upper rungs. The Tzadik does not necessarily have to do something practical to help a Hassid. It is enough that he listens when a man wants to unburden what presses upon his heart and soul.

R. Shimon of Shepetovka, was one of the disciples of the Mezritcher Maggid, and he was sent to Prague to visit its Chief

Rabbi, Ezekiel Landau, to defend the Hassidic movement. When
the Rabbi asked him what was the essence of Hassidut he replied:
"A Hassid is he who corrects his own wrong-doings."

R. Wolf of Zhitomir (? –1800), one of the great preachers
and writers of Hassidut, once explained the comradeship of
Hassidim among themselves:

"When we became Hassidim, we formed a partnership to serve
God collectively. Partners had to put in each his share. The
scholar brought his scholarship; he of noble descent placed into
Hassidut his pedigree, so that he would not use it for the purpose
of pride; and so the rich man brought wealth, and the clever
man, his wisdom. If we saw one among us showing pride in his
portion of the partnership, we told him: "If you take back your
portion, then I'll take back mine, and the partnership will be dis-
solved."

Hassidim dance in circles, each dancer placing his hands on
the shoulders of two others. The Besht explained that a circle
is without a beginning and without an end, and when the Tzadik
dances with his Hassidim, all are equal links in a chain; old
and young, rich and poor, scholars and simple people. In such a
manner of dancing, all differences disappear.

Generally speaking, Hassidism was a youth movement. For the
middle-aged and the elderly it was too big an undertaking, in a
physical sense, to travel by horse and wagon to the various cities
where the Tzadikkim were residing. So, it was usually young
men, one encouraged by others, who wandered in company to visit
the "Rabbi," caring very little that they often had to make the
pilgrimage on foot; that they would have to satisfy their healthy
appetities from left-overs at the master's table; and that they would
have to sleep on the hard benches of Study Houses or in crowded

lodgings in the town. Those of scholarly attainment among the young Hassidim were engaged in spreading the teachings they had heard "at the Rabbi's table," and some of these disciples later became Hassidic leaders themselves, either at the request of their own teachers or by being chosen by fellow-Hassidim after the passing of a beloved teacher who had left no suitable heir.

Since Yiddish has been the language of the Hassidim, the "mother-tongue" has been enriched by a new terminology, based on old Hebrew and Aramaic words and phrases, but revived in a synthesis of original and current meaning.

Talented singers among the young Hassidim, created new tunes and adapted old ones for the purposes of singing specific prayers, chapters from the Psalms and the Sabbath Hymns. The talented singers "cleansed" martial marches, opera music and folk tunes from the secular and from the non-Jewish environment in general, by adopting them in a somewhat changed form for their beloved hymns, prayers and dances. Since it is meritorious to dance before the bride at her wedding, various Hassidic leaders and their followers had wedding dances of their own, accompanied by their own original or adapted tunes.

R. Nathan, the scribe who recorded the tales and sayings of R. Nakhman Bratzlaver, said of a Hassidic dance in which he had participated: "I danced with the soul, and the heart carried my feet." One Tzadik explained that Hassidim use the dance as a means of raising themselves above the material interests on earth. According to Hassidic teaching, sadness closes the Gates of Heaven; song is the key to re-open the Heavenly Gates.

Hassidut united Heaven and earth, connecting this world with the World-to-Come. It emphasized the necessity of observing all the 613 precepts obligatory upon Jews, but it replaced religious rigidity with religious fervor. Hassidism transformed into a mass movement the piety of inspired individuals and of scholars who previously had preferred isolation from the masses.

From the beginning, Hassidut emphasized self-search but disdained philosophical speculation. It reminded the devout that the human eye is able to see everything, but a human being seldom uses the eye to look into his own self. Yes, the thinkers were philosophizing about the secret of life. Had they already discovered the secret of thinking?

In its opposition to pure speculation about God, Hassidut pointed out that if it is difficult to understand an ordinary human being, how more so is it impossible to comprehend the greatness of the Almighty; and he who wishes to comprehend the Creator, is himself nothing more than an ordinary human being. Emphasizing both love of God and love of human beings, Hassidism stressed the teaching that, "we should love human beings because of fear of God, but our love of God should not be a result of our fear of human beings."

Since the days of the Besht, many of the Hassidic teachers have used parables in which a crowned head is the central figure. The king, as hero, is always meant to symbolize the necessity of serving the King of Kings, the Creator, with the same fervor and loyalty that soldiers show in the service of a crowned head who is only a human being. Can there be a greater service than being a soldier in the army of the Almighty?

Hassidism stressed piety and an exemplary behavior that harmonized with true piety. It is true that the Almighty often puts the pious man on trial by sending him against evil men who abuse him, nevertheless, his piety is not weakened, and he even serves

God with greater joy and devotion (*Netiv Mitzvotekha,* by Judah Yitzkhak Yekhiel of Komarna).

Similarly, Hassidism stressed that the world is like a ladder; either one ascends or he descends, because one cannot stand indefinitely on a middle rung of the ladder; he who has good traits, is the possessor of a noble soul; one should remember that life is short and evil behavior makes life much shorter; but one should not become pessimistic and thus be led into constant bitterness. R. Aaron of Karlin emphasized: "Even the minutest bitterness is a result of sadness, and even the coarsest joy is a result of sanctity."

Hassidic teachers stressed that one should fear sin because of its being sinful, and not because of punishment for sin. If man could see his evil inclination in a mirror, he would die of fear. The evil inclination is called "an old and foolish king" (Eccles. 4:13), because it is in constant contact with fools.

If the wicked man realizes that he is wicked, he will not be so wicked, no matter how powerful his evil desires. People who are motivated by evil desires are to be pitied rather than condemned. One is proud, because he lacks in his heart the fear of God; he is envious, so he has no true friends; his anger saps the strength of his body. So finally he has no God, no friends, and to himself he is personally also lost.

Relying on God's compassion in the future, most Hassidim expressed no fear about the days to come, and Hassidic teachers emphasize the necessity of correcting the mistakes of the past instead of looking for signs of what the future may bring. One should rather always seek the truth, because this is something that everybody hides.

Elimination of pride is one of the main teachings of Hassidut. It reminds us that the cemeteries are filled with the graves of people, each of whom thought during his lifetime that the world could not exist without him. "When a person is grown in height, spiritually, he interferes with no one, but when he grows in width, pride, he is pushing me." And he who besmirches the greatness of others, shows by his action how small he is.

Why be boastful altogether? Beauty is seen, kindness is felt, and wisdom is heard. If it is unbecoming to boast of what one knows or what one owns, how more so is it unbecoming to boast of things one has not, or of knowledge one does not possess?

Emphasizing the positive importance of charity and the negative characteristics of those who strive for wealth, Hassidism reminds us that some people are engaged in mining treasures of gold from the earth, and very often the gold buries them. The miser is always worried about money as if all riches were his own, and he is in fear of using it as if his wealth belonged to others. The miser is like a prisoner, because both are linked: the prisoner in chains of iron, and the miser in golden chains. The truth is that only he who gives is rich, and poor is the man whose hand is closed.

"Abolish the lust for money, and the Messiah will come."

Before the coming of the Messiah, falsehood will have greater acceptance than truth, as alluded to in the Scriptural passage: "Grace is deceitful, and beauty is vain" (Prov. 31:30): Falsehood will find grace in the eyes of people, and the stupidity of deceit will be considered as something exceptionally beautiful.

One of the central teachings of Hassidut is the principle that only through love of humans, can one reach the love of God. The Besht told his early followers that one can serve God even in trifling deeds for fellow humans. It is very good to be great, but it is much greater to be good. Some people enjoy the downfall of others because to throw down is easier than to lift.

A good Hassid is he who pleases both his Creator and his fellow-men. Even to smile benevolently when a fool tells an anecdote or uses an epigram is an act of loving kindness.

Eliezer Zvi Zweifel (1815–1888), one of the leaders of the *Haskalah,* the Jewish enlightenment movement in Eastern Europe in the second half of the 19th century, wrote in his book, *Shalom Al Yisrael (Peace unto Israel),* a defense of Hassidut which came under attack by other writers of the Enlightenment Era. He emphasized that the activities and accomplishments of the Hassidic leaders were not inferior to those of the Talmud sages and of the founders of Kabbalah (Jewish mysticism). Furthermore, wrote Zweifel, Hassidut inspired its followers to pray with fervor and to aspire to lofty sentiments. Hassidut received into its ranks the simple masses and treated them with love and understanding; thus doing away with the separation between the scholars and the unschooled in Jewish life, promising everyone the proper Heavenly reward for kind deeds and for unlimited faith in the Creator. The great Jewish historian, Simeon Dubnow, was also the author of a three volume history of Hassidut, written originally in Hebrew. Although his rationalism and intellectualism often interfered with his understanding of specific Hassidic leaders or trends within Hassidism itself, he nevertheless understood its general value, stressing the fact that: "Hassidut is a folk-movement that descended from the heights in the world of Divine Emanation to the lower world of daily life. . . . It came not to mend the faith, but the spirit of the believer, to strengthen within him feeling over reason, the communion with

God over the knowledge of God, the teachings of the heart over the teachings of the book." *(S. Dubnow, Teledoth HaHassidut, Introduction.)*

Eliezer Steinman, who treated Hassidism and its creators in a whole series of books written in Hebrew, formulated in one sentence the character of Hassidut in general: "Human being, you are very, very dear—this is the essence of Hassidism in every detail." *(Eliezer Steinman, Beer HaHassiduth, Introduction.)*

XIV

Gleanings From
The Field of Hassidut

AMONG THE six million Jews who were annihilated by the Nazis during World War II, were a number of great Hassidic teachers. Because of the holocaust, the manuscripts of some of the older masters of this century disappeared, and some of the younger masters were murdered before they had the chance to put their thoughts and teachings on paper.

In order to round out our review of the Hassidic ideas and ideals in regard to universal faith and ethics, the final chapter of this book is devoted to brief characterizations of the teachings of various Hassidic leaders and authors, beginning with R. Israel Baal Shem Tov, founder of Hassidut and his disciples down to the middle of the 19th Century. The Hassidic masters of the 20th Century deserve a special study which is outside the confines of this book.

Hassidism has created, since its beginnings to the present, many concepts of universal faith, ethics and morality, all based on the teachings of Judaism as a religion, a culture and a civilization within the sphere of Jewish peoplehood. The fact that all Jewish spiritual values are rooted in the universality of God and in the brotherhood of humanity made it possible that so distinctly Jewish a book as the Bible should become the most cherished book among many of the peoples which inhabit the globe, and the foundation of two other universal great faiths: Christianity and Islam. One of the foremost Jewish scholars of our time, the late Louis Ginzberg, speaking of post-biblical Jewish creativity, the Talmudic interpretation of biblical law and the Midrashic-Haggadic interpretation of biblical ethics, characterized them all in a single epigram: "The Talmud is the Jewish within the universal; the Midrash is the universal within Judaism." The Sages of the Talmud and the Midrash, many of whom are identical, were quite aware of this, and the world as it was known to them they divided into two separate regions: "From Tyre to Carthage they know respectfully the history of the people of Israel and of their Father in heaven; but from Tyre westward and from Carthage eastward, they know neither Israel nor their Father in Heaven." *(Babylonian Talmud, Tractate Menakhot* or *Meal Offerings 110-A.)*

The post-Talmudic *Geonim* and after them the codifiers, the commentators and the authors of Jewish philosophic and ethical works, added new dimensions to the Jewish universality in faith and morals. All of them served as foundations of Hassidic masters for the formulation of new universal teachings and guides for human behavior, as necessitated by developments and changes in life, Jewish and general, during an era comprising some two hundred years of wars, upheavals and the birth-pangs of new peoples, new countries and new values.

The entire animal world was included in the universalism of Hassidut, and meritorious acts were derived from the actions of such extremes as innocent infants, conniving adults, or personal enemies. Hassidim transmitted the following lessons from generation to generation:

A great teacher said: "The Creator turned to the animals and said: 'Cooperate with Me in forming a higher being, to whom each of you shall donate a desirable characteristic. The cat will contribute modesty; the ant, honesty; the tiger, courage; the lion, bravery; the eagle, diligence, and so forth. Thus will man not only be akin to you, but will also represent the finest in you.' "

R. Dov Ber, the Maggid of Mezritch, successor of R. Israel Baal Shem Tov, directed . . . [a disciple] to learn three things from an infant and seven from a thief. What of the infant? The infant is always merry without even a strain of melancholy; it is never at rest but always moving its limbs, and whenever it desires a thing which is not given it, it bursts into tears. And what of the thief? The thief works at night and if he is unsuccessful one night he tries the next. There is honor among thieves and a measure of unity among them. The thief sells his loot at a low price, and never admits his theft even when beaten; he always claims to have no knowledge about it. The thief is prepared to endanger himself, even when he is doubtful of success. Finally, a thief will not abandon his trade even for all the riches in the world.

The Maggid of Mezritch said: "Every lock has its key which is fitted to it and opens it. But there are strong thieves who know how to open without keys. They break the lock. So every mystery in the world can be unriddled by the particular kind of meditation fitted to it. But God loves the thief who breaks the lock open: I mean the man who breaks his heart for God."

Once he declared; "The whole earth is full of His glory. Even in idolatrous worship there are sparks of holiness."

After the Maggid's death, his disciples came together and talked about the things he had done. When it was Rabbi Shneur Zalman's turn, he asked them: "Do you know why our master went to the pond every day at dawn and stayed there for a little while before coming home again?" They did not know why. Rabbi Zalman

continued: "He was learning the song with which the frogs praise God. It takes a very long time to learn that song."
(Fun Uzer Altn Oitzer, I, p. 8.; Newman: Hassidic Anthology, p. 14; Steinmann: The Garden of Hassidism, pp. 163, 167; Buber: Tales of the Hassidim, Early Masters, pp. 104, 111.)

It was the custom of Hassidic masters of later generations, before expounding ideas, interpretations or commentaries of their own, to relate something about the masters of previous generations and their teachings. Included in such introductory remarks by the later Hassidic leaders, were the matters dealt with in this concluding chapter.

The Besht explained: "And it cast down truth to the ground" (Dan. 8:12): Why should such a gem as truth be cast to the ground? So that man should bend down, because the Almighty wants a person to bend down a bit; but very few people have a desire to lower themselves.

"Who is wise? He who learns from all men" (*Ethics of the Fathers,* 4:1): We can learn even from an evil man, because a bad person also possesses some traits from which one can learn the practice of good deeds.

> From the minute a man passes through the gates of the royal court until he succeeds in entering the palace itself, he is seized by fear and trembling. When a man perceives a great fear coming over him it is a sign that he has come within the gates of the Great King, the King of the Universe. This is the portal of the Lord.

> Everything that a man sees or hears is but a signpost, pointing the way to the worship of God.

> The Besht once said to his followers: "There is a story about a king whose children sat at his table and who, accustomed to the

good fare, took no pleasure in the delicacies with which they were fed. And so the king gave them a piece of advice. He told them to bring bags and to fill them with tidbits from his table and store them away for a time when they would find relish in these remnants from the royal fare. Similarly, make a store of small things such as a parable or a story, for these insignificant matters may, in the length of days, stand you in good stead."

Said the Besht: "Man should learn pride, and not be proud; he should learn anger, but not feel angry. For man should be a complete personality, possessing all human traits. Does not the Torah picture God as possessing both Justice and Mercy?"

The Besht said: "Absolute evil does not exist. When the good man perceives evil-doers, he rejoices in goodness."

"Why does the Bible relate the wrongdoings of good men?" the Besht was asked. "Would it not encourage righteousness to teach that good men are invariably good?" The Besht answered: "If the Bible failed to indicate the few sins of its heroes, we might doubt their goodness. Let me explain this by the following fable:
'A lion taught his cubs that they need fear no living creature, since they were the strongest on earth. One day the cubs went for a walk and came upon a ruin. They entered and saw on the wall of the deserted castle a picture of Samson breaking in twain a lion cub (Judges 14:5–6). In fright they ran to their father, crying out: 'We have seen a creature stronger than ourselves and we are in fear of him.' The old lion questioned them, and on learning what they had seen in the ruin, he said: 'This picture ought to assure you that the race of lions is the strongest of creatures, for when once a stronger creature appears, it is pictured as a miracle. Exceptions prove the rule.' "

Said the Besht: "A king was told that a man of humility is endowed with long life. He attired himself in old garments, took up his residence in a small hut, and forbade anyone to show reverence before him. But when he honestly examined himself, the

King found himself to be prouder of his seeming humility than ever before. A philosopher thereupon remarked to him: 'Dress like a king; live like a king; allow the people to show due respect to you; but be humble in your inmost heart.' "

Said the Besht: "No child can be born except through pleasure and joy. By the same token, if one wishes his prayers to bear fruit, he must offer them with pleasure and joy."

Mind is the foundation of man. If the foundation is solid, the building is secure. By the same token, if a man's mind is filled with holy thoughts, his actions will be sound. But if his mind is occupied with selfish thoughts, even his good actions are unsound, being built on a weak foundation.

Said the Besht: "One who sees faults in another and dislikes him for them is surely possessed of some of these very faults in his own person. The pure and good man can see only the goodness in others. We read (Lev. 19:17): 'Thou shalt not hate thy brother in thy heart: thou shalt surely rebuke thy neighbor and not bear sin because of him.' This teaches us: Rebuke thyself first for seeing faults, and thus being to a degree impure; then thou wilt not hate thy brother, but feel love towards him. If thou rebukest him, it will be in the spirit of love. He will become attached to thee, joining the goodness within him to thine own goodness, and all his faults will disappear."

Said the Besht: "A king built himself a palace and surrounded it with guards. Many of the people came to behold the King, but when they saw the guards, they departed. Others gave presents to the guards, and were permitted to enter. But when they saw the ornaments in the great halls, they halted to look at them and forgot their mission to see the King. Still others looked neither at the guards nor the decorations, but walked straight into the presence of the ruler. Some people," continued the Besht, "who wish to commune with the Lord, retreat at the first hindrance. Others bring the gifts of charity and kind deeds before they commence their prayers, but they become engrossed in a wise comment or fine saying in the Prayer Book. Still others, however, concentrate their minds immediately upon God, and refuse to be diverted by any distraction, however appealing."

A man of piety complained to the Besht, saying: "I have labored hard and long in the service of the Lord, and yet I have received no improvement. I am still an ordinary and ignorant person." The Besht answered: "You have gained the realization that you are ordinary and ignorant, and this in itself is a worthy accomplishment."
(Siakh Sarfay Kodesh, I, p. 99; Keter Shem Tov, 3–A, 13–B, 16–B; Midrash Ribash Tov II, pp. 9, 50, 90–91; Steinman: The Garden of Hassidism, pp. 149, 152, 154; Dubnow: Taledot HaHassidut, p. 54; Newman: Hassidic Anthology, pp. 31, 95, 159, 190, 203, 256, 390, 422, 429.)

R. Yaakov Yoseph, biographer of the Besht and one of his greatest disciples, interpreted a biblical passage:

"Thou shalt surely rebuke thy neighbor" (Lev. 19:17): It means that you "should surely" first rebuke yourself, and after that you may "rebuke thy neighbor."

R. Pinkhas of Koretz, who is considered a contemporary of the Besht rather than a disciple, said of the haughty and of the liars: "He who is filled with self-importance lies to himself and he fools others to believe in his importance."

"Keep thee far from a false matter (Exod. 23:7): The big liars have thoughts of idolatry and heresy, because truth and faith are attached to each other.

Of himself he said: "Nothing was so difficult for me as the work against untruth. This work continued for thirteen years; it broke every member and every bone in my body, until I succeeded."

R. Nakhman of Horodenka (? – ?), whose son R. Simkha became the son-in-law of the Besht's daughter Odell, was among the early Hassidim who settled in the Holy Land. The Hassidic master R. Nakhman of Bratzlav was the great-grandson of R. Nakhman of Horodenka and bore his name.

Commenting on the forms of punishments meted out to culprits, R. Nakhman of Horodenka emphasized:

> "There are two ways of curing offenders. Some claim a cure by inflicting privations, but these usually result in the transgressor becoming embittered against society, and cruel henceforth. Others effect a cure through persuasions which often-times transform the sinner into a man of kindness and helpfulness."
>
> (*Dubnow: Toledot HaHassidut, p. 103; Newman: Hassidic Anthology, p. 312.*)

Related R. Khayim of Krasnah (? – ?), one of the Besht's disciples: "I watched a circus-man walk over a tight rope, and observed how that man concentrated all his thoughts on his deed, otherwise he might have fallen down. Watching him, I realized that when we fulfill precepts or are engaged in a good deed, we should concentrate our thoughts on the specific action, otherwise we might fall down."

R. Shabtai of Rashkov (? – ?) another disciple of the Besht, emphasized the importance of being careful with words. R. Shabtai declared: "He who avoids idle talk for forty days in succession, will undoubtedly be rewarded with the Divine Spirit."

Speaking of R. Yitzkhak of Drohobitch, when he was his opponent, the Besht said: "R. Yitzkhak has been given from heaven the smallest of souls, but as a result of his service and endeavors, he has raised that soul to the greatest heights."

R. Yitzkhak later became a follower of the Besht, and R.

Yitzkhak's son, R. Yekhiel Mikhel, a preacher like his father, is immortal in Hassidic history as R. Yekhiel Mikhel of Zlochov.

R. Yekhiel Mikhel of Zlochov, among the youngest disciples of the Besht and of the early disciples of his successor, R. Dov Ber, the Maggid of Mezritch, interpreted the last of the Ten Commandments, "Thou shalt not covet" (Exod. 20.14): How is it possible for a person to control the desires of his heart? Even if one does not wish to covet what belongs to someone else, it is also difficult to avoid it. But the tenth of the Commandments is an assurance that if one observes nine of the Commandments, he will also be able to observe the tenth.

R. Zeev Wolf of Zbarazh (? –1800), one of the five sons of R. Yekhiel Mikhel of Zlochov and a grandson of R. Yitzkhak of Drohobitch, was in his early youth known as a wild boy who caused his father much pain and heartache. But as soon as he reached his thirteenth year, the Bar Mitzvah age of maturity, he gradually changed his behavior and in time became known as a symbol of love and understanding. He was particularly sensitive about the sufferings of animals, and tried to persuade the teamsters never to use their whips: "If you talk to a horse gently, it will understand and do what you ask. If it is a grave sin even to shout at a horse, how much more sinful is it to cause pain through whipping!"

R. Zeev Wolf was in constant fear that thieves might be tempted to enter his home in order to steal something and thus commit a sin. So every night, before retiring, he declared: "Everything in this house does not belong to me and I have no claim on anything."

In his desire to defend everyone, he even found merit in those who spent their nights at playing cards: "When they become well accustomed to staying up all night, they will certainly repent and make use of the night time for study and good deeds."

R. Zeev Wolf always endeavored to make peace among men. "When two are quarrelling, both are right, and it is of great importance that two rightful people should live in friendship."

FROM THE DISCIPLES OF THE MAGGID

One of the fundamental works of early Hassidic literature is *Or HaMeir (The Radiant Light)* by R. Zeev Wolf, the preacher of Zhitomir. One of the greatest *Magodism* of his time, R. Zeev Wolf was a disciple of R. Dov Ber, the Preacher of Mezritch, the Besht's successor.

It is related that R. Zeev once noticed two drunkards, father and son, walking together. He turned to his own son and remarked: "I envy that drunkard. He managed to educate his son to walk in his ways. How many fathers can say that they have accomplished so much in the education of their own sons?"

Emphasizing repentance, he said: "Instead of worrying what we will do tomorrow, let us correct the wrongs which we committed yesterday."

The redemption from Egyptian bondage was the beginning of individual redemption into all eternity, taught R. Zeev; and anyone who concentrates on this fact will realize that he is on the way to personal salvation.

He interpreted biblical passages to emphasize the importance of fearing God and of the constant struggle against one's own temptations.

"The fear of the Lord is clean, enduring forever" (Ps. 19:10): If one's fear of God is clean and pure, and one is, so to speak, naked in his fear, with no coarse material coverings over it, such God-fearing endures and exists into eternity.

"Mine eye affected my soul, because of all the daughters of my city" (Lam. 3:51): It is the eye that affects the soul more than any other part or sense of the human body.

When R. Elimelekh of Lizhensk and his brother, R. Zusheh of Annipol, were young men and "performed exile" as homeless wanderers, they were given lodging in the home of a poor Hassid whenever they passed through the city of Ludmir. Many years later, after the two brothers had become famous Hassidic masters, they arrived on a visit to Ludmir in a carriage drawn by two horses. The wealthiest man in town invited them to stay at his home, but they rejected his invitation.

"We are now the same men that we were when we used to come here as poor wanderers," said R. Elimelekh to the rich man, "but in previous years you never asked us to come to your house. Evidently, you have changed your attitude because of the carriage and the two horses. If you wish, you can invite them to be your guests. We will stay in the poor Hassid's home."

R. Elimelekh once stated that he was certain he would be granted a share in the World-to-Come. He explained: "When I come before the Heavenly Court and they ask me whether I studied or observed the Law, I will answer with a 'no.' So the Heavenly Court will decide that if a man tells the truth, he deserves a share in the World-to-Come."

In his work, Noam Elimelekh, it is explained: "Words that go out of the heart, enter the heart." These words of wisdom can also be interpreted to mean that the heart from which the words came, is re-entered by the same words to add to its holiness.

In the beginning of the Ten Commandments, it is written: "And God spoke all these words saying: 'I am the Lord, thy God'" (Exod. 20:1–2): The Law was given that all inhabitants of the world might find out that there is a God who rules everyone and everything.

"Can any hide himself in secret places that I shall not see him? saith the Lord" (Jer. 23:24). R. Elimelekh used this verse to castigate a great scholar who was engaged in his studies day and night and acted haughtily in regard to others. Said R. Elimelekh to the proud scholar: "If a man hide himself in secret places to study only for himself, and 'I,' only the 'I,' his personal pride, counts, then God shall not see him."

R. Elimelekh told a group of Jews who were about to make a trip to Warsaw: 'When you reach Warsaw, kindly transmit my regards to my father, your father, everyone's father, the Creator. The whole earth is full of His glory."

R. Zusheh of Annipol, younger brother of R. Elimelekh, constantly emphasized the importance of humility: "For though the Lord be high, yet regarded He the lowly" (Ps. 138:6): The Highness of the Lord can be seen only by those who consider themselves lowly.

R. Moshe of Psheversk (? –1804), a Torah-scribe by profession, was a disciple of R. Elimelekh of Lizhensk. He preferred to be a follower rather than a teacher. Only after his passing, were found the two volumes of his work *Or P'nay Moshe (Radiance on the Face of Moses)*, interpretations of the Holy Scriptures and of Talmudic sayings.

In his chats, R. Moshe emphasized the importance of prayer and of charity. "Human beings were created with mouths so that they may be able to praise the Creator of the Universe. The fact that they can use the mouth for ordinary words and requests, is proof that this is God's charitable gift to humans. One never gets a headache from praying. Prayer is service of the heart, not of the head."

A sack and a stick were hanging in the reception room of R. Shmelke of Nicholsburg. They were his constant reminder to the community leaders that if they pressured him to act against his personal wishes or principles, he was ready to give up the Rabbinate and sustain himself as a wandering beggar.

Rabbi Shmelke interpreted the famous saying of Hillel (Sabbath 31a): "What is hateful to thee do not cause to be done to thy neighbor." He paraphrased it, saying: "What is hateful to thee in thy neighbor, do not do thyself."

Said Rabbi Shmelke: "He who regrets his transgressions may do so for two reasons: one, that he stands in fear of punishments; the other, that he is contrite for having displeased his beloved Father in Heaven. In the first instance, the sin becomes suspended, but a record of it remains. In the second, it is thoroughly erased, and no trace remains, as if no sin had ever been committed."
(Shemen HaTov, pp. 36-154; Newman: Hassidic Anthology, pp. 222; 38.)

R. Moshe Leib Sassover, the great disciple of R. Shmelke of Nicholsburg, constantly emphasized the importance of compassion and brotherly love. He once related: "The meaning of brotherly love I learned from a conversation between two Gentiles. One asked the other, 'Do you really love me?'

" 'Certainly.'

" 'But how can you say that you love me, if you do not know my needs?' "

When speaking of various forms of human behavior and

characteristics, R. Moshe Leib explained: "To overpower anger is of greater importance than to fast a thousand days."

"If you do not like your friend's behavior, examine whether your own behavior is better than his."

"When a man of you bringeth an offering unto the Lord" (Lev. 1:2): When a man is humble, the Lord considers it to be better than any other offering.

"And thou shalt set upon the table of the sanctuary showbread before me" (Exod. 25:30): Showbread is the bread that is constantly ready on one's table for the poor and the hungry.

TEACHERS, ORIGINATORS AND SUCCESSORS

R. Aaron of Karlin, who brought Hassidut to anti-Hassidic Lithuanian Jewry, stressed intellectual awareness, in his teachings, although Hassidut in general made its appeal to the heart rather than to the mind. Said R. Aaron: "When someone is careful not to do evil because of self-compassion, it is also a good trait."

"Of those who built the tabernacle, it is written: 'And Bezallel and Oholiab shall work, and every wise-hearted man' (Exod. 36:1): Wisdom without heart is of no value."

R. Menakhem Mendel of Vitebsk (1730–1788), who had been taken by his father to the Besht when only nine years old, and was later one of the disciples of the Maggid of Mezritch, became the leading figure in the migration of Hassidim to the Holy Land. Before his departure, R. Mendel played a leading role in the strengthening of Hassidut in White Russia, having among his associates several men who later played important roles in the development of Hassidut in general. One of his associates was R. Shneur Zalman of Ladi, founder of the KhaBad intellectual form in Hassidic teaching. From his teachings in the book *Pree*

HaAretz (Fruit of the Land), it is seen that he emphasized proper behavior in ordinary daily life: "Fear of sin means to be afraid of sin itself more than of the punishment for committing a sin."

"Compared to the greatness of God, all human beings, whether saintly or ordinary, are equals."

"The ordinary worm can be higher than I, a human being, for the worm does the will of God without destroying anything or doing harm to anyone."

"God is found within the food, as it is written: 'And they beheld God, and did eat and drink' (Exod. 24:11): One can come nearer to God as a result of the food he eats."

R. Menakhem Mendel of Vitesbsk was a religious poet. Characteristic of his poetic nature are the lines of a Yiddish song he composed:

> If I had wings of gold,
> I would fly to You, my God;
> Had I golden wheels,
> I would in flight go up to You;
> If a saddle and horse had I,
> I would rush to You.
> If I had ink and quill,
> A letter I would dispatch to You,
> Had I a ring in my hand,
> It would be my gift with myself to You.

When R. Shneur Zalman of Ladi was under arrest in St. Petersburg, the chief investigator came into his cell in order to question him. Realizing that the arrested man was a great scholar, the investigator started to discuss with him various biblical problems. He asked:

"Please explain to me the meaning of the Scriptural passage,

'And the Lord God called unto the man and said unto him: Where art thou?' Did not God know where Adam was?"

"This question was addressed not to Adam alone," replied R. Shneur Zalman, "but to every human being since Adam the Lord puts the same question: 'Where art thou, now, at this juncture of your lifetime?' What have you accomplished as regards helping your fellow-man?"

The investigator was very pleased with the answer, and after conversing with R. Shneur Zalman on other subjects, he went to the Czar and pleaded that the arrested scholar be freed since he was innocent of the charges levelled against him. And R. Shneur Zalman was released.

A Mitnaged asked R. Shneur Zalman of Ladi whether the Messiah would belong to the Hassidim or to their adversaries. R. Shneur Zalman replied:

"The Messiah will be an opponent of the Hassidim, because if he were a Hassid, the Mitnagdim would have no faith in him even if he performed such miracles as did Moses."

Speaking on the importance of charity, he said:

"The hand that distributes charity becomes a part of the Almighty's fiery chariot."

In connection with the biblical passage, "Keep far from a false matter" (Exod. 23:7). It is related about R. Shneur Zalman, that he worked for twenty-one years on the matter of truth: seven years to understand what was truth; seven years to drive away falsehood, and seven years that truth should penetrate into himself.

R. Barukh of Kosov (? –1781), a disciple of R. Menakhem Mendel of Vitebsk, explained attachment to God as similar to one's attachment to someone near and dear: "The more one is attached to a person, the greater the other's love for him. And similarly is the result of one's attachment to the Almighty: the more one is attached to Him, the greater is His special interest in and love for such an individual."

In a similar vein, R. Barukh interpreted a passage from the Holy Scriptures: "For the Lord thy God hath blessed thee in all the work of thy hand" (Deut. 2:7): According to the work of your hands in giving charity, the Lord will bless you.

R. Moshe of Kobrin, the great disciple of R. Mordecai of Lekhovitch and of his son R. Noakh, stressed the importance of faith for personal well-being: "I am the Lord that healeth thee" (Exod. 15:26): Meaning, if you will know that "I am the Lord," this alone will be a healing to you.

After the passing of R. Moshe of Kobrin, his followers turned to R. Abraham of Slonim (1802–1884) to be their leader. R. Abraham, the head of a Yeshiva in Slonim, was one of the greatest Talmudic scholars of his time. Since he disdained fame and popularity, it was his plan to publish his work, *Khessed L'Avrohom (Mercy to Abraham,* as based on Mic. 7:20), in thirty copies only.

In his commentaries on the Bible and the Talmud, as well as in his chats with his devotees, R. Abraham often stressed the differences between reason and emotion, wisdom and feeling, as well as the divine and the ethical in daily tasks.

"One's heart is more intimate to a person than his mind," held R. Abraham, "and the heart can influence the mind only according to its strength, which is altogether feeling. The person who is in possession of wisdom, realizes full well that worldly matters are subsidiary, of lesser importance. The heart acts in such matters only in an emotional way, knowing the sweet things in life. But the mind understands both the material and the spiritual, the daily necessities of life and the great value of the service of God. That is why wisdom teaches us: 'It is good that thou shouldest take hold of the one; yea also from the other withdraw not thy hand; for he that feareth God, shall discharge himself of them all' " (Eccles. 7:18).

"He standeth at the right hand of the needy" (Ps. 109:31): He who mistreats the needy and does not permit them to enter his house, is also guilty of turning away the Almighty who always escorts the needy, being at their right hand.

"Who is wise? He who learns from all men" (Ethics of the Fathers 4:1): The adage says that 'every fool has his own wisdom', but not the wisdom of others; but the wise person learns from others, so that in addition to his own wisdom, he uses the wisdom of others. That is why he is really wise.

R. Nathan the Scribe recorded also the following biblical comments by R. Nakhman of Bratzlav, the Besht's great-grandson:

"And God Almighty give you mercy" (Gen. 43:14): That you be able to understand what mercy is. It is possible that the great sufferings of an individual are a result of the Almighty's mercy, because whatever God does to an individual, is in his favor. But our understanding is too limited for evaluation, and we wish that the Creator should place mercy in our hands, according to our conceptions, simple mercy which can protect against pain and trouble. And this is what Jacob meant when he said to his sons: "And God Almighty give you mercy."

Moses said: "How can I myself alone bear your cumbrance, and your burden, and your strife" (Deut. 1:12): Our Talmudic sages said that the generation consisted of heretics which is the heaviest burden a person has to carry. The believer leans upon his trust and faith in the Almighty, and this makes his life easier. But the heretic wrangles constantly with his own doubts, he has no strong foundation in life, and is burdened by his own skepticism.

The modern American Yiddish poet Yaakov Glattstein, wrote a whole book entitled *The Bratzlaver to His Scribe*. The fragment quoted below, is characteristic of the entire book which is symbolic of R. Nakhman's great spiritual influence on Yiddish creativity in general. The quoted fragment is called "There Is a Dish Called Hunger":

How did this loaf of bread come upon my table, Nathan?
Why have I not thought of it ever before?
I get up, chirp my prayers like a birdie,
And my crumb is there.
In the meantime I fill up my gut,
Should I be considered of nobility?
There is a dish like hunger,
Taste it!

Well, surely you will say,
I fast, fast days much too many,
But they are not fastings for the stomach,
But, so to speak, for God.
I will begin to fast of hunger,
Simply of hunger.
I'll make a pact with all the hungry, a brotherhood.
All the fastings have no value,
Because they are for the own soul.
But the body remains outworn and rags.

We are being tried in the joy of easy little precepts,
And we believe, living we live it up.
We immerse ourselves, so to speak, in noble-mindedness
And we let ourselves become coarse.
It is a pleasure to purify oneself
And to remove oneself from this earthliness.

We'll get horse and wagon,
Onward; We have left the stomach.
You have a double pleasure:
You left not only your own,
But the others' empty stomach as well.
And the earth, the ground is ours.

I will fast into my body deep,
And fall even lower than earthly desire,
That the simple piece of bread should become
The cherished saucer from the sky.
I want to become a hungry animal,
That seeks to devour.

I wish to see how long I can be trusted.
I want to reach the trial of hunger,
And feel how piously just
A hungry human being can be,
If he doesn't take a knife in his hand
And does not become a robber.

Nathan, let's permit ourselves a bit of misery, a bit of pain,
On the contrary, let's not Good-Luckify our lives,
Let's not skin pieces from the World-to-Come,
Even because of hunger.

Let's sink deeper into body-hunger,
And devote a Tuesday, or perhaps
An ordinary Wednesday
To the hunger of man,
Be speechless all day long,
And later say Grace-in-Company,
At a shamed table,
I, you, he, the hungry human.

R. Nakhman once stated:

"When someone realizes that by his actions he can do wrong

and spoil things, he should also realize that by his actions he can do good and correct things."

R. Yehuda Tzvi Brandwein of Stretin (? —1844), was a disciple of R. Uri of Strelisk, and, like his master, was the spiritual leader of the poorest among the Hassidim, and lived the same life of austerity as his devotees. R. Yehudah Tzvi left no books, but his teachings are recorded in the collection *Deggel Makhne Yehudah, (The Standard of the Camp of Judah,* based on Num. 2:3).

In his interpretations of Biblical passages, R. Yehudah Tzvi emphasized the differences between the spiritual and the material:

"Of the fat places of the earth shall be thy dwelling, and of the dew of heaven from above" (Gen. 27:39): This is how Isaac blessed his son Esau. But when Isaac blessed Jacob he said: "So God give thee of the dew of heaven, and of the fat places of the earth" (Ibid., 27:28): Isaac said to Esau: "Of the dew of heaven from above," meaning that spiritual, heavenly things are above him and far from him; but to Jacob he said: "Of the dew of heaven and of the fat places of the earth," blessing him with both spiritual and material wealth.

"This word is very nigh unto thee, in thy mouth and in thy heart that thou mayest do it" (Deut. 30:14): There is a difficulty in this passage, because, since thoughts come from the heart into the mouth, the heart should have been mentioned first. But the difficulty disappears when we understand the passage as meaning that when one attempts to teach others morals and ethics, he should first make sure that what he wishes to say with his mouth, is also found within his heart.

R. Abraham (? —1865), the son and successor of R. Yehuda

Tzvi, often repeated his dictum: "Love of human beings is the surest way to attain love of God."

R. Mordecai of Chernoble used to say: He who wants to serve the Almighty with fear and love, must first of all understand why one should love and fear Him."

R. Mordecai's son, R. David Talnah (1808–1882), a great Hassidic master in his own right, emphasized the importance of charity by pointing at the difference between human beings and angels, giving the human being greater importance in the field of deeds:

"It is related in the Midrash that in Heaven there is one angel who has a thousand mouths, and in each mouth he has a thousand tongues, and with all of them he sings praises to the Holy One, Blessed be He. But that remarkable angel does not have a single pocket to keep there some coins for distribution among the poor."

A Hassid of R. David of Talnah came to the master and complained that he was in great need. R. David cut the conversation short, and this caused the Hassid much grief because before him the master had conversed for a long time with a man known for his wealth. R. David understood that the needy Hassid felt hurt, so later he said to him: "I did not have to talk to you long in order to know that you are poor. But the other man whom everybody considers wealthy, I had to talk to him for quite a long time until I realized that he is just as needy as you are."

R. Yokhanan of Rakhmistrivka, one of R. David's brothers, stressed the differences between lip-service to truth and the practice of truth:

"Those who love the truth often talk so much about the importance of truth, that they are not careful enough about mixing truth with untruth; but those who hate lies, are careful not to talk too much about the truth, because of fear that they might stumble over an untruth."

R. Nakhum of Stephanesht (? –1869), one of the successors of his father, R. Israel of Rhuzin, consoled troubled individuals by using folksy moral tales and similes. His use of popular sayings included the following:

"If every human being's troubles were put separately on a hook, everyone would rush to get back his own share after realizing that the troubles of others are bigger and worse than his own."

R. Yaakov Koppel Hassid, one of the early disciples of the Besht, became the father of a boy who was later the founder of a Hassidic dynasty. R. Yaakov Koppel's son was R. Menakhem Mendel Hager (? –1825). After his marriage, R. Menakhem Mendel became a business man, but later he accepted the rabbinic chair at Kosov. A follower of R. Moshe Leib of Sassov, R. Menakhem Mendel was greatly admired by a number of important Hassidic leaders of the generation after R. Dov Ber and his disciples. They prevailed upon him to leave the world of commerce and devote himself exclusively to spiritual leadership. His teachings are recorded in the work *Ahavat Shalom (Love of Peace)*.

Emphasized R. Menakhem Mendel:

"Every day is a separate garment for the human being. According to the importance of his deeds are the looks of his garments. Good deeds, done without a warm heart and without inspiration, also create garments, but they are not the property of the person, because his heart is not in them.

"When someone distributes charity, the Almighty rewards that person as if he brought his own body and soul as an offering upon the altar of God."

R. Menakhem Mendel interpreted a biblical passage regarding truth:

"Keep thee far from a false matter" (Exod. 23:7): In the whole world there isn't a single human being who tells only and just the truth. In reality one is either nearer to falsehood or farther from falsehood.

R. Shlomo Leib of Lentchno (? –1843) was one of the most unusual teachers who followed in the footsteps of R. Moshe Leib Sassover, the Seer of Lublin, and the masters of the Pshyskha trend in Hassidut. It is related that he never looked at anything that might be considered unclean; he never gazed at coins or banknotes, and he took only what was handed to him, never taking anything on his own initiative. He warned his Hassidim:

"The evil spirit is full of eyes. From this we can assume how many eyes a human being needs in order to be saved from the evil spirit."

R. Shlomo Leib once complained: "How can I fulfil the precept 'Thou shalt love thy neighbor as thyself' (Lev. 19:18), when I cannot even tolerate myself and I am constantly engaged in arguing against myself?! But I am repenting so I should be able to look at myself, and the same thing I am obligated to do as regards my fellow humans until they repent."

Characteristic of R. Shlomo Leib are his interpretations of biblical passages:

When some one remembers at the beginning of every day that "In the beginning God created the heaven and the earth" then all earthly matters are to him "unformed and void" (Gen. 1:1–2).

"Dan shall judge his people" (Gen. 49:16): God blessed the tribe of Dan that it should dispense judgment impartially, flattering no one.

"And the Lord said unto Moses: 'Write this for a memorial in the book, and rehearse it in the ears of Joshua' " (Exod. 17:14): It is written in a book, so why was it necessary to repeat it unto Joshua's ears? The passage teaches us that sometimes when one hears something by word of mouth, he remembers it longer than something read in a book.

"And I besought the Lord" (Deut. 3:23): The most important aim of prayer is to beseech the Lord.

"And this is the blessing wherewith Moses, the man of God, blessed" (Deut. 33:1): He blessed that every one become a man of God.

"All the rivers run into the sea, yet the sea is not full" (Eccles. 1:7): No matter how much wealth certain people accumulate, their passion for wealth is never satisfied and they feel that their pockets are not yet full.

R. Issakhar Ber of Radoshitz (? –1843), a disciple of the Seer of Lublin, preferred to be a Hassid rather than a master, and the only pride he permitted himself was the statement that in his lifetime he had visited 120 Hassidic leaders. Being himself a very poor man, he understood the complaints of his poor devotees whose search for a livelihood interfered with their desires to dedicate themselves more to worship and study rather than to small material matters. He consoled them:

"One is rewarded much more for the little he accomplishes under difficulties than for those large accomplishments which come to him easily."

R. David of Lelov (? –1813), a great lover of nature sustained himself and his family from the income of a small grocery store. The moment he saw that his daily income was about to reach more than was necessary for the upkeep of his household, he closed the grocery store and devoted himself to study and to charitable activities. R. David later liquidated his business altogether in order not to cause other storekeepers feelings of jealousy.

R. David, a disciple of R. Elimelekh of Lizhensk and of the Seer of Lublin, influenced many people to become followers of Hassidut. Among those who had been led by R. David to the path of Hassidut, was a non-believing physician who practiced his heresy openly. That physician later became the Hassidic master of Pietrkov, popular as R. Khayim Leib Doctor.

R. David's teachings were published after his death in the collection *Migdal David (The Tower of David)*.

R. David was particularly fond of children, and his associations with youngsters enabled him to imagine that he was of their age-group. It is related that whenever he visited a town, he would gather a group of young children and give each of them a small flute. Then he would hire a horse and wagon and drive the children all over town, encouraging them to use the flutes and rejoice in merriment. He used to say: "Kind words and regard for another person's feelings, rather than harsh reproof, influence people to repentance and to good deeds."

He interpreted a biblical passage as proof that not all people have the same ability to perceive and understand:

"Now Jetro, the priest of Midian, Moses' father-in-law, heard of all that God had done for Moses and for Israel His people" (Exod. 18:1): Others also heard the same, but they were not influenced to change their ways. But Jetro heard and he became convinced that "the Lord is greater than all gods" (Exod. 18:11).

Love, compassion, understanding and encouragement of the troubled and the needy—these were the main characteristics of R. Yitzkhak Kalish of Wurka (? –1848). He possessed the foresight, the insight, the humility of his three masters: the Seer of Lublin, R. David of Lelov and R. Simkha Bunim of Pshyskha. R. Mendel, who later became the Hassidic master of Kotzk, was one of his closest friends, although they were opposites in attitude: R. Mendel being demanding while R. Yitzkhak was full of understanding. R. Yitzkhak left no written works. His teachings and tales about him are recorded in the two-part volume *Ohel Yitzkhak (Isaac's Tent)*, the title being based on Gen. 24:67.

Once a man desired to create dissension between R. Yitzkhak and his Hassidim, so he related to the master some unbecoming deeds of a number among them. R. Yitzkhak retorted: "Why should you tell me things that are untrue? I'll relate to you some bad deeds and negative characteristics of my own, so you will not have to invent attributes that I do not possess."

One of R. Yitzkhak's Hassidim was very wealthy but notorious as a miser. The master advised the man to stop sustaining himself on bread and herring, but eat regular meals of the choicest foods and drink good wines. Other Hassidim heard the advice, and they later asked the master to explain the reason. He explained: "When the miser becomes accustomed to eating good food and drinking the best of wines, he will give a poor person at least bread and herring. If he himself eats bread and herring only, what will his miserly heart let him give to a needy person?"

Once he was asked by the Hassidim why the text of the Confessional on the Day of Atonement enumerates the sins in alphabetical order. "So that the confessors know when to stop," replied R. Yitzkhak.

Following are some of his biblical interpretations, as recorded in *Ohel Yitzkhak:*

"And they saw him afar off, and before he came near unto them, they conspired against him to slay him" (Gen. 37:18): Scripture teaches us that Joseph's being distant, and estranged from his brothers, gave them a desire to kill him. Two people, even if they carry in their hearts resentment against each other, so long as they continue to engage in conversations eventually see clearly that their mis-understanding is a result of rumors. But if they become estranged and cease to speak to each other, their hatred grows to such an extent that one is ready to murder the other.

"And Pharaoh commanded: '. . . Ye shall no more give the people [the Israelites] the straw to make brick . . . and the tale of the bricks ye shall not diminish naught thereof' " (Exod. 5:6–8): Would it not have been more logical to give them the straw so that they could double the amount of bricks? From this we learn that preoccupation of the mind and trouble and worries of the heart are more burdensome to the body than hard labor.

"All the commandment which I command thee this day" (Deut. 8:1): Today, tomorrow, the day after tomorrow, everywhere and always.

"King Solomon made himself a palanquin of the wood of Lebanon. He made the pillars thereof of silver, the top thereof of gold" (Song of Songs 3: 9–10): How could one lie on a palanquin made of gold? The end of the passage explains: "The inside thereof inlaid with love" (Ibid.): When there is love, one can sleep even on gold.

R. Yitzkhak was succeeded by his son R. Menakhem Mendel (? –1868). He interpreted biblical passages in a way similar to his father's:

"And God heard the voice of the lad [Ishmael]" (Gen. 21:17): Scripture did not tell us before that the lad was crying. But there is a form of crying without voice, and this is the kind of crying that splits the heavens and only God hears it.

"And they drank [with Joseph] and were merry with him" (Gen: 43:34): Not the wine made them drunk and merry, but the feeling of brotherhood. The drinking brought joy to them and joy intoxicated them.

The older brother of R. Menakhem Mendel, R. Yaakov David (? –1876), became the Hassidic master of Amshinov. Like his father and younger brother, he devoted his energies to the welfare of the needy and those beset by various difficulties, imbuing them with optimism.

> The Amshinover said: "To sin against a fellow-man is worse than to sin against the Creator. The man you harmed may have gone to an unknown place, and you may lose the opportunity to beg his forgiveness. The Lord, however, is everywhere and you can always find Him when you seek him."
> (Siakh Sarfey Kodesh, IV, p. 119; Newman: Hassidic Anthology, p. 124.)

R. Yitzkhak of Wurka and his successors were great lovers of song as a stimulant to joy and hope. R. Yitzkhak was the author and composer of the Yiddish song "Why Worry?", which gained great popularity:

Why worry what will happen tomorrow?
Better correct the wrongs of yesterday.
No drink, no food, but not to forget the Creator,
To pray, to study in order to please Him.

R. Moshe Teitelbaum (? –1841), born in the Eastern
Galician city of Pszemysl and in his early youth a scholarly opponent of Hassidut, later became a disciple of the "Seer" of
Lublin. He was a man of great imagination and lofty longings,
as can be seen from the four volumes of his main work *Yismakh
Moshe (Rejoicing of Moses)*. When he became spiritual leader
of the Jewish community in Uhel, Hungary, he gained a great
Hassidic following. Because of his great fame, many non-Jews
also came to him for blessings, assistance and advice.

Thanks to the popularity of his main work, the master of
Uhel is mentioned in the scholarly world of the Jews, not by
his own name, but is called "The Author of Yismakh Moshe."

The following quotations are characteristic of the author and
his work:

"And God said: 'Let us make man' " (Gen. 1:26): God took
council with the angels before creating man, and prepared for
him the teaching about the attribute of humility, that the great
should ask the advice of the small.

"And thou shalt rejoice in all the good which the Lord thy
God hath given unto thee and unto thy house" (Deut. 26:11):
Just as there is no full satisfaction in the possession of wealth, so
there is no full satisfaction in various forms of joy. The more
joy one has, the more he wants.

After the demise of the Seer of Lublin, many of his Hassidim
became devotees of R. Meir Halevy of Apta (? –1831), a

scholar of renown although an opponent of the intellectual trend in the Hassidic movement. R. Meir did not wish to be an innovator, but rather stressed the teachings of his own master and of Hassidut in its original simplicity. R. Meir preached humility and peace among men. He said to one of the opponents of the ways of the Pshyskha Hassidim: "If you lived alone in a forest, you would quarrel even with the trees."

R. Meir's interpretations of biblical passages and Talmudic teachings, were a synthesis of explanatory and mystical comments. They are included in his work, *Or L' Shamayim (Light in the Heavens)*.

Commenting on humility, he wrote:

"The main service of God is to be humble in the presence of every person; this humility should be a source of the greatest joy."

"The importance of humility we learn from the testimony of the Torah as regards Moses: 'Now the man Moses was very meek, above all the men that were upon the face of the earth' " (Num. 12:3).

"The evil inclination sometimes leads one to sadness and pessimism. But when one derives joy from the source of humility, he cannot be overpowered by evil desires to turn from the ways of being a true servant of the Almighty."

Preaching humility, R. Meir of Apta often repeated the teachings of his forerunners in Hassidut, that one should never be haughty in dealing with another human being, even when the other person is considered a sinner, because it is possible that the evil man has a single good trait that he who is haughty does not possess.

R. Shlomo Hakohen (1801–1867), son of the spiritual head of the Jewish community of Balshavetz, gained fame as a scholar in his early youth. His sensitive soul longed for the poetic, ethical depths within the Talmudic laws and his singing voice sought ways to reach heavenly heights. He had several teachers in Hassidut. Foremost among them was R. Meir of Apta. R. Shlomo was for thirty-two years Rabbi of the Jewish community of Radomsk, and as a Hassidic master he was known as R. Shlomo Radomsker. He did not wish to become a Hassidic teacher of the masses and preferred rather to have fewer devotees but greater scholars among them. His two-part work *Tifereth Shlomo (The Beauty of Solomon)* is chiefly a collection of biblical interpretations and commentaries on Jewish festivals.

R. Shlomo was a man of great worldly wisdom, and his replies to specific questions were often witty and ironic.

A young Hassid consulted the Radomsker about the problem of divorcing his evil and cruel wife. The young man was a scholar, and quoted the Talmudic statement that "when someone divorces his first wife, even the altar in the Holy Temple sheds tears."

"It is better that the altar shed tears rather than that you should be crying all your life because of a cruel wife," R. Shlomo told him.

A well-known heretic, who had taken special pleasure in abusing pious people, died suddenly, and representatives of the burial society came to R. Shlomo to ask whether to place him in a grave at the gate of the cemetery, according to the custom as regards sinners; or should he be interred in a grave in the regular rows?

"Bury him wherever you like, as long as you bury him," replied R. Shlomo.

A notorious informer came to invite R. Shlomo to the circumcision ceremony of his son. "If you do not come, you will transgress the command not to put people to shame," emphasized the man.

"You, as an informer, break so many laws," said R. Shlomo to him, "why do you begrudge me one small transgression?"

Following are comments on two biblical passages taken from the work *Tiferet Shlomo:*

"And thou shalt rejoice in all the good which the Lord thy God hath given unto thee and unto the house" (Deut. 26:11): You should rejoice in all the good, not simply because it is good, but because God has given it to you.

"Rob not the weak because he is weak, neither crush the poor in the gate" (Prov. 22:22): If the poor is poor, what can he be robbed of? There are evil people who do not wish to give charity, and they use the pretext that a specific individual, who is considered poor, is not poor at all and has sizable savings. Thus the poor man's chances are hurt in the eyes of others. That's why it is written that the weak and the poor should not be crushed, meaning they should not be robbed of their need which is the only "wealth" they possess.

MOGELNITZA, ALEXANDER, GOSTININ, SOKHATCHOV AND PILOV

R. Khayim Meir Yekhiel of Mogelnitza (? –1849), known in Hassidic lore as the "Seraph," was the grandson of R. Israel, the Maggid of Kozhenitz. The grandfather was his first teacher. Later he became a devotee of several Hassidic masters of his time. It was only on their insistence that he agreed to lead others in the ways of Hassidut.

The Seraph once made the following observation:

"A person must live very long in order to learn how to die properly."

The biblical interpretations of the Seraph reflect his personal hopes, wishes and desires in the service of the Almighty:

"Now the man Moses was very meek" (Num 12:3): Why is Moses praised so much for being meek? Because all the precepts aim at teaching humility, thus meekness is the greatest of all human attributes.

"Thou shalt surely rebuke thy neighbor" (Lev. 19:17): Rebuke him according to his own standards, and not in accordance with the standards of your own.

"Ye shall be holy, for I, the Lord your God, am holy" (Lev. 19:2): Everyone can easily practice holiness, if he only wishes. He can be holy by overpowering his anger, by not engaging in gossip and evil talk and by doing the opposite of what the evil inclination incites him to do.

"But from thence you will seek the Lord thy God and there thou shalt find Him" (Deut. 4:29): If you call to God, He will reply.

"Because thou didst not serve the Lord thy God with joyfulness and with gladness of heart" (Deut. 28:47): Just as a person who is hungry eats with great desire, passion and joy, so must one serve the Almighty with great desire, passion and joy.

R. Khanokh Henikh of Alexander (1799–1870), held rabbinic positions in two cities of Poland, Novidvor and Proshnitz, preferring to be a Hassidic disciple rather than a master. He was a devotee, first of R. Bunim of Pshyskha, later of R. Mendel of Kotzk and lastly of R. Yitzkhak Meir of Ger. When R. Itzkhak Meir passed away, many of his Hassidim turned to R. Khanokh

Henikh for leadership. He moved to Alexander, where he held Hassidic court for several years only. Before he was "called to the Academy-on-Most-High," R. Khanokh Henikh devoted all his energy to impressing upon his Hassidim the importance of humility and the service of the heart. He left no written records of his teachings, but what his devotees recalled of his statements was published in the collection *Khoshvoh L' Tovah (Meant for Good)*, based on Gen. 50:20.

Chatting with his closest Hassidim about human weaknesses, R. Khanokh Henikh asked: "Jealous? Over what? Passion? What for? Honors? Why?"

He once criticized a Hassid for avoiding gatherings of fellow-Hassidim. The man replied that "no one regrets it if he avoids such gatherings."

"Yes, yes, you are right," commented R. Henikh, "if one avoids such gatherings, he does not regret . . . his transgressions."

In his chats on the subjects of pride, repentance and the power of physical passions, R. Khanokh Henikh emphasized:

"When a person grows in height, spiritually, he interferes with no one; but when he grows in width, pride, he is pushing me."

"One should confess his sins in a quick manner so as not to remain too long in the swamp of transgression."

When R. Khanokh Henikh was asked why the Talmud uses the synonym "grave" for the woman's womb, he replied: "Many a man has been buried because of it."

Like all the other Hassidic teachers, the master of Alexander used the interpretation of biblical passages to convey his own ideas and ideals:

"In the beginning God created the heaven and the earth. Now

the earth was unformed and void" (Gen. 1:1–2): If at the beginning of the day one takes into his mind the thought that "in the beginning God created the heaven and the earth," then he really feels all day long that the earth is unformed and void.

"And Joseph said unto his brethren: . . . And now be not grieved" (Gen. 45:4–5): Grief is not a transgression, but the most serious transgression cannot bring one to the thick-heartedness that is the result of melancholy and sadness. Where does melancholy come from? A person thinks that he should be privileged to have this or that, either materially or spiritually, and can't think of anything else but of himself alone.

"And the Lord said unto Moses. . . . Lift thou up thy rod, and stretch out thy hand over the sea and divide it" (Exod. 14:15–16): According to the Midrash, Moses pleaded with the sea to divide itself so that the Israelites might cross over on dry land. But the sea answered Moses with pride: "I am older than you. I was created on Tuesday and the human being was created on Friday." When the Almighty heard the prideful statement of the sea, He said to Moses: "Lift up thy rod and divide the haughty sea." Those bloated with pride, are punished for it.

"Thou shalt not covet" (Exod. 20:14): Desires are things of the heart; so how could there be a command about the heart's desires? But a person should be able to control the heart. Just as it would never occur to a simple peasant that he could marry a princess, so one should never permit the feelings of his heart to covet what belongs to someone else.

"And the mountain burned with fire unto the heart of heaven" (Deut. 4:11): Until the heart became heavenly.

"Depart from evil and do good" (Ps. 34:15; 37:27): Departing from evil will abolish it, and this means doing good.

"By understanding (He) made the heavens" (Ps. 136:5): God created the heavens so that humans can look at them with the use of understanding and thus comprehend the greatness of the Creator.

"His greatness is unsearchable" (Ps. 145:3): The greatness of God cannot be understood by those who rely only upon their own researches.

"Let thy garments always be white; and let thy head lack no oil" (Eccles. 9:8): A person should always imagine that he is wearing clothes of white silk; that a pitcher of oil is standing upon his head, and that if he turns his head the wrong way, the pitcher will turn over and the oil will soil his costly garments.

"The good way to which a man should cleave . . . R. Eliezer said: 'A good eye'" (*Ethics of the Fathers* 2:13). Instead of seeking faults in your neighbor, look for his virtues.

R. Yekhiel Meir of Gostinin (1816–1887) became a Hassidic master at the age of sixty, after the passing of his own revered teacher, R. Abraham of Chekhanov. Before that he had been a disciple of R. Mendel Kotzk and later of R. Yitzkhak Meir of Ger. R. Yekhiel Meir was born in Opotchno, becoming an orphan very early in life, and a maternal uncle became his guardian. Later he became the son-in-low of a wealthy man in the city of Gostinin, and this enabled R. Yekhiel Meir to devote himself to a life of piety and study.

When R. Yekhiel Meir first visited R. Mendel—the master was then residing in Tomashov, before moving to Kotzk—the young man from Gostinin was full of trepidation. R. Mendel calmed him by saying: "Don't fear. We here are not creating something new. We are just realizing what is in the power of every individual to accomplish."

As a Hassidic master, R. Yekhiel Meir was known as the "Psalms Reciting Jew" and he used to say: "There is no better medicine book than the Book of Psalms." Other devotees called him "The Good Jew of Gostinin." Whenever he wished to reprove someone for a misdeed, he did not do it immediately, but postponed it for a day or more and then he expressed his reproof by saying: "You displeased me yesterday" or "You caused me displeasure several days ago."

Speaking of learning and knowledge, he said: "Who is a thief? Not he who knows how to steal, but he who does the stealing. Who is a scholar? Not he who knows how to learn, but he who sits and studies."

Before he died, R. Yekhiel Meir called together his children and read with them the Ten Commandments (Exod. 20:2–14). When he reached the commandment, "Thou shalt not steal," he said to them: "Remember, it makes no difference whether one steals a sackful of gold or a piece of paper."

R. Yekhiel Meir's noble character found its loftiest expression in his interpretations of biblical passages:

"And it shall come to pass when he crieth unto Me, that I will hear, for I am gracious" (Exod. 22:26): One may be right in a controversy with a poor man, nevertheless one should realize that the poor person has many grievances, and his cries reach the Almighty. That is why God himself warns us: "And it shall come to pass when he crieth unto Me, that I will hear, for I am gracious."

"Moses was very meek" (Num. 12:3): If there were a special command on humility, it would be impossible to know who was really humble, and who was meek for the purpose of fulfilling a command.

"Judges and officers shalt thou make thee in all thy gates" (Deut. 16:18): Everyone should be the judge and the watchman of his own body, search the gates of its members, as is the duty of a judge and court officer.

"Cast me not off in the time of old age" (Ps. 71:9): So that I be in possession of strength to overpower my evil passions, and cast me not into the hands of my evil inclination.

R. Abraham Bernstein (1839–1910), who became famous as the Hassidic master of Sokhatchov, was a great scholar and the son of a great scholar. His father, R. Zeev Nakhum, was the spiritual leader of the Jewish community of Byala and the head of its Rabbinical Academy. The father was a disciple of R. Mendel of Kotzk. When still in his early teens, Abraham became a son-in-law of the Kotzker, marrying his daughter Sarah Tzeenah. R. Abraham never thought of himself as qualified to be a Hassidic leader, and he preferred to occupy a Rabbinic position as spiritual head of a specific community. But R. Abraham was a short-tempered man. He quarrelled with the community leaders, to whom his demands often seemed extreme. Before becoming the spiritual head of the Jewish community of Sokhatchov, he had held a similar position in three other communities. In regard to his quarrels with community leaders, he once stated ironically:

"If I lived in the forest, the branches of the trees would persecute me."

After the death of his father-in-law, R. Abraham became a disciple of R. Yitzkhak Meir of Ger, and after his passing, he declared himself a devotee of R. Khanokh Henikh of Alexander. Only after the death of the Alexanderer, did he agree to Hassidic leadership, on condition that only scholars be his Hassidim and that he should not be interfered with in his tasks as the head of a rabbinic academy. He left two scholarly works which are studied to this very day: *Tiferet Shlomo (The Beauty of Solomon)* and *Eglay Tahl (Drops of Dew)* based on Job 38:28.

The master of Sokhatchov emphasized:

"The Almighty makes use of broken vessels. He dwells with him 'that is of a contrite and humble spirit' " (Isa. 57:15): The poor man has a broken heart, therefore he is nearer to God.

He who has only personal interests at heart, is in a worse position than a blind man. The blind man sees nothing, but the one with a personal interest in a matter, sees everything upside down.

R. Khayim Israel of Pilov (? –1906), a grandson of R. Mendel of Kotzk, was saddened by the reality of Jewish life in the Russian Empire, and he was one of the first Hassidic masters who believed that before the arrival of the Messianic Era, practical steps should be taken to settle Jews in the Holy Land. His love of the biblical homeland of the Jewish people and his ideas in regard to practical measures for its rebuilding, are embedded in his work *Shlom Yerusahalayim (Peace of Jerusalem)* published posthumously.

Many Hassidic masters of the era doubted whether the time had come for the realization of the idea of resettling the Holy Land. Commenting on a biblical passage, he philosophized about deed and realization in general:

"And Aaron spoke unto Moses: 'Behold this day have they offered their sin-offering and their burnt-offering . . . and if I had eaten the sin-offering today, would it have been well-pleasing in the eyes of God?' And when Moses heard that, it was well pleasing in his sight" (Lev. 10:19–20): When someone has to do something, he is often hesitant because it is unclear to him whether to do it or not. But when the deed is in process, then it really becomes clear enough whether it is worthy of realization.

R. Khayim Israel of Pilov stressed that the individuals of the simple masses possessed the idealism to transform into reality the visions of dreamers. The basis of this conviction, which was later substantiated during the great efforts of the Zionist movement, he also found in a verse of the Holy Scriptures:

"For God shall save Zion and build the cities of Judah. . . . The seed also of His servants shall inherit it; and they that love His name shall dwell therein" (Ps. 69: 36–37): First usually come the "seed of His servants," the simple people, and they are followed by those who are the spiritual lovers.

R. Mordecai Yoseph Leiner of Izhbitza (? –1854), who had led the revolt against R. Menakhem Mendel of Kotzk, when the latter wanted to transform Hassidut from a mass movement into an order of chosen scholars, emphasized the importance of self-elevation by means of attachment to the Almighty in a human way. Simultaneously he stressed fear of God as an antidote to fear of human beings. The teachings of the master of Izhbitza were gathered in the collection *MaY Ha Shiloakh (The Waters of Shiloa* based on Isaiah 8:6); the first word of the title in the original being an abbreviation of the name Mordecai Yoseph. Two of his many comments on biblical passages will suffice to illustrate his basic teachings.

"And God said: 'Let us make man in our image'" (Gen. 1:26): This means that the Almighty turns to everyone and says:

"Let's make a man, the man who should include the positive to be found in all human beings. Everyone should contain in himself all of humanity."

"And it came to pass, because the mid-wives feared God, that He made them houses" (Exod. 1:21): Fear of human beings never brings tranquility, but fear of God does, because of reliance on His mercy. Because the mid-wives had fear of God, they were not afraid of Pharaoh, King of Egypt, and God rewarded them with houses, since possession of a house signifies tranquility.

R. Mordecai Yoseph's son Yaakov, known as the author of the scholarly work *Bait Yaakov (House of Jacob),* preferred study in solitude to Hassidic leadership. The devotees of R. Mordecai Yoseph chose two of his disciples, both residing in Lublin, to become their leaders. The first was R. Leibeleh Eiger, grandson of a Talmudic giant; and after R. Leibeleh's death, R. Tzadok HaKohen, a religious philosopher of great stature.

R. Leibeleh (1816–1888) had been a disciple of the Kotzker before he joined the ranks of the rebellious R. Mordecai Yoseph. Since the Hassidim of the Kotzker usually delayed their daily prayers, R. Leibeleh asked the master:

"When I will be in the World-to-Come, what answer should I give my grandfather if he asks me why I prayed later than the prescribed hours for the morning devotions, having spent too much time in preparation to pray?"

"You should tell him," replied R. Mendel, "that according to Maimonides, if a worker sharpens his saw all day long, and only in the last hour of the working day he begins to saw, he has to be paid for a whole day's work."

R. Leibeleh Eiger's teachings are to be found in his two volume work *Torat Emmet (Torah of Truth)*. He stressed the difference between human beings and the creatures of the animal world:

"The human being possesses powers, senses and passions that are similar to those of the lowest animals. The difference between the human being and the animal is that the human being has the power of choice to sanctiy the physical needs and desires that are necessary for procreation and for reasons of health. Every human being should try to sanctify the desires and lusts that he has in common with the animals."

R. Tzadok HaKohen (1823–1900), R. Leibeleh's successor, was a prolific writer, the most popular among his works being *Pree Tzaddik (Reward for the Righteous,* the title being based on Ps. 58:12). Wrote R. Tzadok:

"And they believed in the Lord and His servant Moses" (Exod. 14:31): Just as a person must have faith in the Lord, he must also have faith in his own abilities. It means: Just as a person believes in God, so he should also believe in himself, be certain that God is interested in him, and that there is a reason for his coming into this world. A person should believe that he is not like an animal, which ceases its existence after its death. On the contrary, he should be convinced that his soul comes from the Divine Source of Life, and that the Creator gets pleasure from his soul when he does His will.

"I am the Lord thy God" (Exod. 20:2): The First Commandment is not in the imperative mood, because when someone is lacking in faith, no imperative statement will change his mind.

The main secrets of the Holy Scriptures are difficult to penetrate, but everyone imagines them within his heart. "The heart is the main hiding place of a human being's true character. Pride, for instance, is not always in the form of open haughtiness in regard to others. A person's pride is sometimes shown only to himself, because the essence of pride is in the heart."

More than has been related in this
book is to be found in the
teachings of Hassidut.
As for the rest,
dear reader,
go and
learn.

TAM VeNISHLAM

Completed and concluded.
Praise and Thanksgiving.

TO THE CREATOR OF THE WORLD

Bibliography

A selective list of works dealing with the Hassidic movement, its masters, and their teachings. It does not include earlier works by and about Hassidic leaders, most of which have been mentioned in the text of this book.

AGNON, SHMUEL YOSEPH. *Ha-Esh Veha-Etzim;* Jerusalem, 1957.

————. *Sifrehem shell Tzadekim;* Jerusalem, Tel-Aviv, 1951.

————. *Sifrehem shell Tzadekim;* Jerusalem, 1965.
Tales about the books by Hassidic Masters.

ALFASI, YITZKHAK. *Tiferet She-Ba-Malkhut;* Tel-Aviv, 1951.
The Masters in the cities of Kosov and Vizhnitz.

————. *HaRabbi MiKotzk;* Tel Aviv, 1962.
The life of R. Mendel Kotzker.

————. *Goor;* Tel-Aviv, 1954.
The Masters of the Alter dynasty of the city of Gher.

————. *Ha-Savah Ha-Kadosh Me-Radoshitz;* Tel-Aviv, 1957.
The Master of Radoshitz.

————. *Toldot Ha-Hassidut;* Tel-Aviv, 1959.
A history of Hassidism.

————. *Safer Ha-Ademorim;* Tel-Aviv, 1961.
Contains a bibliography of books by Hassidic Masters.

————. *Ha-Kohzeh Me-Lublin;* Tel-Aviv, 1969.
Life and teachings of the "Seer of Lublin," Rabbi Yaakov Yitzkhak Halevi Horowitz of Lublin.

BELLOW, SAUL, editor. *Great Jewish Short Stories;* New York, 1963.

BEN MENAKHEM, NAPHTALI. *B'Shaarey Sefer;* Jerusalem, 1956.
Includes reviews of books dealing with the Hassidic movement and its leaders.

BEN YEKHEZKEL, MORDECAI. *Sefer Ha-Maasyot* (six volumes) Tel-Aviv, 1965.
Jewish tales, including many about Hassidic leaders.

BENARI, NAKHUM. *Eshkolot;* Tel-Aviv, 1955.
Includes Hassidic interpretations of biblical books.

BERBER, MENAHEM, editor. *May HaYam;* New York, 1954.
The life and teachings of R. Yekhiel Meir of Gostinin.

BERL, KHAYIM YEHUDA. *Reb Yitakak Isaac Me-Kamarnah;* Jerusalem, 1965.

BRATZLAVER, R. NAKHAM. *Sippuray Maasiot;* Buenos Aires, 1967.
The Yiddish tales of R. Nakham of Bratzlav.

BROMBERG, RABBI A. O. I. *Mi-Gedolay Ha-Tarah Ve-Ha-Hassidut* (twenty volumes); Jerusalem.
A series of biographies of the great men of Torah-learning and Hassidism.

BUBER, MARTIN. *The Tales of Rabbi Nachman;* Trans. by Maurice Friedman; New York, 1956.

———. *Darko Shell Adam Al Pee Torat Ha-Hassidut;* Jerusalem, 1957.
Human behavior according to Hassidic teachings.

———. *Pirkay Hassidut;* Jerusalem, 1957.
Hassidic tales.

———. *Or Ha-Ganuz;* Jerusalem, 1965.
Hassidic tales.

———. *Tales of the Hassidim* (two volumes) translated by Olga Marx; New York, 1966.
Early Masters and Late Masters.

BURSTYN, AVIEZER. *Tzidkat Ha-Khakham;* Haifa, 1966.
Biography of R' Naphtali Horowitz of Ropshitz.

CAHANA, DAVID. *Toledot Ha-Mekubalim Ha-Shabtaim Va-Hassidim*
(two volumes); Tel Aviv, 1926–27.
History of Jewish mysticism, the false Messiah, Shabbtai Tzvi, and
his movement, and of the Hassidim.

DAWIDOWICZ, LUCY S. *The Golden Tradition. Jewish Life and Thought
in Eastern Europe;* New York, 1967.

DON, YOSEPH. *Hanovellah Ha-Hassidit;* Jerusalem, 1966.
The Hassidic novel in modern Jewish Literature.

DRESSNER, SAMUEL H. *The Zaddik;* New York, 1960.

DVORKES, YESHAYA A. *Massekhet Avot Imm Peirushay Rabbenu Israel
Baal Shem Tov;* Jerusalem, '65.
The Baal Shem Tov's commentaries to *Ethics of the Fathers.*

DUBNOV, SHIMON. *Toldot Ha-Hassidut;* Tel-Aviv, 1960.
History of Hassidism by the eminent historian.

———. *Toldot Ha-Hassidut;* Tel Aviv, 1960.
Also available in Yiddish translation.

ECKSTEIN, MENAKHEM. *Mavoh Le-Torat Ha-Hassidut;* Tel-Aviv, 1960.
An introduction to Hassidism.

EHRENBERG, RABBI E. *Arzay Ha-Levanon;* Jerusalem, 1967.
On the dynasty of Rabbi Khayim Halberstam of Tzanz.

EISENSTEIN, J. YEHUDA DAVID, editor. *Otzar Yisrael* (five volumes);
New York, 1951.
Jewish Encyclopedia, includes biographies of Hassidic Masters.

ENGELSHER, ABRAHAM. *Der Yiddisher Vitz;* Brooklyn, New York.
(year of publication not given).
Humorous tales about Hassidic teachers.

ERLICH, Y. *R' Mendel Me-Kotzk;* Tel-Aviv, 1952.

FEDERBUSCH, DR. SIMON, editor. *Ha-Khassidut Ve-Tzion;* Jerusalem, 1963.
A collection of monographs by various authors on the teachings of the Hassidic masters regarding the Jewish revival in the Holy Land.

———. *Ha-Hassidut Ve-Tzion;* New York, 1963.
Collective work on the attitude of Hassidic Masters to the Holy Land.

FOX, YOSEPH. *Rabbi Mendel Me-Kotzk;* Jerusalem, 1967.
Biography of the Master of Kotzk and review of his teachings.

FOX, DR. JOSEPH. *Rabbi Menachem Mendel M'Kotzk;* Jerusalem, 1967.

FRENKEL, RABBI I. *Men of Distinction* (two volumes); Tel-Aviv, 1967.
English version of previous book.

———. *Yekhiday Segulah;* Tel-Aviv, 1957.

FRIEDMAN, ALEXANDER. *Zusia*s *Wellsprings of Torah* (two volumes); translated from the Yiddish by Gertrude Hirschler, New York, 1969.

FRIEDMAN, ALEXANDER. *Zusia: Wellsprings of Torah* (two volumes);
———. *Der Toreh-Kvall* (five volumes); Warsaw, 1930–39.
Commentaries on biblical portions of the week. An English translation was published in New York and a Hebrew translation in Jerusalem in 1967.

GERSTENKORN, YITZKHAK. *Amuday Ha-Hassidut Le-Sefer Thillim;* B'nei Brak, 1967.
Commentaries of Hassidic Masters to the Book of Psalms.

GHESHURI, M.SH. *La-Kassidim Mizmor;* Jerusalem, 1936.
On the songs and melodies of the Hassidim.

———. *Entzychlopedyah Shell Ha-Khassidut;* Tel-Aviv, 1959.
On Hassidic song and dance.

GLITZENSTEIN, AVROHOM KHANOK. *Rabbi Yisrael Baal-Shem-Tov;* Kfar Khabod, Israel, 1962.
> Biography in Hebrew, with views on the Besht by the masters of the Khabod trend in Hassidism. A Yiddish translation by Uriel Zimmer appeared in New York in 1960.

GORDON, MOSHE HA KOHEN. *Va-Yakhel Moshe* (two volumes); Brooklyn, New York, 1956.
> Includes Hassidic interpretations of the Five Books of Moses (the Pentateuch).

———. *Yalkut Moshe Al Ha-Torah;* Tel-Aviv (year of publication not given).
> Supplementary volume to two volumes mentioned above.

GREENBERG, AARON YAAKOV. *Itturay Torah* (four volumes—Genesis-Leviticus); Tel-Aviv, 1965–68.
> Includes Hassidic commentaries on the biblical portions of the week.

GUTTMAN, J. Y. *Sefer Derakh Ha-Emunah U'Maaseh Rav;* Warsaw.
> Photo reprint edition.

GUTTMAN, RABBI M. Y. *Gezah Kodesh;* Tel-Aviv, 1951.

———. *Kodesh Ha-Kodoshim;* Tel-Aviv, 1951.

———. *Belz;* Tel-Aviv, 1952.
> On the Hassidic Masters of the Rockeach dynasty of Belz.

———. *Oneg Shabbat;* Tel-Aviv, 1954.
> Biblical interpretations of Hassidic leaders.

———. *Rabbi Pinkhas Me-Koretz;* Tel-Aviv, 1960.

———. *R'Mendel Me-Remanov;* Tel-Aviv.

———. *Mi-Gibboray Ha-Hassidut;* Tel-Aviv.
> Some Hassidic Masters and their followers.

Ha-Encyclopedia Ha-Ivrit; Jerusalem, 1964.
Volume 17, cols. 756–821. Essay by Y. Tishbi on Hassidism with a bibliography.

HORODETZKY, SHMUEL ABBA. *The Leaders of Hassidism;* London, 1928.

———. *Ha-Hassidut Ve-Hassidim* (three volumes); Tel-Aviv, 1923. A major source on the history of Hassidut.

———. *Ha-Hassidut Ve-Toratah;* Tel-Aviv, 1944.
The teachings of Hassidism.

———. *Shivkhay Ha-Besht;* Tel-Aviv, 1947.
The traditions of the founder of Hassidism.

HOROWITZ, NAPHTALI. *Hassidut un Ettik;* New York, 1965.
Ethical statements by Hassidic masters of various generations.

HOWE, IRVING, and GREENBERG, ELIEZER, editors. *A Treasury of Yiddish Stories;* New York, 1954.
Includes Marie Syrkin's translation of C. C. Peretz's "If Not Higher."

ISRAELI, RABBI SAUL. *Perakim M'Makhshevet Yisrael;* Pardes Khanna, Israel, 1954.

KASHER, MOSHE SHLOMO, editor. *Prakim Be-Torat Ha-Khassidim;* Jerusalem, 1968.

KASHER, S. Y., editor. *Baaley Tshuvah;* Jerusalem, 1969.
Stories of repentance and repentants.

KATZ, BENZION. *Rabbanut, Khassidut, Haskalah* (two volumes); Tel-Aviv, 1956.
The Rabbinic, Hassidic, and Enlightenment trends in Judaism.

KARIV, AVRAHAM. *Shabat U'Moed Be-Drush Uba-Hassidut;* Tel-Aviv, 1966.
Hassidic commentaries on the Sabbath and Jewish holidays.

KESHET, YESHURUN. *Parshuyot;* Jerusalem, 1968.
A study on R' Nakhman of Bratzlav (pp. 77–103).

KIRSCHENBAUM, RABBI DAVID. *Fun di Khasidishe Oitzres;* New York, 1948.

KI-TOV, ELIYAHU. *Be-Khessed Elyon;* Jerusalem, 1960.
On Hassidic masters.

———. *Ke-Khudo Shel Makhat* (two volumes); Jerusalem, 1962.

KLEINMAN, MOSHE KHAYIM. *Sefer Le-Yesharim Tehillah;* Jerusalem (year of publication not given).

———. *Sefer Mazkeret Shem Ha-Gedolim;* Bnei Berak, 1967.
Stories about Hassidic masters, with a list of the dates of their passing.

KORMAN, ABRAHAM. *Zramim Ve-Kitot BiYahadut;* Tel-Aviv, 1966; pp. 57–118.
Trends and movements in Judaism.

LANDAU, BEZALLEL. *Ha-Besht Uvnei Heykhallo;* B'nai Brak, 1961.
The founder of Hassidism and his disciples.

LAVY-YAZKIROWITZ, ELIEZER LIPMAN. *Otzar Maamorim;* Jerusalem, 1952.
Essays on Hassidic thought.

LEFTWICH, JOSEPH. *The Golden Peacock;* New York, 1961; pp. 695–700.

LEVIN, MEYER. *Classic Hassidic Tales;* New York, 1966.
Marvelous Tales of Rabbi Israel Baal Shem Tov and of his great-grandson, Rabbi Nachman, retold from Hebrew, Yiddish and German sources.

LEVINE, YEHUDA LEIB. *Bayt Kotzk;* Jerusalem, 1959.

———. *Bait Sapinka;* Tel-Aviv, 1959.
Tha Masters of the Sopinka dynasty.

————. *Ha-Saraph;* Tel Aviv, 1959.
A Hassidic Master, his life and teachings.

————. *Bait Kotzk;* Jerusalem, 1959.

LIPSON, MORDECHAI. *Mi-Dor Dor* (four volumes); Tel-Aviv, 1968.
Includes anecdotes about Hassidic teachers and their followers.

MAHLER, RAPHAEL. *Ha-Hassidut Veha-Haskalah;* Merkavia, 1961.
Hebrew version of the Yiddish book on Hassidism and the
Yiddish Enlightenment Movement.

————. *Der Kampf Tzvishn Haskoleh un Hassidus in Galitzyeh;* New
York, 1942.
History of the struggle between the Enlightenment movement
and Hassidism in Austro-Galician Jewry.

————. *Ha-Hassidut Veha-Haskalah;* Merkavia, 1961.
Hebrew version of the above-mentioned book.

MAIMON, RABBI YEHUDA LEIB, editor. *SeferHa-Besht;* Jerusalem, 1960.
A collective work on the founder of Hassidism, his teachings and
his followers.

————. *Miday Khodesho* (eight volumes); Jerusalem, 1968.
Includes biographies and tales about Hassidic Masters.

————. *Saray Ha-Mayah* (six volumes); Jerusalem, 1968.
Includes biographies of Hassidic Masters and their teachings.

MANDELBAUM, BERNARD. *Choose Life;* New York, 1968.

MEISELES, MEIR. *Judaism: Thought and Legend;* B'nei Berak, Israel.
Anthology translated from the Hebrew by Rebecca Schoenfeld-
Brand and Aryeh Neuman.

MENCHER, DR. ARYEH. *Parshiyot Be-Toldot Yisrael Be-Zman Ha-
Khadash;* Jerusalem, 1967.

MINKEN, J. S. *The Romance of Hassidism;* New York, 1935.

MINTZ, JEROME R. *Legends of Hasidism;* Chicago and London.

NEWMAN, LOUIS I. *The Hasidic Anthology;* New York, 1944.
Tales and teachings of the Hassidim. Extensive bibliography.

NIGER, SHMUEL. *Bletter Geshikte fun der Yiddisher Literatur;* New
York, 1959.
Monographs on history of Yiddish literature, containing study on
R. Nakhman of Bratzlav's tales.

OPATASHU, YOSEPH. *Maises fun Baal Shem Tov;* New York, 1957.
Retold tales about the founder of Hassidism and of his closest
disciples.

ORYAN, MEIR. *Mistorin Ba-Hassidut,* in vols. 14–15 of the Annual
Carmelit; Haifa, 1959 (pp. 338–348).
Mysticism in Hassidic teachings.

————. *Sneh Boair Be-Kotzk;* Jerusalem, 1961.
R' Mendel of Kotzk and his disciples.

PERETZ, Y. L. *In This World and Next;* New York, 1958.
Selected writings translated from the Yiddish by Moshe Speigel.

RABINOWITZ, HAYIM REUVEN. *Dyokenaot Shel Darshonim;* Jerusalem,
1965.
Portraits of Jewish preachers, among them masters of Hassidut.

RABINOWITZ, Z. M. *Ha-Maggid Mi-Kozhenitz;* Tel-Aviv, 1947.
The life and teachings of R' Israel, the Preacher of Kozhenitz.

RABINOWITZ, AVI MEIR. *Rabbi Yaakov Yitzkhak of Pshyskhah;* Tel-
Aviv, 1960.
Biography of the "Holy Jew."

RAPHAEL, YITZKHAK, editor. *Sefer Ha-Besht;* Jerusalem, 1951.

————. *Sefer Ha-Hassidut;* Tel-Aviv, 1962.
Anthology of one hundred Hassidic teachers, biographies and
bibliography.

RECHT, BERL. *Mi-Sippuray Ha-Hassidim;* Tel-Aviv, 1960.
Hassidic tales.

SCHARFSTEIN, ZVI. *Otzar Ha-Raayonot Ve-Hepizgamim* (two volumes); Tel-Aviv, 1965.
Includes sayings and teachings by Hassidic Masters.

SCHNEUR ZALMAN, RABBI OF LIADI. *Liqutei Amarim.* Translated from the Hebrew by Nissan Mindel, Nisen Mangel, Zalman I. Posner, Jacob Immanuel Schochet; Brooklyn. New York, 5725–5628; 1965–1968.
Four parts. The original of the work is named *Tanya.* Introduction to the English translation of Iggereth Hakodesh . . . *Tanya,* Part Four, by Jacob Immanuel Schochet, 5728–1968, pp. 93.

SCHOLEM, GERSHON. *Major Trends in Jewish Mysticism;* 1961.

SCHWARTZ, LEO. W., editor. *The Jewish Caravan;* New York, 1935; pp. 373–405.
Great stories of twenty-five centuries.

SCHWARTZMAN, RABBI MEIR. *Ha-Rav Mi-Goor;* Jerusalem, 1958.
The life and teachings of R' Isaac Meir, the first Master of Gher.

————. *Esh Tamid;* B'nei Brak, 1962.
Chapters on the history and teachings of Hassidism.

SHEMEN, N. *Dos Gezang fun Hassidut* (two volumes); Buenos Aires, 1959.
Dealing specifically with the Hassidic music and the influence of Hassidism in general.

————. *Shivkhey Ha-Besht;* Tel-Aviv, 1960.
The traditional tales about the founder of Hassidism.

SHOENFELD, M. *Emmet Me-Kotzk Titzmakh;* Tel-Aviv, 1951.
The teachings of R' Mendel of Kotzk and of his disciples.

SHUNAMI, SHLOMO. *Maftayakh Ha-Maftaykhot;* Jerusalem, 1965.
"Bibliography of Jewish Bibliographies" published by the Magnes Press of the Hebrew University in Jerusalem. A special section is devoted to Hassidic bibliography.

SILVERSTONE, ABRAHAM. *Mimainay Ha-Hassidut;* New York, 1957. From the wells of Hassidism and its teachings.

SPIEGEL, SHALOM. *Hebrew Reborn;* Cleveland and New York, Jewish Publication Society of America, Philadelphia, 1957. (paperback) Chapter VI, pp. 119–159; Notes pp. 446–450.

STASHEVSKY, GERSHON EMANUEL. *Sefer Gedulat Mordecai, Gedulat Tzadikim;* Warsaw, 1934.
Reprinted in Israel. Tales about Hassidic masters.

STEINMAN, ELIEZER. *Beair Ha-Hassidut* (ten volumes); Tel-Aviv. Anthology of Hassidic teachings with evaluations and biographies of the Masters.

———. *Shaar Ha-Hassidut;* Tel-Aviv, 1957.
Introduction to Hassidism, with biographies, characteristics, and selections.

———. *Gan Ha-Hassidut;* Jerusalem, 1957.
Hebrew original of *The Garden of Hassidism.*

———. *Yalkut Le-Am U'Lenoar;* Tel-Aviv, 1958.

———. *Rabbi Israel Baal Shem Tov;* Jerusalem, 1960.

———. *The Garden of Hassidism;* translated from the Hebrew by Hayim Shachter; Jerusalem, 1969.

———. *Studies in Judaism, Vol I;* New York, 1896.
A special chapter on Hassidism.

SURSKY, AARON. *Dmuyot Hod;* B'ne Brak, 1967.
Includes portraits of Hassidic Masters who settled in the Holy Land.

———. *Tiferet Bayt Ha-Levy;* Jerusalem, 1965.
The life and teachings of R' Levi Yitzkhak of Berdichev.

TWERSKY, YOKHANAN. *Ha-Baal Shem Tov;* Tel-Aviv, 1965.
Biography of the founder of Hassidism, written by an author who was a descendant of R' Nakhum of Chernoble, a disciple of the Baal Shem Tov.

TUMIM, FRENKEL YEHUDA ARYEH. *Ohalay Shemen;* Bilgoray, 1911.
Reprinted in Israel.

UFFENHEIHER, RIVKA SHATZ. *Ha Khassidut K'Mystikah;* Jerusalem, 1968.
On the mystic elements in Hassidic thought, with a bibliography of Hassidic works.

UNGER, MENASHE. *Pshyskhe un Kotzk;* Buenos Aires, 1949.
The biographies and teachings of the Masters of Pshyskhe and Kotzk.

————. *R' Yisraoel Baal Shem Tov;* New York, 1963.
The biography, teachings and disciples of the founder of Hassidism. Yiddish.

————. *Hassidut un Yom-Tov;* New York, 1958.
Views of Hassidic masters on Jewish holidays.

WALDEN, AARON. *Shem Ha-Gedolim He-Khadash;* Lvov, 1906.
Hassidic masters, their lives and deeds.

WAXMAN, DR. MEYER. *A History of Jewish Literature;* Vol. III, Ch. I; New York, 1945.

————. *Moray Ha-Dorot;* Tel-Aviv, 1964.

WEINSTOCK, RABBI MOSHE YAIR. *Kodesh Hillulim;* New York, 1959.
Biographies.

WEISBROD, RABBI DAVID. *Arzay Ha-Levanon;* Tel-Aviv, 1956.

WEISS, SHABTAI. *Me-Otzar Hamakhshavah Shell Ha-Hassidut;* Tel-Aviv, 1951–1965.
Highlights of Hassidic thought.

WERTHEIM, RABBI AARON. *Halakhot Ve-Halikhot Ba-Hassidut;* Jerusalem, 1960.
Interpretation of Hassidic teachings.

YAAKOV, ISRAEL. *Kol Sippuray Baal Shem Tov* (three volumes); Tel-Aviv, 1969.

YEUSHSON, B. *Fun Unzer Altn Oitzer;* New York, 1954.
Comments on Bible and on Jewish holidays, including interpretations of various Hassidic Masters.

ZARITZKY, DAVID. *Otzar Mishlay Hassidim* (three volumes); Tel-Aviv.
Anthology of Hassidic parables.

ZEITLIN, HILLEL. *Arainfir in Khassidut un der Veg fun Khabad;* New York, 1957.
Introduction to Hassidism and the Khabad school of Hassidic teaching.

———. *Be-Pardes Ha-Hassidut Veha-Kabbalah;* Tel-Aviv, 1965.
In the Paradise of Hassidism and Jewish mysticism.

ZELIG, YAAKOV HAYIM. *Sefer Merom Harim;* Jerusalem, 1965.

ZEVIN, RABBI SHLOMO. *Sippuray Hassidim* (two volumes); Tel-Aviv, 1965.
Tales about Hassidic Masters in connection with biblical portions and Jewish holidays.

ZINBERG, ISRAEL. *Geshikhte fun Literatur bai Yidn* (new edition); Buenos Aires.

ZIPPER, YAAKOV. *Ish Hayah Be-Aretz;* Tel-Aviv, 1955.

Index of Names

Index of Place Names

347